HACKED

HACKED

The Inside Story of America's Struggle to Secure Cyberspace

Charlie Mitchell

ROWMAN & LITTLEFIELD
Lanham • Boulder • New York • London

Published by Rowman & Littlefield
A wholly owned subsidiary of The Rowman & Littlefield Publishing Group, Inc.
4501 Forbes Boulevard, Suite 200, Lanham, Maryland 20706
www.rowman.com

Unit A, Whitacre Mews, 26-34 Stannary Street, London SE11 4AB

British Library Cataloguing in Publication Information Available

Library of Congress Cataloging-in-Publication Data

Names: Mitchell, Charlie, 1962- author.
Title: Hacked : The inside story of America's struggle to secure cyberspace / Charlie Mitchell.
Description: Lanham : Rowman & Littlefield, 2016. | Includes bibliographical references and index.
Identifiers: LCCN 2016006180 (print) | LCCN 2016016849 (ebook) | ISBN 9781442255210 (cloth : alk. paper) | ISBN 9781442255227 (electronic)
Subjects: LCSH: Internet--Government policy--United States. | Computer security--Government policy--United States. | Cyber intelligence (Computer security).
Classification: LCC TK5105.875.157 M575 2016 (print) | LCC TK5105.875.157 (ebook) | DDC 384.30973--dc23. LC record available at http://lccn.loc.gov/2016006180

Printed in the United States of America

For Andrew, Benjamin and Joaquin.
May their futures be cyber-secure.

CONTENTS

Foreword   ix

1   "Carry Out Our Demand If You Want to Escape Us"   1
2   The First Cyber President   15
3   Sirens on Capitol Hill   25
4   To Build a Framework   41
5   The Department of Insecurity   81
6   The Telecom Challenge   111
7   The FTC, "Protecting America's Consumers"   129
8   Fear and Failure, Again, on Capitol Hill   143
9   The Information-Sharing Matrix   155
10   A New Congress Brings a New Energy to Cyber Debate   167
11   The Promise and Peril of "Strong Encryption"   189
12   Cyber Tensions Define the U.S.-China Relationship   197
13   Help Wanted, Desperately, for Cybersecurity   209
14   Senate Debate Takes Shape, Then—Surprise!—Stalls   215
15   At Long Last, the Political System Arrives at an Answer   243

16 The Unfinished Journey   255

Author's Note   275
Bibliographical Essay   279
Index   295
About the Author   301

FOREWORD

In October 2015, as the Senate prepared to take a historic step on cyber-security, news broke that a teenager had hacked the private e-mail account of the Central Intelligence Agency's director. Like many Americans, John Brennan stored a collection of sensitive documents in his e-mail account that provided a virtual user's guide to his personal life as well as sensitive government documents. The hacker revealed his actions, though not his identity, to the *New York Post*, which broke the story.

"The hacker said he used a tactic called 'social engineering' that involved tricking workers at Verizon into providing Brennan's personal information and duping AOL into resetting his password," the paper reported. The hacker said he got into Homeland Security Secretary Jeh Johnson's Comcast account as well.

Anyone and everyone is at risk in cyberspace. The risk rises exponentially if you use common passwords across sites and services. Cyber crooks and hackers employed by foreign intelligence services make fast work of passwords that use proper names, birth years, or other easily obtainable personal information. Once in, hackers can silently bleed funds from bank accounts or cause any number of personal headaches.

But that's the lower end of the cybersecurity threat facing the United States and the rest of the world. At the upper end, you'll find the destruction of industrial control systems, fried computer networks, and disabled electric power grids. All of those types of cyber attacks have already taken place. Much worse could be in store.

The effort to secure cyberspace, by government and industry, remains in the embryonic stages.

Cybersecurity is about the vulnerability of the computers and cyber networks that run every aspect of life in the United States and other technology-based countries. It's about potential threats on a grand scale to the global economy.

The U.S. government defines cybersecurity as "The activity or process, ability or capability, or state whereby information and communications systems and the information contained therein are protected from and/or defended against damage, unauthorized use or modification, or exploitation."

The "extended definition" puts it fully in a policy context:

> Strategy, policy, and standards regarding the security of and operations in cyberspace, and encompass[ing] the full range of threat reduction, vulnerability reduction, deterrence, international engagement, incident response, resiliency, and recovery policies and activities, including computer network operations, information assurance, law enforcement, diplomacy, military, and intelligence missions as they relate to the security and stability of the global information and communications infrastructure.

The federal government identifies sixteen critical infrastructure sectors within the U.S. economy. Each one touches every American in some way. The information technology sector, the telecommunications industry, the financial sector, and gas and electric utilities are obvious targets for cyber attacks and cyber theft. But each of the other critical infrastructure sectors—transportation, water works, chemical facilities, the health-care system, seaports, nuclear power plants, the emergency services system, the so-called defense industrial base and even "smart" buildings, dams, and agriculture—has its own vulnerabilities in cyberspace.

As the first decade of the twenty-first century ended and the second decade began, the political class was beginning to get it. But political leaders and government policymakers had barely scratched the surface on any of the policy elements described above.

"Cyber is deeply ingrained in virtually every facet of our lives," Rep. Mac Thornberry of Texas said in 2011, after chairing a congressional Republican task force on the subject. "We are very dependent upon it, which means that we are very vulnerable to disruptions and attacks. Cyber threats pose a significant risk to our national security as well as to our economy and jobs."

Thornberry pointed to the policy rub: "At least 85 percent of what must be protected is owned and operated by the private sector. Government must tread carefully in this area or risk damaging one of our greatest strengths—dynamic, innovate companies and businesses that are the key to our economy and to cybersecurity advances."

But tread it must. Republican and Democratic politicians alike were realizing that cybersecurity was an issue that couldn't be avoided, and that sculpting answers would be an arduous and frequently thankless task.

A glance at the statistics told the story.

The FBI's Internet Crime Complaint Center received 269,422 complaints in 2014. Those cyber crimes came with a price tag of over $800 million. Social media platforms were an increasingly popular entry point for crooks, according to the bureau.

Every stolen electronic record carried an average cost of $154, IBM and the Ponemon Institute declared in the tenth annual Cost of Data Breach Study released in 2015. Millions upon millions of records were being stolen at lightning speed. Do the math, and the potential economic cost shoots way over FBI estimates based on formal complaints. PricewaterhouseCoopers did the math in 2015 and found 1 billion compromised records.

And that was just the garden-variety criminal side of the cybersecurity equation. The Department of Homeland Security's center for monitoring computer networks for cyber attacks would record 350,000 attacks or intrusions in a six-month period between October 2013 and May 2014. That was 120,000 more incidents than in the entire previous twelve-month period. Intruders remained on infected systems for months or even years.

They scooped up the most sensitive of personal information, swiped the keys into databases containing valuable intellectual property and trade secrets, and slipped past security obstacles to map industrial control systems in preparation for future attacks. Darker still, there were politically inspired distributed denial of service, or DDoS, attacks launched by rogue 'players and aimed at bringing down systems critical to the U.S. economy.

NBC News in July 2015 obtained a National Security Agency map showing "more than 600 corporate, private or government 'Victims of

Chinese Cyber Espionage' that were attacked over a five-year period, with clusters in America's industrial centers."

Red dots represented the location of each attack; the Northeast Corridor, Silicon Valley, Southern California, and the technology-rich northwestern corner of the United States were lost in blurs of red. But dots spread from coast to coast, popping up wherever China, a commercial rival and potential military adversary, might find value.

A month later, NBC News reported the Chinese had infiltrated the e-mails of top Obama administration officials.

Cyber attacks and breaches were not just an inconvenience; in total, the attacks by criminals, terrorists, and nation-states threatened to pull apart the Internet itself. They set the stage for future attacks, the "cyber Peal Harbors" foreseen by ex-defense secretary and CIA director Leon Panetta that could blind the nation and grind its economy to a halt. The insurance firm Lloyd's calculated in 2015 that a determined assault on the U.S. electric grid could cause between $250 billion and $1 trillion in damage. Others postulated mind-boggling body counts. Yes, cyberspace could be deadly on a massive scale.

With that in mind, approaching cybersecurity as simply a technology problem is a mistake. It's a people problem, rooted in the freewheeling online habits of consumers and employees that can undermine the safety of vitally important national assets. "We all expect businesses to protect our sensitive information," Sen. Charles Grassley (R-Iowa) told an audience at Iowa State University in 2014. "But, we as consumers simply can't stick our heads in the sand and assume that we don't also share some responsibility. The fact of the matter is that there are simple steps that can be used to strengthen the security of online information."

It's a motivation problem, with cyber attackers and criminals enjoying an abundance of incentives: Cyber saboteurs can unleash terrible high-tech mayhem; cyber crooks can make enormous illicit profits. Deterrence, detection, and law enforcement are still spotty or nonexistent in cyberspace. Even worse, it may be easier and cheaper for honest citizens and companies to absorb the attacks—even if they do gradually expose our nation to possible catastrophe.

Technologists say the problem is that business executives and government representatives aren't listening to—or paying for—the skilled technology experts who could apply solutions. Experts in security technology and processes look around the meeting halls during cybersecurity conferences sponsored by the government and they see mid-level corporate managers, vendors pushing their products, lawyers worried about liability, and lobbyists worried about government rules. They don't see very many of the people who actually devise cybersecurity solutions down in the corporate boiler room or at research universities. Some are in the hall, to be sure: the veterans of the Y2K scare in the late 1990s and the people who built up frontline cybersecurity structures like the U.S. Computer Emergency Response Team. But those folks are outnumbered and underrepresented in this policy discussion, in their own eyes.

There's no disputing that cybersecurity is a process problem: Entities, ranging from major corporations to small companies to government offices, need to empower someone at a high, influential level with responsibility for ensuring that the enterprise as a whole accounts for the cybersecurity of all the component parts.

The government and private sector response to cybersecurity challenges is often shockingly inept. But trying to identify root causes triggers defensive reactions, finger-pointing, and endless disputes in policy circles. That helps explain why cybersecurity is such a difficult issue for the U.S. political system to sort out. Politicians hear mixed messages on the nature of the problem and on the business community's needs and responsibilities. Is it a military or a law enforcement problem? Is it industry's responsibility to secure cyberspace, or is it government's?

The answers easily fall into the "all of the above" category.

As politicians and policy stakeholders struggle to define the problem, they naturally struggle to spell out what "success" might look like. "Attacks averted" is an extremely hard metric to produce. A successful cyber breach, in fact, actually might demonstrate the process is working as planned. Attacks and breaches will occur; the policy goals, therefore, must be based on management and mitigation.

That, however, is an extremely hard argument to make, convincingly, in political circles. And yet, there is truth to it.

The underlying policy challenge, according to Dave Oxner of the Securities Industry and Financial Markets Association, is getting the government side, the private sector, and the public all to realize that cyber risks can be mitigated but not eliminated. "We need to change the mindset that this can be solved," Oxner said. A longtime congressional aide before moving over to the financial sector, Oxner could testify on both the difficulty of selling that message and on how difficult it is to actually get solutions, even partial solutions, through the political process.

As a result of this unavoidable ambiguity, politicians and policymakers often fall back into preconceived answers formulated in response to entirely different questions: We need regulation, for instance, or we need tax breaks. But whatever the answer, it has to fall within the jurisdiction of my congressional committee!

Cybersecurity, as a policy issue, also frequently lands next to the unsettled debate over the government's anti-terror surveillance powers. The conflation of the two issues is often, but not always, an unfair distortion. But it makes the development of national cybersecurity policies a delicate dance through privacy and civil liberties issues, with all of the accompanying political fireworks.

Policy development on cybersecurity inches through the process at glacial speeds that would dismay any self-respecting tech entrepreneur. As perhaps should be expected, Congress chews over policies, but can't keep up with the policy demand. The tech sector offers brilliant products, including security systems. Its major customers in the private sector—manufacturers, bankers, everyone else—engage on the issue and show flashes of innovative and organizational brilliance. But keeping pace with the cyber challenges and attacks is a daunting, expensive prospect as the bad guys get their hands on the same technological innovations that fuel economic growth.

Time is working against our political system writ large: the elected officials, the federal bureaucracy, and the industry stakeholders who interact with government over cybersecurity on a daily—if not hourly—basis.

In the face of such a monumental challenge, the political system's response has been muted, and perhaps even negligent. What exactly has government done to protect cyberspace and what are our elected officials doing?

And why is cybersecurity policy so hard to make? The warning flags are clear, so this is not a problem sneaking up on the nation. There won't be a "cyber Pearl Harbor" for one simple reason: In this case, we see the enemy fleet just off our shore and can hear the opponent's attack bombers warming up their engines.

Technological tools and computer network security doctrines and guides are available to counter these attacks. Increasingly, the will is there too, at the highest levels of government as well as in corporate boardrooms. But transferring tools and desire into effective policy doesn't come easily. There are legal, political, and financial barriers; there are philosophical differences to bridge and gaps in awareness and comprehension. As we shall see, the nation is only just beginning a journey into a policy realm unlike any other seen before.

As befits a great democracy, the U.S. strategy on cybersecurity, such as it is, is a compromise between the demands for security and for economic and personal liberty. The current operating philosophy underlies a "voluntary" cybersecurity strategy in which industry has much responsibility and a degree of flexibility, while government maintains much coercive power that it exercises cautiously, for now.

The system is voluntary because political efforts to establish a mandatory regime of cybersecurity controls for industry failed. But even hardcore opponents of command-and-control government regulation concede that more must be done, particularly in the private sector.

"[T]he risk calculus some private-sector entities employ does not adequately account for foreign cyber threats or the systemic interdependencies between different critical infrastructure sectors," Director of National Intelligence James Clapper warned lawmakers in September 2015. But was building defenses against foreign enemies really the responsibility of the private sector? Many on the industry side argued that they were being placed in an unprecedented position of responsibility to perform a national security function.

Clapper wasn't finished with his stinging critique of the private-sector targets of cyber attacks. "The muted response by most victims to cyber attacks has created a permissive environment in which low-level attacks can be used as a coercive tool short of war, with relatively low risk of retaliation," he told the lawmakers.

The result of this push and pull has been a sometimes strange amalgamation of private-sector initiative and government guidance and threats. It has played out at agencies such as the National Institute of Standards and Technology, the Federal Communications Commission, and the Federal Trade Commission. It has played out—incompletely—on Capitol Hill.

Congress's inability to put a legal stamp on a national cybersecurity strategy and philosophy permitted federal bureaucracies and activist agencies to set the policy course, often with industry hanging on desperately. It also spurred cottage industries around business-sector sharing of cyber threat indicators, for instance, and groundbreaking initiatives from places like the insurance sector. It motivated major industry groups to produce strategies and self-policing tools to encourage cyber best practices for warding off hacks and monstrous cyber attacks.

But is a semi-voluntary approach to securing cyberspace going to be effective? And if it isn't, can the U.S. political system manage to respond and recalibrate?

Is there an alternative?

1

"CARRY OUT OUR DEMAND IF YOU WANT TO ESCAPE US"

I am sympathetic to Sony's situation. The hit they have sustained from a perception and a cost perspective is substantial. But if there is one good thing to come of all this, I hope it is the increased awareness of how serious this problem is. It is not a problem to be solved, but one to be managed, and if we are going to do that, we need to take action today. The Internet was not built with security in mind, but security must be on our minds going forward.
—Rep. James Langevin (D–Rhode Island),
co-chairman, Congressional Cybersecurity Caucus,
December 22, 2014

By late 2014 and early 2015, lawmakers on Capitol Hill were getting restless about cybersecurity and that posed both a danger and an opportunity for the Obama administration.

For almost two years congressional squabbles and distractions left the White House firmly in charge of cyber policy. In 2013, President Barack Obama signed an executive order on cybersecurity that unfurled a panoply of initiatives at the Departments of Commerce and Homeland Security, and throughout the government.

Most significantly, it directed the National Institute of Standards and Technology to build a "framework of cybersecurity standards," which was released February 12, 2014, and instantly became the focus of government–private sector interaction on cyber policy.

But one year later members of Congress were already clamoring for results, even lawmakers who were anxious to preserve the collaborative approach embodied in the framework.

"And the problem right now is simple," Sen. Bill Nelson of Florida, the top Democrat on the Senate Commerce Committee, said at a hearing in early 2015. "As strong as the framework is, and as much as I trust that companies and industry sectors are working towards adopting it, there is no way to actually verify that progress. . . . How [can] you say everything's working?"

Dr. Charles Romine, director of the NIST Information Technology Laboratory, gamely tried to address the impatience. "We're one year in, we haven't seen an entire culture shift, but the conversations are taking place," Romine told Nelson and other senators on the Commerce Committee. Moreover, industry's willingness to engage and actually move on the issue of improving cyber defense was "astonishing," he added.

Romine, and NIST, enjoyed tremendous respect in Congress. But scientists tended to get trampled when impatient lawmakers began chasing an issue.

Democrats, including consumer-rights firebrand Sen. Elizabeth Warren (D-Massachusetts), in the fall of 2014 sent sharply worded letters to sixteen banks and other financial firms asking for details on their cyber breach experiences.

The hacks kept coming. One of the Department of Homeland Security's own contractors was breached. The Postal Service revealed a breach in November 2014. The "cloud" was hacked and nude celebrity photos came tumbling out. Home Depot said 56 million credit and debit card numbers and 53 million e-mail addresses were exposed in a hack on its network. The hack at the health insurer Anthem struck close to home for many consumers and employees of the federal government.

The crime wave was beginning to make cyberspace look and feel as dangerous as New York City's streets in the 1970s.

And then there was Sony Pictures.

In the late fall of 2014, the movie studio was preparing to release *The Interview*, a clownish farce about a fictional assassination attempt against North Korean leader Kim Jong-un. A group calling itself the Guardians of Peace first sent e-mails trying to blackmail the studio, then began disabling computers and destroying data on Sony's computer networks, leaking embarrassing information about the company and its executives, and threatening violence against American moviegoers. U.S. law enforcement agencies quickly traced the attack back to North Korea.

"As a result of our investigation, and in close collaboration with other U.S. government departments and agencies, the FBI now has enough information to conclude that the North Korean government is responsible for these actions," the bureau announced on December 19, 2014.

The FBI offered a nod to Sony Pictures for swiftly notifying law enforcement about the breach. "Sony reported this incident within hours, which is what the FBI hopes all companies will do when facing a cyber attack," the FBI said in its statement. "Sony's quick reporting facilitated the investigators' ability to do their jobs, and ultimately to identify the source of these attacks."

But Sony Pictures co-chairwoman Amy Pascal was mortified by leaked e-mail exchanges in which she made jokes about Obama with racial overtones. She would lose her job in the uproar.

All of Sony Pictures would be mortified when Obama publicly lambasted the studio for delaying the release of *The Interview*, suggesting the company had abandoned American principles in a cowardly retreat.

"We cannot have a society in which some dictator someplace can start imposing censorship here in the United States," Obama said at an end-of-year news conference. The president spoke on the same day the FBI identified North Korea as the culprit in the Sony Pictures attack.

"Because if somebody is able to intimidate folks out of releasing a satirical movie," Obama said, "imagine what they start doing when they see a documentary that they don't like or news reports that they don't like."

To many on the business side, the president's comments came off as blaming the victim, a common industry refrain when companies were vilified after hacks.

Sen. John McCain (R-Arizona), soon to take over as chairman of the Senate Armed Services Committee, laid blame at the president's own feet, saying the Obama administration had failed to articulate a policy of deterrence against cyber foes.

The episode triggered concerns among cybersecurity experts and policymakers that went far beyond the fate of a silly movie or even the threat to the First Amendment or determining the proper response to cyber blackmail.

It wasn't a "cyber Pearl Harbor," but it gave hints at the destructive potential of cyber attacks. And the North Koreans, while active players in the cyber-war space, were not even considered top-tier combatants by cybersecurity authorities. If a peeved minor power could attack a company in the United States, make it flinch in the face of violent threats, and spill the secrets in its computer files, what kind of damage could the big players—say, China, Russia, or Iran—render if they really wanted to do so?

"Sony really threw the administration for a loop and showed significant gaps in the policy," said a financial-sector expert on cybersecurity. The Sony Pictures attack demonstrated how cyber vulnerabilities almost anywhere could have a dramatic impact on the United States as a whole. It also suggested that the Obama administration's overall cyber strategy had "varsity" and "junior varsity" components: Critical infrastructure like power systems was varsity; the retail economy was important, but not in such a life-threatening way.

In October 2014, before Sony Pictures, the administration announced plans for a "summit" with financial-sector and technology industry leaders to address consumer data security issues. The plan was to show off tools being developed by the government and private sector to confront all of those annoying, costly hacks at places like Home Depot, Target, Neiman Marcus, and so many others. The event would be oriented around the administration's "BuySecure Initiative" aimed at preventing identity theft in commercial transactions and protecting citizens' personal data during interactions with the government. It was to be an important "junior varsity" event, though the administration certainly didn't phrase it that way.

The White House realized it had to broaden the summit's scope and related policy steps following the violent cyber attack on Sony Pictures. Almost immediately the administration began work on a new executive order on cybersecurity, this one addressing the sharing of cyber threat indicators between government and the private sector. The White House planned for a major rollout around the annual State of the Union address in January 2015; the promised summit would follow in February, almost two years to the day from release of the Obama administration's first cybersecurity executive order.

Those hacks at JP Morgan, Target, and other companies might elicit a quick look and then a collective yawn from most of the public, and not much more from Congress.

Sony Pictures was just a movie studio, and yet the cyber attack there quickly became a public sensation and preoccupied the policy discussion in Washington. There was a sense of outrage at a brazen foreign attack, it was relatively easy to understand, at least in its consequences, and it was scary.

Sen. Ron Johnson (R-Wisconsin), who would ride the Republicans' November 2014 electoral victory into the chairmanship of the Senate Homeland Security and Governmental Affairs Committee, told InsideCybersecurity.com that the hack had upended his plans.

"Before Sony, I thought we'd have a little time to address other issues," Johnson said in a late December interview. "But I want to take advantage of the public awareness" generated by the cyber assault on Sony.

The restlessness, and anxiety, wasn't confined to Capitol Hill. It was particularly acute across the Potomac River at the Pentagon.

"The country is more vulnerable than it should be," Gen. Martin Dempsey, chairman of the Joint Chiefs of Staff, said in a February 2015 speech.

Dempsey wasn't so worried about movie studios. He was worried about what North Korea or China or some other adversary could do to Internet service providers or the civilian electricity companies that supplied all of his domestic military bases.

"And I'm telling you this because it's not a military issue uniquely or solely," Dempsey said in that speech to an audience in Texas. "Ninety percent of my logistics enterprise, 90 percent of . . . our ability to flow forces and to distribute this incredible network of aircraft that we have— 90 percent of that rides on commercial Internet providers. And so if they're vulnerable, I'm vulnerable. And I don't like being vulnerable."

As lawmakers reorganized and launched the new 114th Congress in January 2015, the Obama administration prepared to get out in front, again, with the new executive order on information sharing and a package of legislative proposals on cybersecurity issues. The administration was doubling down on its cyber strategy.

Congress was welcome to play in the cybersecurity space, the White House seemed to be saying, but we like our approaches much better than anything you can offer.

With a nudge from the Sony Pictures affair, a lame-duck session of Congress passed a flurry of minor cyber bills in December 2014. These measures tidied up government lines of authority for addressing cyber issues and gave a stamp of approval to what the executive branch was already doing. Five cyber bills were signed into law as the 113th Congress expired, essentially housekeeping measures on government roles, research, and hiring cybersecurity personnel.

They were important as foundations, and they showed that Congress could actually pass bills with "cybersecurity" in the title. That was never a sure thing after the notorious leaks by fugitive ex-National Security Agency contractor Edward Snowden revealed previously unknown details about the scope and often embarrassing substance of U.S. government electronic surveillance.

But business groups like the U.S. Chamber of Commerce, and many of their allies on Capitol Hill, wanted something more, a new law that would clear the way for better information sharing on cyber threats between the government and industry, and among companies themselves. Liability protection was the key. This was the top cyber policy priority for much of the business community, and had been for several years.

It made sense and the administration didn't disagree with the need for such a law. The government often had information on imminent cybersecurity threats, but what it could share with the private sector was limited by law or national security constraints.

On the other side, U.S. businesses had technical clues that could help thwart or limit the damage from a cyber attack—whether it was a nation-state sponsored act of aggression or a criminal hack. But industry was often reluctant to share those clues amid fears of possible legal liability. The perceived risk of government penalties, shareholder lawsuits, and public disclosure dominated the discussions among corporate executives, security officers, and lawyers whenever information sharing came up.

Phyllis Schneck, the Department of Homeland Security's top cybersecurity deputy during Obama's second term, saw firsthand how companies hesitated before sharing timely data on cyber threats during her previous career as a senior security executive with McAfee.

"The next day we were not able to share information about certain oil and gas companies in the sector being targeted," Schneck testified before a congressional panel in 2013, describing an episode faced by McAfee's security professionals. "Our lawyers didn't let us because they worried we'd get sued the next day if the stock prices of the energy sector went down."

A small number of very large companies were engaged in extensive sharing by 2013, but that could provide only a partial view of the threat environment. The question, an industry source said, is "How do you get the thousands of other companies over the hump so they'll participate? How do you allow the government to really pull the pieces together?"

There were limits on what industry could and would share on its own, with no further guidance and protection from government. Those exemptions from lawsuits, regulatory action, and public disclosure were incentives only government could provide. "We need many more private entities participating but that won't happen without liability protection," the industry source said.

Determining the appropriate level of liability protection, while ensuring the sanctity of privacy and civil liberties, hobbled efforts to pass a cybersecurity information-sharing bill in 2012, 2013, and again in 2014.

The Obama White House simply wouldn't support the leading congressional proposals to address the issue, which would have provided extensive legal immunity for companies engaged in the sharing of cyber threat indicators. Despite its public embrace of the need for an information-sharing law, White House cybersecurity coordinator Michael Daniel signaled in January 2014 that the administration was in no hurry to back information-sharing legislation.

Daniel told audiences he wanted to "really drill down" on the policy changes that were actually necessary to spur more sharing. "Everyone loves information sharing," Daniel said, "and no one knows what it means."

Before signing off on any legislation—and giving away a valuable incentive such as liability protection—the White House wanted to understand "the core barriers" to information sharing and what could be addressed unilaterally through executive action.

"What information do we need to move between government and the private sector?" Daniel asked. "Or between companies? First we need to make it more specified, then we need to make it automated."

Daniel put together "a small group" of staffers to work on information-sharing policy questions. He wanted to engage in a "structured conversation with industry . . . [and] avoid unintended consequences and figure out what the real barriers are," Daniel said.

That did not suggest a speedy embrace of the legislation, or ready acceptance of industry's prescription for addressing cyber problems.

A bill championed by Intelligence Chairman Mike Rogers (R-Michigan) passed the House twice with a solid bloc of Democratic votes. Known as CISPA, for the Cyber Intelligence Sharing and Protection Act, it didn't pass the White House test for ensuring the protection of privacy and civil liberties. The Snowden leaks, beginning in June 2013, spelled doom for that bill.

"Snowden killed information sharing," said Brian Finch, a Washington, DC, attorney. Finch was an adamant supporter of Rogers's information-sharing bill, but said Snowden's inflammatory disclosures about government cyber-snooping poisoned the well for all kinds of cyber legislation.

Snowden's leaks, Finch observed, had little or nothing to do with the type of information-sharing legislation industry was seeking. But they created a political environment of heightened sensitivity that made it impossible to get near the issue. Skeptics looked at CISPA and other proposals and asked: What exactly would the government and big corporations be doing with the data they wanted to share, behind a wall of legal immunity and a shield from the disclosure requirements of the Freedom of Information Act?

Sens. Dianne Feinstein (D-California) and Saxby Chambliss (R-Georgia), the leaders of the Senate Intelligence Committee, produced a cybersecurity information-sharing bill in the summer of 2014 that they thought would meet the demands of the White House and soothe privacy concerns stoked by the Snowden leaks.

They were wrong.

Their bill, the Cybersecurity Information Sharing Act, or CISA, passed the Senate Intelligence Committee by a twelve-to-three vote on July 8, 2014. The overwhelming bipartisan vote for the bill was hailed by groups including the U.S. Chamber of Commerce, the American Bankers Association, the Financial Services Roundtable, energy groups, manufacturers, and other industries on the cybersecurity frontlines.

In the House, Rogers slapped his hands together, disavowed any pride of authorship and said he would gladly bring the Feinstein-Chambliss bill to the House floor. If, that is, they could get it through the full Senate.

"We had to make compromises between what the business sector wanted and what the privacy folks wanted," Chambliss told reporters after the committee vote. "Now we think we have a done a very good job in achieving compromises on significant issues. Will there be complaints? Sure. Because it's not perfect for anybody."

One complaint was over Feinstein's decision to hold the vote behind closed doors, even though everything in the bill would be publicly released and other congressional committees were discussing the exact same issues in open session. Supporters of the bill said opponents were exaggerating its flaws and misrepresenting its impact on citizens' privacy and civil liberties. The secret markup did little to ease those concerns, even if it was standard operating procedure for the congressional intelligence panels. It wasn't standard operating procedure for a broader audience where buy-in was needed before this legislation could move any further through Congress.

The seeds of the bill's ultimate demise were evident in those three lonely votes against it in the Senate Intelligence Committee.

"We agree there is a need for information-sharing between the federal government and private companies about cybersecurity threats and how to defend against them," Sens. Ron Wyden (D-Oregon) and Mark Udall (D-Colorado) said in a joint statement after the vote.

But Snowden's baleful influence was hanging over the bill.

"However, we have seen how the federal government has exploited loopholes to collect Americans' private information in the name of security," Wyden and Udall said. "The only way to make cybersecurity information-sharing effective and acceptable is to ensure that there are strong protections for Americans' constitutional privacy rights. Without these protections in place, private companies will rightly see participation as bad for business."

The senators added: "We are concerned that the bill . . . lacks adequate protections for the privacy rights of law-abiding Americans, and that it will not materially improve cybersecurity. We opposed the bill for these reasons, but we stand ready to work with our colleagues to address its shortcomings."

The third no vote came from Sen. Jay Rockefeller (D-West Virginia), though he never publicly acknowledged it. Rockefeller was retiring at the end of the year, so he could've said anything he wanted to say about what happened in the Intelligence Committee. But he was a senator from the old school and why have a secret vote if you're going to talk about it?

What Rockefeller said publicly, on multiple occasions, was that corporations didn't really need all that liability protection they were clamoring for.

Wyden was an iconoclastic voice on the Intelligence panel and, along with Udall and Rockefeller, uncompromising on civil liberties issues. The Intelligence Committee as a whole was much more favorable than Wyden, Udall, and Rockefeller to the views of the intelligence services like the National Security Agency.

By the terms of their membership on the secretive committee, there was often little they could say in public about its work. But because of the nature of the Senate, the three could cause massive headaches on the Senate floor for the bill's sponsors. With Democrats fearing catastrophe in the upcoming elections, Senate Majority Leader Harry Reid (D-Nevada) showed no interest in dealing with the Feinstein-Chambliss bill, or the divisions it caused within his own caucus, in the fall of 2014.

Feinstein, a twenty-two-year Senate veteran, knew that moving major cybersecurity legislation was a long shot. But she was a powerful figure in the Senate, who built up reservoirs of respect for taking on difficult issues, like the federal ban on assault weapons in the 1990s. As a longtime member of the Intelligence Committee, she wasn't afraid to stand up for the National Security Agency, which didn't endear her to civil liberties groups. Snowden was a traitor, in Feinstein's eyes, not some kind of self-styled hero of the U.S. Constitution.

She characterized her committee's cybersecurity bill as a first step "in a very difficult area." The policy would evolve and be revisited, she stressed. But the first step was needed, and quickly, to begin reorienting the government and industry's resources and thinking toward this cybersecurity challenge.

Her homestate *Los Angeles Times* editorialized against the proposal.

"Although the bill . . . is better than the House proposal and some of the previous versions, it still leaves too many openings for personal information to be shared with government agencies that don't need to see it, and that could use it for too many purposes beyond cybersecurity," the

Los Angeles Times wrote. "In fact, it requires that information shared with the government be sent automatically to the Department of Defense and, presumably, the National Security Agency, given the latter's interest in cyberattacks. For that reason, it feels too much like a bill to deter hackers by expanding the surveillance of ordinary Internet users."

Feinstein responded forcefully in a letter to the *Los Angeles Times*. "First, the legislation is purely voluntary," she wrote.

"Second, the bill already includes numerous privacy protections. These include requirements that companies strip out personally identifying information before sharing, that the government destroy information it receives after a specified time and that the information sharing program is reviewed by the Privacy and Civil Liberties Oversight Board, inspectors general and many others."

On Capitol Hill, Feinstein expressed hope that the bill would move to final passage and asked for patience as cybersecurity officials tried to implement a complex policy.

Her patience with privacy advocates, on the other hand, was beginning to wear thin. The privacy community, and trial lawyers, wanted "more, more, more," she said in an October 2014 speech at a U.S. Chamber of Commerce cybersecurity conference.

Feinstein and Chambliss felt they had bent over backward to accommodate privacy concerns. After all, the criminal hacks, cyber espionage, and waves of attacks were a far greater threat to privacy than law enforcement activities. Now, Chambliss complained to InsideCybersecurity.com after a Ripon Society breakfast, the privacy and civil liberties folks were moving the goal posts "a little bit."

Groups like the American Civil Liberties Union (ACLU) and Center for Democracy and Technology were unapologetic.

Gabriel Rottman of the ACLU said the Feinstein-Chambliss bill would allow "auto-sharing" of cyber threat information among various federal agencies "without any mitigation or 'sorting' by DHS."

By contrast, Rottman and others felt they received a better bargain on privacy and civil liberties protections from both the House and Senate homeland security committees.

The small-bore bills mentioned earlier were mostly the work of those homeland security committees rather than the intelligence panels. They may have been "low hanging fruit," as some in industry dubbed them, but they were a big deal in the way they established a Department of Homeland Security entity, the National Cybersecurity and Communications Integration Center (NCCIC), as the forum for sharing cyber threat indicators between government and the private sector.

The NCCIC (pronounced N-KICK in policy circles), could receive threat indicators from industry and go through steps to ensure the elimination of personally identifiable information before that data went to intelligence services or law enforcement. That scrubbing stage was critical to the Obama administration and online privacy advocates.

The Feinstein-Chambliss bill allowed direct information sharing, with liability protection, between industry and other government entities beyond the NCCIC, including the intelligence community and FBI. The senators said multiple privacy safeguards were included. Industry said having multiple avenues for private sector-to-government sharing was crucial and would allow existing cybersecurity relationships to flourish and fight the bad guys.

The ACLU saw it differently.

"So," Rottman said, "you're talking about the entire SIGINT, HUMINT (military and civilian), counterintelligence, and federal law enforcement communities receiving this information either automatically or permissively (and without any check in the law)."

Rottman added: "There's potentially a serious amount of communications content that the government would be unable to get without a subpoena, court order, warrant or other process that will flow freely to the government under this new privacy exception."

What followed were five months of on-again, off-again discussions involving the White House and Feinstein, Chambliss, Rogers, and Dutch Ruppersberger, the top Democrat on the House Intelligence Committee. Chambliss and Rogers were retiring at the end of 2014 and Ruppersberger expected to be "term-limited" off the intelligence panel. All were desperate to get an information-sharing bill into law before they left.

The White House declined official comment on the Senate Intelligence Committee-passed bill, even though it had formally threatened to veto the House-passed version by Rogers and Ruppersberger. An unnamed "senior official" told Information Security Media Group in July 2014 that privacy issues must be resolved before the administration could support Feinstein-Chambliss.

Publicly, administration officials pointed favorably to those small-bore bills produced by the House and Senate homeland security committees and the Senate Commerce Committee, the housekeeping measures that would put into law things the Obama team was already doing.

"While deliberations continue on other areas of cybersecurity, don't wait on areas where there is consensus," Department of Homeland Security undersecretary Suzanne Spaulding urged senators in September 2014.

In December 2014, that's exactly what happened. The Obama administration-backed bills, reflecting Obama administration policies, passed both the House and Senate without debate and were signed into law. Lobbyists and lawmakers said the bills represented a series of "first downs" on cyber policy, incremental progress down the field.

The Obama administration praised Congress for its work and, just slightly disingenuously, urged Congress to take the next step and pass a cyber information-sharing bill.

"One of the things in the new year that I hope Congress . . . is prepared to work with us on is strong cybersecurity laws that allow for information sharing across private-sector platforms, as well as the public sector, so that we are incorporating best practices and preventing these attacks from happening in the first place," Obama said at his 2014 end-of-year news conference.

New Republican chairmen at both the House and Senate intelligence committees, and the new Republican chairman of the Senate Homeland Security Committee, were promising to do just that. House Homeland Security Chairman Michael McCaul (R-Texas), who deferred on the issue to the House Intelligence Committee in 2014, by December was already writing his own information-sharing bill with liability protection for industry.

Jurisdictional fights on Capitol Hill might be in the offing, but the issue was already engaged by the close of 2014.

And once again, the Obama administration would move to get out in front of Congress. The administration prepared its executive order and legislation on information sharing, as well as new law enforcement tools to fight hackers and a proposal for a national consumer data-breach notification law.

And, in a bit of déjà vu, administration witnesses and the leaders of the House and Senate homeland security committees seemed to share at least some common ground on information-sharing during the first cybersecurity hearings of the new 114th Congress. By contrast, the administration appeared to be turning a cold shoulder to the intelligence committees in both chambers.

Congress had been working on all of these issues in fits and starts, but the administration had its own timetable. Why wait for them?

2

THE FIRST CYBER PRESIDENT

It's the great irony of our Information Age—the very technologies that empower us to create and to build also empower those who would disrupt and destroy. And this paradox—seen and unseen—is something that we experience every day.

—President Obama, May 29, 2009

In April 2009, news reports revealed that cyber intruders were detected maneuvering through the computer systems that run the great American electricity grid, the power system that lights our cities and charges our laptops. The *Wall Street Journal* said the hacks originated in Russia, China, and other countries. What was the point? They were preparing the ground for a future war. In a hypothetical conflict between the United States and China, the grid would be target number one. The adversary would attempt to plunge the United States into darkness. And in 2009, such an attack would carry a high probability of success.

President Obama publicly claimed ownership over the cybersecurity issue in a seventeen-minute speech to a White House audience on May 29, 2009. The top news story that morning concerned whether nominee Sonia Sotomayor had the right temperament to serve on the Supreme Court. A few articles mentioned that Obama would make a cybersecurity speech that day; most of those focused on whether he would name a "cyber czar."

The stock market was on tenuous footing and the U.S. economy was shaky following the collapse of the previous year that helped catapult Obama into office. The economy was priority number one for the Obama administration, but the new president saw cybersecurity as a foundational issue and an existential challenge to be confronted immediately.

"It's no secret that my presidential campaign harnessed the Internet and technology to transform our politics," Obama said that day in May. "What isn't widely known is that during the general election hackers managed to penetrate our computer systems."

The issue had the president's personal attention, but addressing cybersecurity would require nothing less than a cultural change, a dramatic evolution in the public's conception of cyberspace. The problem, in part, was people: the daily practices and habits of consumers, employees, profit-driven business executives, and budget-conscious bureaucrats.

It was technological, in the rapid dissemination of tools that could be used to pilfer and destroy, as well as in the very construction of an Internet economy with insufficient consideration to security.

It was a military/diplomatic problem with poorly defined rules of engagement or standards of conduct. And it was a political problem, as the executive branch and Congress groped for appropriate answers within governing systems not designed to confront a challenge that showed no regard for lines of authority or jurisdiction.

Obama was clearly intrigued by this challenge and was well-aware of the dangerous state of the playing field, former administration officials would say. The president and other policymakers knew there were three grades of "bad" when it came to cyber attacks.

The nation and its citizens were vulnerable in each category: the common, though quite sophisticated, cyber thievery; cyber espionage carried out by the vastly talented armies and intelligence arms of China, Russia, and Iran, and aimed at America's secrets, its infrastructure, and, for often mysterious reasons, even the personal data of its citizens; and then there was "the Big One," the cyber attack built to destroy and perhaps kill.

The threat was overshadowed during much of the first decade of the twenty-first century by two wars in the Middle East. But even as the George W. Bush presidency was engulfed and defined by those wars, the forty-third president was also intrigued by this new front in cyberspace and Bush's White House would get the policy gears moving on cybersecurity.

Director of National Intelligence (DNI) Mike McConnell briefed Bush on the severity of the cyber challenge, particularly the vulnerability of the defense industrial base to cyber attacks. That got the president's attention and DNI McConnell was ordered to come up with a plan. "President Bush was very easy to persuade on national security issues," commented one source active on cyber policy within the Bush II White House.

Mike McConnell put Melissa Hathaway in charge as Cyber Coordination Executive and director of a first-ever interagency task force on the issue. The task force included the departments of Defense, Homeland Security, and Treasury; the FBI; and other agencies. Members devised a "one team, one fight" strategy that the president and all of the cabinet secretaries signed off on over the summer of 2007. Hathaway and her colleagues put together a strategy to get the entire program funded in an unprecedented way: as a single budget item even though it cut across agencies.

"If you killed funding for one part, you'd have to zero everything out—that was my strategy to ensure that Congress didn't pick and choose, because that wasn't going to work," Hathaway recalled. "This was one team, one fight."

In January 2008, President Bush signed two policy directives that would establish for the first time a "Comprehensive National Cybersecurity Initiative." It was classified secret and revealed to lawmakers only in closed settings. That reflected the security-minded atmosphere of the time, but it also fueled lawmakers' interest in putting together a cybersecurity policy that the public could understand and, hopefully, support.

One of President Obama's earliest moves on cyber was to publicly release a description of the 2008 directives, signaling at least a new atmosphere around cybersecurity policy discussions. But the policy pieces developed by the Bush team would heavily influence Obama's approach.

In particular, the Bush initiative called for strenuous efforts to secure the government domain along with policies to increase "situational awareness," encourage new "leap-ahead" technologies, and define the federal role in protecting critical infrastructure, which was, of course, mostly in private hands.

After at least 150 briefings, Bush administration officials persuaded Congress to go along with upward of 80 percent of the program elements in the budget that year, according to Hathaway. The foundation for engaging on cybersecurity policy was now in place for the first time in the executive branch.

As a bookend to the year 2008, the Center for Strategic and International Studies (CSIS) produced a nonpartisan report on cybersecurity for the forty-fourth presidency that would provide more pieces of the policy template for the new administration.

The commission that wrote the report, "Securing Cyberspace for the 44th Presidency," was co-chaired by Reps. Michael McCaul (R-Texas) and James Langevin (D-Rhode Island), along with Scott Charney of Microsoft and retired Air Force Lt. Gen. Harry Raduege.

CSIS's own James A. Lewis was the project director.

The report became a well-thumbed desktop reference for Obama's policy advisers and industry leaders alike, and commission members would play important roles in the coming years.

McCaul, a conservative Texan and former federal prosecutor, became a key cybersecurity policy liaison on Capitol Hill for an administration generally viewed by Republicans—especially Texas Republicans—with hostility. Charney was a frequent witness at congressional hearings on cyber policy and a point of contact for the administration in the tech community. Lewis would help make CSIS one of the premiere locales for the cybersecurity dialogue that Obama hoped to foster among government, industry, academia, and others.

The ninety-six-page CSIS report emphasized the need for government-industry partnership on cybersecurity and to develop regulations for critical infrastructure. The report had an animating effect within the new White House and many of its conclusions would feed directly into Obama's first legislative proposal on cybersecurity in 2011. That included a regulatory aspect that would be swept under the rug after a historic run at cyber legislation collapsed in the Senate at the end of 2012.

As the 2008 election neared, Hathaway was assigned to the transition team developing policy books for either Obama or Republican nominee John McCain. She created a catalogue of what the George W. Bush administration had done on cyber, and worked assiduously to ensure that cybersecurity was listed as one of the top three priorities in the separate transition books on policy issues facing the Department of Defense, Department of Homeland Security, and the FBI.

After his election, Obama kept Hathaway in the White House and placed her in charge of a pivotal sixty-day review of cybersecurity policy. Hathaway was an American University graduate who studied advanced strategic issues at the U.S. Armed Forces Staff College. She brought a ferocious passion to the task and liked to say she was running the cyber-security initiative like a business. That is, it was as if she were spending her own money: There would be no waste, no diversions into extraneous areas, and every aspect of the policy would be meticulously accounted for and documented.

Her review fed directly into President Obama's May 2009 speech.

"The Bush guys laid the foundation and Obama was first to build off that. . . . There was momentum in the work by Melissa and so the Obama administration was off to a running start," said Bruce McConnell, who served as chief cybersecurity strategist at the Department of Homeland Security during Obama's first term and into his second.

Based on the Hathaway-led sixty-day review, the White House would propose a strategy grounded in partnerships with the private sector, measurable results, research into new technologies, and a commitment to protecting citizens' online privacy even as the government and industry battled cyber attackers.

The demands of this approach could be contradictory at times, and there was a fierce battle within the administration and on Capitol Hill between what Bruce McConnell characterized as "command-and-control" and "laissez-faire" factions.

The debate began during the final years of the George W. Bush administration and carried over into the new administration. Some of that was traditional turf squabbling among agencies, some was deeply philosophical, and some a potentially toxic combination of the two.

A top cybersecurity official at the Department of Homeland Security (DHS), Rod Beckstrom, resigned in March 2009, citing the National Security Agency's dominance over cyber policy. The nation's founding fathers would surely object to this subjugation of a civilian agency to military control, Beckstrom told United Press International.

But Philip Reitinger would assume some of Beckstrom's responsibilities and help secure DHS's place in the government's cybersecurity hierarchy over the next two years. Reitinger fit well into the young Obama administration's cast. The one-time member of the Vanderbilt fencing team knew his way around the skirmishing in both government and the highest levels of the technology sector: He served in both the defense and justice departments, and had been a senior strategist at Microsoft. Reitinger was also a graduate of Yale Law School.

Hathaway herself would resign in August 2009 after waiting for months to get the nod as Obama's White House cybersecurity czar, a position that would go to Howard Schmidt, another former Microsoft executive.

"There were some differences between the Obama and Bush approaches," said Bruce McConnell, who helped coordinate the federal response to the Y2K challenge during the Bill Clinton administration, and returned to government eight years later to work on Obama's cyber policy team from a billet at the Department of Homeland Security.

From her perspective, Hathaway said the new administration tilted so heavily toward economic considerations that it was unwilling to take tough stances on national security. "It was a challenge," she said. "The Clinton [administration] veterans in the new administration saw all the benefits of the Internet and thought the Bush people were overblowing the security threat."

John Brennan, then as White House homeland security adviser, was a champion of cybersecurity issues in the early days of the Obama administration, according to Hathaway. But it was a complicated issue to explain within the White House policy councils, and economic adviser Lawrence Summers almost always had the last word. "Economic growth trumped national security," Hathaway said. "It was a source of tension. They had Recovery Act money to spend and they didn't want to hear things like 'Don't build a smart grid without security.' It was hard to bring the economic people [in the White House] along on cybersecurity policy."

Bruce McConnell downplayed tensions between security and economic issues. "The Obama administration was more sensitive to privacy and there was more emphasis in the Bush administration on traditional security roles," McConnell said. "But Bush left the institutional framework for developing the policy, and the approach was similar."

Most importantly, McConnell said, many officials in both administrations were grasping an emerging consensus on the direction the government should take with cyber policy. Part of that was a decision regarding what exactly the government should focus on protecting. Was it "lifeline industries" that provided the blood and oxygen to the rest of the economy? Or was it all of critical infrastructure? The Obama administration decided on the latter, and the result would be a cybersecurity strategy of use to virtually every type of business.

American military leaders weren't necessarily in agreement with that consensus, which was taking shape in the private sector and among civilian security officials. In fact, the generals and admirals warned loudly that the private-sector operators of power plants and other critical infrastructure weren't doing nearly enough to protect cyberspace. The military was reliant on these private companies to power its bases and provide other services.

The sense of vulnerability in the uniformed ranks was acute and—as evidenced by Gen. Dempsey's remarks in early 2015—would remain so throughout the years of the Obama administration. Military leaders believed electric power companies and others simply must be required to follow increasingly stringent, mandatory standards.

Many of the bright new faces and canny cyber veterans in the Obama administration countered with a practical argument: How could top-down regulations possibly keep pace with this threat?

And to top it off, 85 percent or more of the nation's critical infrastructure—the vulnerable power lines, financial systems, wireless networks, and water works—was in private hands. A regulatory regime would have to be massive, and would enormously intrude into U.S. business operations.

The new administration had to quickly resolve this debate between "command-and-control" and "laissez-faire" factions. It was dawning on many that it was a mistake to view cybersecurity as a technical issue. It was about people, process, and commitment. Some policymakers got that distinction during Obama's first term, and some didn't.

By the spring of 2009, the Obama administration was ready to embark on what a few of its cyber policy leaders referred to as the "laissez-faire" approach to cybersecurity, a colorful if not-fully complete description of a strategy it would follow through two terms. Regulation was part of the equation under the Obama team's initial approach, but it wasn't solely or even predominantly based on setting hard and fast cybersecurity rules for industry.

On May 29, Obama announced that he would create a new White House position, cybersecurity coordinator, but didn't name the person who would take on the role. Of greater importance, Obama for the first time publicly sketched out his administration's cybersecurity philosophy.

"This new approach starts at the top, with this commitment from me: From now on, our digital infrastructure—the networks and computers we depend on every day—will be treated as they should be: as a strategic national asset," Obama said. "Protecting this infrastructure will be a national security priority. We will ensure that these networks are secure, trustworthy, and resilient. We will deter, prevent, detect, and defend against attacks and recover quickly from any disruptions or damage."

Obama announced that a comprehensive cyber strategy would be developed in collaboration with industry and other stakeholders. He released a report detailing the findings of Hathaway's review and how the administration would proceed.

"One element of the strategy clearly differed from that established by the Bush administration in January 2008," the *New York Times* reported. "Mr. Obama's approach is described in a 38-page public document being distributed to the public and to companies that are most vulnerable to cyberattack; Mr. Bush's strategy was entirely classified."

Obama also wanted to trumpet the role—and leadership—of the private sector in his cyber strategy.

"[W]e will strengthen the public/private partnerships that are critical to this endeavor," Obama said. "The vast majority of our critical information infrastructure in the United States is owned and operated by the private sector. So let me be very clear: My administration will not dictate security standards for private companies. On the contrary, we will collaborate with industry to find technology solutions that ensure our security and promote prosperity."

That was welcome news to industry lobbyists, many of whom saw the new Obama administration as regulation-happy and predisposed to fight the business community rather than partner with it. Despite the words, industry leaders still saw the lurking hand of regulation behind the administration's highly public embrace of private-sector solutions. Many thought Obama's commitment not to regulate was strictly aimed at his friends in the tech sector, not the broader business world.

On the other side of the policy fence, the military brass continued to lament the seeming inability of civilians to confront the true danger.

"Let me also be clear about what we will not do," Obama said. "Our pursuit of cybersecurity will not—I repeat, will not include—monitoring private sector networks or Internet traffic. We will preserve and protect the personal privacy and civil liberties that we cherish as Americans."

Media coverage of the speech was mildly positive, as was the business community's public reaction. But the mainstream media wasn't quite convinced there was any substance there. Who was this coordinator? Would she, or he, have clout? *Time* called the whole speech "cyberhooey."

It was often the case in cyber policy that the "forest" eluded media and political onlookers who fixated on individual "trees" like the desired personality in a White House cyber coordinator or the lack of meaty rules or even tax breaks to get businesses out of their seats and working to build a stronger cyber network.

Cybersecurity was complicated, tangible signs of progress were elusive, and it was often difficult to distill cyber policy developments into interesting news stories. But in the spring of 2009, even some astute security experts were questioning whether the Obama administration's entire exercise was more public relations than cybersecurity. The administration was asking industry, and Congress, to stand up and take responsibility for cybersecurity, but all of these stakeholders were extremely curious to see what the administration itself was bringing to the game.

Obama provided the beginning of an answer in his May 2009 speech. But the new administration wasn't quite ready to drive policy, yet. Roles within the executive branch still needed to be fleshed out, and members of Congress still planned to define the policy direction. It would take several years, actually, for the White House to slide into the driver's seat.

3

SIRENS ON CAPITOL HILL

People say this is a military or intelligence concern, but it's a lot more than that. It suddenly gets into the realm of traffic lights and rail networks and water and electricity. . . . It's not a problem that will ever be completely solved. You have to keep making higher walls.
—Sen. Jay Rockefeller (D-West Virginia), interview with the
Washington Post, April 1, 2009

Congress was trying to play catch-up, but the cyber threat environment was already quite severe in 2009, evidenced by a numbing succession of breaches and attacks.

As senators knew and a Senate committee report would later point out:

In 2007, TJX Corporation—the parent company of T. J. Maxx and Marshall's department stores—experienced a breach in its wireless networks that left about 45 million credit and debit card numbers exposed to theft and cost the company about $25 million to resolve. In early 2009, Heartland Payment Systems learned they had suffered a breach that allowed criminal access to in-transit payment card data, requiring them to spend $32 million in the first half of 2009 to resolve.

The hacks were hitting American citizens in their wallets.

There were other, even more troubling episodes for lawmakers to ponder. As noted, foreign powers were detected mapping out the computer controls for U.S. electricity grids and natural gas pipelines. There was nothing hypothetical about the threat posed by such activities: The Russian military successfully used cyber attacks as part of its 2008 invasion of neighboring Georgia.

Later in 2009, Google and other tech companies would be hacked in a sophisticated operation allegedly originating from China. American citizens' browsing habits and every other aspect of the cyber lifestyle were now the targets of bad actors with unknown, but clearly sinister, motives.

It would take several more years before the idea took hold on Capitol Hill that "higher walls" probably weren't the answer to the nation's cybersecurity challenge. But in the spring of 2009, many influential lawmakers were aware of the growing cyber threat as the new administration settled in, and were sorting through legislative responses. The problem was, with dozens of committees claiming jurisdiction over cybersecurity, urgent economic issues taking precedence, and the White House focused on passing health reform, cybersecurity was at the top of very few to-do lists for members of Congress.

It was also still a bit of a mystery issue to many in Congress. Republican lawmakers fretted over giving President Obama a "kill switch" to cut off the Internet. Democrats postulated elaborate regulatory schemes. Lawmakers like Sens. Jay Rockefeller (D-West Virginia), Olympia Snowe (R-Maine), Joseph Lieberman (D-Connecticut), and Susan Collins (R-Maine) were eager to develop a major bipartisan policy response. Intelligence Committee leaders like Dianne Feinstein and Saxby Chambliss in the Senate, and Mike Rogers and Dutch Ruppersberger in the House, wanted to move quickly on legislation to get ahead of the threat.

The need for a legislative response was becoming increasingly apparent. But as always, the jurisdictional lines in Congress played an outsized role in structuring the response. Rockefeller and Snowe, in April 2009, came out first with a bill designed to fall within the Commerce Committee's jurisdiction. The bill called on the National Institute of Standards and Technology to create industry standards on cybersecurity that could be audited, a huge red flag for business groups. It called for a certification process for cyber professionals, another red flag. Some lawmakers were also fixated, for a while, on creating a congressionally chartered White House office on cybersecurity as a way of elevating the issue as a policy priority. It would also give congressional committees access to a White House official who was subject to confirmation—and to lawmakers' demands for testimony. The Obama White House didn't much care for that idea, or for Congress telling the White House how to organize itself.

After several rounds of revisions, the Senate Commerce Committee passed its cyber bill in March 2010.

Members of the Senate Homeland Security and Governmental Affairs Committee believed the first pieces of legislation should clarify the Department of Homeland Security's (DHS) cybersecurity responsibilities. Collins's staff took the first shot at drafting language in 2009, beginning a collaborative if lengthy process with Lieberman's staff. It would take over a year before the committee was ready with a bill.

Senate Majority Leader Harry Reid (D-Neveda) began showing interest in the issue as the commerce, homeland security, and intelligence committees got rolling. Reid didn't know much about cybersecurity, but he did know that conflicting jurisdictional claims by committees could create major problems for leadership. At one point he suggested a special committee on cybersecurity, but the chairmen of the existing committees quickly shot down that idea. The next step, then, was for the commerce, homeland security, and intelligence panels to resolve their differences, which they would do in a long series of negotiations. Still, Senate leaders wouldn't find time on the floor for cyber legislation during a lame-duck session at the end of 2010.

The new year brought a new Republican majority to the House, which was the most direct political fallout from President Obama's health care push and the emergence of the conservative Tea Party. Amid this, the Obama administration was putting the final touches on its own bill defining the government's response to cybersecurity and charting a path forward, based on the principles outlined by Obama in the spring of 2009. The Obama administration's bill was finally unveiled in May 2011. It took nearly two years to write—"about twice as long as it should have," according to Bruce McConnell, the former DHS cyber strategist.

But it strived to encompass the latest thinking and consensus on cyber policy, and, in the words of White House officials, kick off an unprecedented dialogue on the topic. The administration had identified the need for a collaborative approach, at least in rudimentary form, and now wanted to encourage the political process to catch up. That would take some time; four years and two election cycles later, many of the same aspects were still subjects of debate.

The Obama bill would update laws on securing the government's own computers and networks. It called for a uniform national data-breach reporting standard and tougher criminal penalties for hackers. It called for

DHS to offer assistance to industries that asked for help in securing their networks and called for voluntary information sharing.

That was a mixed bag from businesses' perspective; the voluntary aspects were welcome, while the others were sources of division or outright opposition within industry. Language on "robust privacy protection" triggered a bout of nerves: A whole new framework on privacy protections and civil liberties threatened to upend established law and precedent and create a legal nightmare for industry groups, at least in their eyes.

But here's where the Obama administration plan went completely off the rails, from industry's perspective:

"The Administration proposal requires DHS to work with industry to identify the core critical-infrastructure operators and to prioritize the most important cyber threats and vulnerabilities for those operators," according to the May 12, 2011, White House fact sheet.

"Critical infrastructure operators would develop their own frameworks for addressing cyber threats," according to the White House. And the hook: "Then, each critical-infrastructure operator would have a third-party, commercial auditor assess its cybersecurity risk mitigation plans. Operators who are already required to report to the Security and Exchange Commission would also have to certify that their plans are sufficient."

A mandatory auditing process was akin to regulation from industry's perspective and would lead inevitably to a costly, check-list approach that was the antithesis of good cybersecurity practice.

Further, the White House said,

> A summary of the plan would be accessible, in order to facilitate transparency and to ensure that the plan is adequate. In the event that the process fails to produce strong frameworks, DHS, working with the National Institute of Standards and Technology, could modify a framework. DHS can also work with firms to help them shore up plans that are deemed insufficient by commercial auditors.

The bill was a big bite, coming at a time when ascendant Republicans were muscling Congress away from such comprehensive approaches to virtually any policy question. Obamacare, the signal issue of the previous two years, convinced a new generation of Republicans that big was bad when it came to legislation. The Obama proposal would not find a sponsor for its bill on Capitol Hill, but elements would be folded into the bipartisan work underway in the Senate.

The new year was, in fact, bringing a new interest in cybersecurity from House Republican leaders. They empowered a task force on cybersecurity that ultimately would tilt the playing field in ways that reflected the new majority's bite-sized approach to legislation.

The 2011 House Republican Cybersecurity Task Force included twelve Republican lawmakers and was chaired by Rep. Mac Thornberry of Texas. The group's report, released in October 2011, drew an enthusiastic response from industry as a departure from the command-and-control approaches being pursued in the Senate and contemplated by both the Bush and Obama administrations.

The GOP report urged leaders of the relevant House committees to move legislation that would encourage development of voluntary industry standards on cybersecurity, backed by incentives including liability protection. An agency such as the National Institute of Standards and Technology should collaborate with industry on developing the voluntary standards. Regulations on information security should be streamlined. Government grants and tax credits should be tweaked to encourage better cybersecurity practices. Congress should consider the role of insurance.

Targeted, limited regulation—promulgated by *existing* regulators— could be considered in certain critical infrastructure sectors, the Republicans said. Congress should discuss the desirability and usefulness of mandatory reporting of cyber incidents. The task force also suggested a uniform national consumer data-breach notification requirement to replace the dozens of state laws on the topic.

The government's own systems needed better security. And criminal law should be updated. Information sharing should be encouraged, again, with liability protection.

It was mostly a forward-looking report—many of the recommendations would be melded into Obama's 2013 cybersecurity executive order, and many would still be the subject of debate in Congress in 2016.

But significantly, it did not call for a restructuring of congressional jurisdiction and responsibilities. After all, the majority-ruled House didn't face the same kind of obstacles that routinely stifled legislative efforts in the Senate. And the GOP leadership didn't need to kick up a fight with the newly empowered Republican committee chairmen who had received their coveted gavels just months earlier. Those chairmen wouldn't be interested in ceding any of their jurisdictions, in any policy area.

There were sound reasons for the task force's decision on congressional restructuring. Two House committees—Intelligence and Homeland Security—ultimately would be able to fulfill their responsibilities under the report. But it was a missed opportunity to put Congress ahead of the curve on cyber policy, for once, by facing up to the fact that jumbled and duplicative lines of authority made it impossible to craft a comprehensive cybersecurity strategy—in the Senate or in the House. Cases in point: The tax-writing Ways and Means Committee never got around to taking up the recommendations on tax breaks; the commerce, banking, and judiciary committees couldn't settle on data-breach legislation; and the committees with jurisdiction over particular critical infrastructure sectors rarely if ever discussed the cybersecurity regulations applicable to those industries.

A month after the task force report, in November 2011, House Intelligence Committee leaders would follow up with their first pass at a cybersecurity information-sharing bill. Intelligence Chairman Rogers and ranking member Ruppersberger collaborated on a measure that would allow sharing of cyber threat data with federal agencies including law enforcement and the National Security Agency. It allowed the government to use the data for a variety of law enforcement purposes beyond cybersecurity, and gave a scant nod to the privacy and civil liberties concerns that would ultimately shape the debate over information-sharing legislation. The key, to industry, was liability protection for companies that shared data with the government.

This was a security bill, with a law enforcement component, its sponsors believed. But cybersecurity, like the Internet itself, always spawned unexpected issues and policy twists.

The Cyber Intelligence Sharing and Protection Act, H.R. 3523, known as CISPA, would pass the House in April 2012 on a 248 to 168 vote, with strong industry support and vehement opposition from the online privacy community. Voting in favor were 206 Republicans and 42 Democrats; 28 Republicans and 140 Democrats voted no.

Immediately, it was linked to other debates in the unsettled areas of Internet rights and privacy.

"Did Congress really not pay attention to what happened with SOPA?" the Web site TechDirt asked, incredulous that lawmakers were treading this turf after a recent net-roots uprising thwarted congressional plans to pass a "Stop Online Piracy Act" bill supported by much of the business community.

"Like SOPA early on, it appears that Congress simply takes for granted that if you call something one thing (whether it's 'stopping piracy' or 'protecting cybersecurity') no one will bother looking at the details to realize just how problematic the bill actually is," TechDirt wrote. "But this is a bad, bad bill, which effectively will lead to significant spying on Internet usage and private communications by the government with little to no oversight—and that includes not just domestic law enforcement, but military spying as well," according to TechDirt. "The whole thing is absolutely crazy (especially when there are less onerous bills that are much more sensible)."

Web sites with names like "TechDirt" didn't have a lot of currency among lawmakers prior to the online piracy "SOPA" debate, and the concerns cited still didn't particularly register in congressional committees worried about providing security tools for companies. But more easily recognizable names like the American Civil Liberties Union (ACLU) were weighing in as well on the Rogers–Ruppersberger bill.

"We urge you to amend the bill to include explicit collection and use limitations and rigorous oversight mechanisms," the ACLU wrote in a letter to Rogers and Ruppersberger just before the House vote. "In the absence of such amendments, we will vigorously oppose this legislation as inconsistent with the long tradition of Americans' reasonable expectations of privacy."

Rogers was a media-savvy former FBI agent and Ruppersberger was a street-smart politician from Baltimore. So it was a bit surprising to find the duo so utterly tone deaf on the politics of this one, at least in 2012. But they wised up quickly and over the coming months would propose dozens of changes to the legislation to meet privacy advocates' concerns. It was to no avail: CISPA had joined SOPA as fighting words for many in the digital-rights community.

The White House didn't like the CISPA bill either, citing the scale of liability protection and the scope of information that could be shared, and threatened to veto the measure. The White House also, very publicly, wanted to be seen as the champion of online privacy and civil rights. It was a matter of legacy.

The veto threat for the first time drew a line in the sand between the White House and lawmakers over cyber policy, but it would never have to be carried out. In the Senate, Intelligence Chairman Feinstein had drafted a similar information-sharing bill in early 2012, and merged it into the effort to advance a comprehensive cybersecurity bill along with Lieberman, Collins, Rockefeller, and Tom Carper of Delaware.

The broad Senate bill included elements on federal network security, the role of the Department of Homeland Security, and the responsibilities of critical infrastructure operators. Language on emergency powers spurred fears of an Internet "kill switch" that the sponsors scrambled to swat away. Likewise, Lieberman and others stressed it was a completely different animal than the SOPA anti-piracy measure that had stoked so much antipathy. But separating cybersecurity issues from other policy disputes related to the Internet would be an enduring problem for sponsors of cyber bills—in 2012 and in subsequent years.

On January 30, 2012, the U.S. Chamber of Commerce (Chamber) weighed in with the first of two letters to Senate leaders that would largely frame the debate that year. Majority Leader Harry Reid would fume for years afterward that the Chamber used its muscle to crush the legislation. But Matthew Eggers, a top cybersecurity strategist and lobbyist at the Chamber, recalled that the business group was trying hard to reorient the discussion, not kill legislation.

"It wasn't the typical Hill letter," he said several years later. "It was lengthy and we wanted to be very clear that this [emerging bill] would be something we'd challenge. But we didn't want to 'just say no.'"

What Chamber Vice President R. Bruce Josten spelled out in the letter to Reid and Minority Leader Mitch McConnell (R-Kentucky) was the consensus position of much of the business community on the appropriate approach to cyber policy. First, business leaders were worried that Reid was using the sense of urgency around cybersecurity to push through a bill with vast, untold consequences for the economy. "Rushing forward with legislation that has not been fully vetted would be a major mistake," Josten wrote.

"Since 2009, the Chamber has consistently said that it will support legislation that is carefully crafted and narrowly tailored toward effectively addressing the complex cyber challenges that businesses are experiencing," Josten wrote. "However, the Chamber strongly opposes new regulations and compliance mandates that would drive up costs and misallocate business resources without necessarily increasing security. More top-down regulations would significantly restrict necessary opportunities for the public and private sectors to work together collaboratively against our mutual adversaries."

Instead, the Chamber called for voluntary information sharing with legal protection, improvements to the security of the government's own networks, a national research and development project, public awareness campaigns, and "international cooperation against cybercrime."

Tellingly, many of these positions would be part of a broad consensus within the coming years. But a trust deficit in 2012—attributable to stakeholders on all points of the political compass—meant policymakers focused more heavily on differences than areas of agreement.

"The Chamber takes the issue of cybersecurity very seriously, and we believe that the best solution to improving America's cybersecurity will not be found in additional regulation," Josten wrote.

> Instead, legislation should support efforts that genuinely enhance collaboration between industry and government partners and that foster mutually agreed-upon solutions targeted at increasing collective security. Layering new regulations on critical infrastructure will harm public-private partnerships, cost industry substantial sums on compliance, and not necessarily improve economic and national security.

In February, Lieberman held a hearing on the Cybersecurity Act of 2012, the joint work of the leadership of his Homeland Security Committee, Rockefeller's commerce panel, and Feinstein's Intelligence Committee. The maverick Connecticut senator's tone was a bit defensive, according to CSOonline.com, a CXO Media Company.

"Lieberman began the hearing by stating that the proposed law wouldn't tell companies how to meet security requirements, that they could use any hardware or software they chose, and that all indications were that the law would enhance security innovations," CSO's Wayne Rash reported. "Lieberman also said that despite rumors that have been circling the Internet, there is no Internet 'kill switch' in the bill that would allow the President to seize control of the Internet, and there is nothing in the bill that touches on the balance between intellectual property and free speech. He specifically pointed out that there is nothing related to the ill-fated SOPA and PIPA bills in his legislation."

Collins echoed Lieberman's assessment and appeared to put the bill on solid bipartisan footing. But many Republicans backed by their leader, Sen. McConnell, would object to both the substance of the bill and Democratic plans for quickly moving it across the floor.

Sen. John McCain (R-Arizona) signaled the brewing opposition during that first hearing in February. McCain, along with Sens. Charles Grassley (R-Iowa), Kay Bailey Hutchison (R-Texas), Saxby Chambliss (R-Georgia), Mike Enzi (R-Wyoming), Jeff Sessions (R-Alabama), and Lisa Murkowski (R-Alaska), had all written to Majority Leader Reid ahead of the hearing warning him not to short-circuit the process by quickly bringing the bill to the floor.

McCain said the measure would turn the Department of Homeland Security into a "super regulator."

McCain's problems with the bill ran deep, according to the *Daily Caller* news site. "Additionally," McCain said at that first hearing, "if the legislation before us today were enacted into law, unelected bureaucrats at the DHS could promulgate prescriptive regulations on American businesses—which own roughly 90 percent of critical cyber infrastructure."

The Lieberman-Collins bill would go through several permutations in search of a formula that could pass the Senate. Before February was over, McCain and his GOP allies would put out an alternative bill, "SECURE IT," based on information sharing and voluntary collaboration. Ominously, cybersecurity had cleaved along largely partisan lines studded with a variety of philosophical differences. Partisan considerations and the substantive policy disagreements were defining the issue for lawmakers on Capitol Hill, despite the striking similarities in how a McCain, a Lieberman, or a Rockefeller would tackle the issue.

There was a general sense of agreement on the need for stronger criminal laws and better information sharing, and for government to get to work on shoring up its own networks and clarifying DHS authority. The need for government–private sector collaboration was readily apparent to everyone.

But all of that common ground couldn't make up for a crucial dispute: Should government ultimately have some kind of hammer to force private companies to better secure their own systems?

Obama administration officials in March held a secret briefing for senators, walking them through a mock cyber attack that cut off power to New York City. The scenario was frightening but didn't move the political needle. After months of stalemate, Lieberman, Collins, Rockefeller, and Carper offered a revised version of their combined cyber bill in July 2012.

"We are going to try carrots instead of sticks as we begin to improve our cyber defenses," Lieberman said in a statement to BloombergBusiness. "If that doesn't work, a future Congress will undoubtedly come back and adopt a more coercive system."

Bloomberg reported that the new version would "create a National Cybersecurity Council, led by the secretary of Homeland Security, to work with industry groups to develop voluntary standards on the best ways to defend against computer attacks. It would offer benefits, such as liability protection and expedited government security clearances, to owners of critical infrastructure who meet those standards, according to Lieberman's statement."

President Obama wrote a supportive op-ed in the *Wall Street Journal*. Privacy groups expressed satisfaction with the changes. But as Senate floor debate neared, it wouldn't be enough.

Former DHS official Paul Rosenzweig, writing for the conservative Heritage Foundation, said the voluntary aspects of the legislation were a fraud and painted Lieberman–Collins as outright regulation.

"The revised bill still requires the creation of industry best practice standards for protecting critical infrastructure," he wrote on July 23, 2012. "Instead of making those standards mandatory, it pushes the owners of critical infrastructure to adopt new 'voluntary' standards. Those incentives include liability protection, priority assistance for cyber threats, and access to classified information about threats."

The government shouldn't use access to threat information as a hammer to force adoption of the voluntary standards, Rosenzweig wrote. "Second, the liability protections provided as an incentive are far too weak. If a company adopts the voluntary standards, it could still be sued for consequential damages." Further, "voluntary standards would stifle innovation and likely be obsolete by the time they are written."

The kicker from Rosenzweig: "Finally, a voluntary standard system is a short step from a mandatory one. Senator Lieberman has already said that if industries do not adopt the voluntary standards, Congress will make them do so."

And, though Rosenzweig didn't mention it, the bill contained a carve-out for the information technology sector from regulatory and mandatory reporting requirements. "That embittered a lot of the other sectors and contributed to the hostility against the bill," a business source observed. Representatives of other industries lined up outside Senate leadership suites and the Homeland Security and Governmental Affairs Committee's offices in futile bids to obtain a similar exemption.

On the sidelines, Rockefeller and GOP Sen. Kay Bailey Hutchison of Texas were quietly discussing a way out of the political jam: a compromise legislative solution that would rely on the National Institute of Standards and Technology to develop a voluntary approach to boosting industry cyber standards. "This was going on under the radar," according to one source, a Senate aide at the time, "and it was largely unreported."

The growing partisan strife around the cyber legislation was drawing plenty of media attention though. Harry Reid on one side, and Mitch McConnell and John McCain on the other, exchanged accusations on what seemed a daily basis over who was stalling cybersecurity. In the midst of this, *Politico*'s Jennifer Martinez noted a call for calm from Hutchison.

"We do hope to come to terms with the bills," Hutchison told Martinez. "I think that everybody is serious about this, and there's no reason to start throwing political punches."

Unmentioned was that Rockefeller and Hutchison were trying to come to terms outside the main body of negotiations. The effort was "scuttled" by the prevailing politics of the Senate, the source said, "but that's where we'd end up in 2014."

On August 1, 2012, as the end neared for the Senate cyber bill, Rogers penned an op-ed in *Politico* ripping Senate Democrats and the president.

"The reason the Senate is likely to fail is many senators (along with the majority of the House) understand that massive federal regulation—particularly in this troubled economy—is the wrong answer to these problems," Rogers wrote.

"The Senate's inability to find middle ground here can be traced directly back to the president's failure to exercise serious leadership," Rogers charged. "The White House launched its push last May to get Congress to legislate on cybersecurity. The administration sent up a proposal that was so regulation-heavy and weak in other areas that not a single House or Senate member would support it."

Obama took his turn, posting a blog on the White House Web page that would also run in the *Wall Street Journal*. The cyber threat was real and the stakes were huge, Obama wrote. Comprehensive cybersecurity legislation was essential.

On August 2, the Senate voted fifty-two to forty-six on ending the GOP filibuster of the cyber bill, eight votes short of the sixty needed to advance the bill under the Senate's rules. Cybersecurity legislation was stalled and Congress headed home for its August recess.

The U.S. Chamber of Commerce was cast as the villain—or hero—of the episode.

"The politics of obstructionism, driven by special interest groups seeking to avoid accountability, prevented Congress from passing legislation to better protect our nation from potentially catastrophic cyberattacks," the White House said in a statement.

The *New York Times* reported:

> The bill's most vocal opponents were a group of Republican senators led by John McCain of Arizona, who took the side of the U.S. Chamber of Commerce and steadfastly opposed the legislation, arguing that it would be too burdensome for corporations.
>
> At a meeting last week, Mr. Lieberman got into an argument with Mr. McCain, his closest ally and friend in the Senate, about his opposition to the bill. Mr. Lieberman questioned why Mr. McCain was doing the bidding of the U.S. Chamber of Commerce and asked what Mr. McCain would say if the nation was crippled by a cyberattack.
>
> Mr. McCain angrily said his reputation on national security issues was unquestionable.

"The administration took something of a hands-off approach," Bruce McConnell said of the Senate end game that summer. "They didn't want to spend a lot of political chips on something that looked like it might be unsuccessful and was going to be unpopular with the private sector."

After Congress left town for its summer recess, the U.S. Chamber's cybersecurity policy team hammered out a twenty-three-page critique of the Senate bill. "We weren't just saying no because of regulations or because it would be too burdensome to deal with cybersecurity—that's a simplistic view," Eggers said later. "We wanted to say we were *already* being burdened, by cyber attacks, and our sectors—banking, chemicals, utilities—were *already* regulated on cyber."

The business community wanted to separate out and act on the information-sharing piece of the legislation. It wanted to maintain and enhance existing government-industry collaborations like the National Infrastructure Protection Plan, which might be marginalized by the approach in the Senate bill. The Chamber expressed deep alarm over giving the Department of Homeland Security regulatory authority.

The one place where DHS already tried to exercise such power—in the chemical sector—was an unmitigated disaster, the industry group said. The Chamber quoted Sen. Grassley saying he was "baffled why we would take an agency that has proven problems with overseeing a critical infrastructure and give them chief responsibility for our country's cybersecurity."

There would be a Senate re-do in the late fall, with similar results. The arguments were familiar, including a fight over the majority leader's insistence on restricting amendments.

On November 14, 2012, Reid brought the bill up again, but the motion to invoke cloture came up nine votes short of the sixty needed to limit debate. "The bill that was and is most important to the intelligence community was just killed, and that's cybersecurity," Reid said, according to the *Hill* newspaper. "Whatever we do for this bill, it's not enough for the U.S. Chamber of Commerce. So everyone should understand cybersecurity is dead for this Congress. What an unfortunate thing, but that's the way it is."

"Before the vote, Republican senators argued that Reid was playing politics by trying to jam the sweeping cybersecurity bill through the Senate without holding an open amendment process," the *Hill* reported. "They also argued that industry still held legitimate concerns with the measure and it would not adequately address the rising cyberthreat." The paper quoted Sen. Chambliss as saying: "Frankly, the underlying bill is not supported by the business community for all the right reasons. They're the ones that are going to be called to comply with the mandates and the regulations, and frankly it's just not going to give them the protection they need against cyberattacks."

When the Lieberman–Collins bill went up in flames on the Senate floor in late 2012, there were crocodile tears at the White House. Congressional Republicans had missed a chance to bolster the nation's cybersecurity, the White House would charge, perfectly content to pin the failure on GOP obstructionism. On the other hand, Congress's failure handed the ball to the president and he was ready to advance a cyber policy initiative with or without the legislative branch.

That was a happy, ironic outcome for the White House, which helped set the stage for this failure by steadfastly refusing to engage with the congressional Republican leadership. And Obama wasn't going to negotiate with McCain, his erstwhile presidential opponent, on cybersecurity either before or after the 2012 election. The politics of cybersecurity often could be subtle, but deep down, they were as bare-knuckled as on any other issue between the Obama White House and congressional Republicans.

For its part, the business community had dodged a potential regulatory bullet, but there wasn't much celebration over the fact. "We weren't spiking any footballs," said Eggers of the Chamber. "We still had the problem."

4

TO BUILD A FRAMEWORK

It is the policy of the United States to enhance the security and resilience of the Nation's critical infrastructure and to maintain a cyber environment that encourages efficiency, innovation, and economic prosperity while promoting safety, security, business confidentiality, privacy, and civil liberties. We can achieve these goals through a partnership with the owners and operators of critical infrastructure to improve cybersecurity information sharing and collaboratively develop and implement risk-based standards.

—Presidential Executive Order 13636, February 12, 2013

Was anything safe in cyberspace? The hacker group Anonymous seized the State Department's Web site in February 2013. Total hack attempts around the world crossed the 1 billion mark in 2012, NCC Group, the British security firm, reported in a study. The Internet was under siege.

By the beginning of 2013, the Obama administration was well on its way with an alternative plan for advancing the president's policy agenda on cybersecurity just as it was doing in other areas, such as immigration, where Republicans were blocking legislative progress. President Obama had just been re-elected to a second term, but the House of Representatives was in Republican hands and the Democrats' narrow majority in the Senate promised to keep the legislative process at a standstill.

The answer on cybersecurity would be Obama's Executive Order 13636, an ambitious, detailed policy document that spelled out the administration's cybersecurity principles and priorities. It was focused on protecting critical infrastructure but administration officials never hid the idea that this should be the basis for cybersecurity across the economy.

The executive order began taking shape in the late summer and early fall of 2012. The administration knew Obama's legislative proposal on cyber "was a dead letter," former Department of Homeland Security (DHS) official Bruce McConnell recalled. "But the ideas made it into the executive order."

Eggers of the U.S. Chamber of Commerce (Chamber) called the executive order "a graceful off-ramp to Plan B" following the failed legislative debate. "And Plan B was a winner."

The U.S. Chamber may have been battling with the administration across a broad range of policy areas, and delivered a heavy blow against the Senate cyber legislation the previous year. But the GOP-leaning business group's leaders chose to rally behind the president's approach to cybersecurity as embodied by the executive order. In fact, Eggers said, the administration's embrace of a strong private-sector role "allowed the government and industry to rally together."

The Obama administration had stepped away from a "top-down" approach, Eggers said, and of similar importance, was eyeing a strategy that would play well in the international policy arena. The U.S. approach, whatever it was, would set the tone for cyber policies across the globe; if the United States opted for a command-and-control system, other powers would do the same—and would create their own, rival regulatory regimes. U.S. business groups saw the prospect for multiple, conflicting regulatory requirements in different parts of the globe, at huge cost to American industries.

White House cybersecurity coordinator Michael Daniel organized listening sessions over several months with industry groups, online privacy advocates like the Center for Democracy and Technology, representatives of industry-based cyber information sharing and analysis centers, or ISACs, and any other stakeholder with a piece of the cybersecurity policy equation.

Daniel moved into the Executive Office of the President as cyber coordinator in 2012 after seventeen years at the Office of Management and Budget (OMB), replacing Howard Schmidt. Cyber policy initiatives had been lagging at the White House since the development of the ill-fated legislative proposal, and the policy area was in need of a jolt.

After largely ceding the issue to Congress—more specifically to Senate Democrats—cybersecurity had faded as a top-tier issue within the White House. "There was no unity of purpose within the administration or between the administration and Congress," Hathaway charged later. Amid other crises and substantial personnel turnover in the upper ranks of the national security team, cybersecurity wasn't consistently in the top-three security issues on the administration's radar between 2010 and 2012.

Daniel was an unlikely character to help deliver the needed jolt but he would play an instrumental role in bringing the issue back to the top tier of White House priorities. He had a master's degree in public policy and national security from the John F. Kennedy School at Harvard University. His undergraduate degree was from Princeton University in 1992. More surprising, perhaps, was his turn in musical theater with the Princeton University Players. He also practiced martial arts. Daniel appeared quietly at public events and his manner was deferential. However, the stage experience and martial-arts discipline provided effective tools in dealing with industry lobbyists and lawmakers.

Daniel was a budget guy, observers noted, not a cybersecurity guy. Perhaps that was a shortcoming from a technologist's viewpoint, but having someone in an influential spot who could protect cybersecurity funding priorities was definitely a plus. It also fit into the emerging mantra that cybersecurity was more a process and risk-management issue than a technology issue. If that was true, Daniel's OMB pedigree might make him the perfect candidate for the coordinator job.

Other personnel moves were afoot as the administration geared up for a White House-directed push on cyber in 2013.

Ari Schwartz moved from the Commerce Department to the White House to work on cybersecurity issues, particularly privacy aspects. He was an invaluable link to online privacy advocates, after spending twelve years as a senior leader at the Center for Democracy and Technology. Likewise, industry groups considered him a trustworthy and open-minded source within the White House. Schwartz, a 1993 Brandeis University graduate, would continue moving up the ladder by taking over as senior director for cybersecurity at the National Security Council (NSC) in early 2014, just as key aspects of the executive order were hitting the implementation stage.

Samara Moore, who specialized in systems and technology within the energy sector, was detailed to the NSC staff from the Department of Energy. Daniel, Schwartz, and Moore spearheaded upward of 1,600 "conversations" with stakeholders during development of the executive order.

There was substantial skepticism in the business community when the executive order effort got rolling in the fall, but one development in particular helped smooth the way for success. When a draft leaked out in November, industry groups were alarmed and asked for a chance to provide input. Daniel and the National Security Council staff agreed. "That was very positive and helped create trust," an industry source said.

Presidential Executive Order 13636 was signed by President Obama on February 12, 2013, a few months after cyber efforts fizzled on Capitol Hill. The order declared cybersecurity to be a top national priority and the president flagged the issue in his State of the Union speech that night.

"The cyber threat to critical infrastructure continues to grow and represents one of the most serious national security challenges we must confront," according to the executive order. "The national and economic security of the United States depends on the reliable functioning of the Nation's critical infrastructure in the face of such threats."

The executive order identified the economic infrastructure of the nation that was vulnerable to attack, "so vital to the United States that the incapacity or destruction of such systems and assets would have a debilitating impact on security, national economic security, national public health or safety, or any combination of those matters."

That could be electricity or natural gas systems, communications networks, the banking system and more.

The order called for increased information sharing on cyber threats between government and the private sector, and it ordered new "enhanced cybersecurity services" be provided to industry.

It included a lengthy section on protecting the privacy and civil liberties of Americans, an Obama administration mantra that would be repeated even more fervently after the Edward Snowden leaks began in June 2013.

And it called on the National Institute of Standards and Technology (NIST) to create "a baseline framework to reduce cyber risk to critical infrastructure."

The framework was to be flexible, cost-effective, and voluntary. Unspecified government-provided incentives would encourage its use by businesses. It would be developed in an open, collaborative process with industry and other interested stakeholders.

It would be completed within one year, by February 12, 2014.

Daniel, two weeks after the release of the order, stressed the importance of the private sector's role in making the whole thing work.

"I can't emphasize enough that it has to be a collaborative process. It has to be industry-driven," Daniel said at the annual RSA Security conference in San Francisco. "It won't work unless we get very heavy participation and really enthusiastic participation from industry."

The outreach to industry was key to the executive order's success, a telecom industry source said. "There was a desire for there to be minimum opposition and maximum support when the executive order came out. They accomplished that."

The order reserved the right to regulate, if necessary, "but they used the things that caused Lieberman–Collins to fail as positive lessons learned," the telecom source said. "They moved away from all that Lieberman–Collins stuff except in one small piece."

That would be section 9, which discussed that most vital of all critical infrastructure. The section required specific information from a handful of companies operating that vital infrastructure; the identity of the companies was a national secret. "Otherwise," the source said, "it was all consultative."

Creating a policy that assures security, resiliency, efficiency, innovation, and prosperity at the same time is difficult enough for the political machinery in the nation's capital.

Getting the private sector to "buy in"—to actually co-pilot a vast new federal policy initiative—is virtually unheard of. The first, and in many ways most important, question would be who was to lead the construction of the cybersecurity framework within the federal bureaucracy.

If it were a regulatory agency, industry would greet the endeavor with battalions of lawyers and a defensive mind-set that would probably doom the enterprise from day one.

"The administration wasn't going to put regulation in the E.O.," Bruce McConnell observed. "There is a regulatory dimension but it's written in a way that's less scary."

If it were the Department of Homeland Security, the initial skepticism and mistrust from industry and civil liberties groups alike might be too much to overcome. DHS would have an important role to play in carrying the plan out to the critical infrastructure sectors and in areas like exchanging information on cyber threat indicators. But it would not be the organization to build a cyber framework for industry.

Plus, Bruce McConnell said, DHS in early 2013 was still more of "an idea" when it came to cybersecurity; it didn't yet represent a real "capability" to take on immense new cyber responsibilities.

Instead, Obama's announcement in the winter of 2013 that he was handing responsibility for the heart of his cybersecurity program to an obscure federal agency in Gaithersburg, Maryland, was one of the most significant of his administration. It led to a framework of cybersecurity standards that guided government–industry relations on cyber in the coming years.

The telecom source said there was never any question that major industry groups would play ball on the executive order once they understood the administration's direction. The reason for the buy-in could be found in Obama's preamble to the executive order. "The president said the owners and operators of critical infrastructure have to be partners," the source said. "You can't do that and threaten a regulatory overhang at the same time."

The National Institute of Standards and Technology is a rare breed among government agencies: It's genuinely well-liked and appreciated among industry groups, academia, and members of Congress. It doesn't provoke jealousy or underhanded attacks from other government agencies because it's not a regulator and has no interest in bureaucratic turf wars.

Since 1901, NIST has shepherded the formulation of industrial measurements and standards. In the early 1900s that meant standardizing the length of a foot and the weight of a gallon. By the second decade of the twenty-first century, NIST was at the leading edge of research into nano technologies, advanced manufacturing, bioscience, and many other areas including computer security.

NIST is a part of the Department of Commerce. Tucked away on a large bucolic campus in suburban Maryland, it seems far from the cacophony and battles of the federal center of Washington, DC. NIST is a flyspeck on the federal government's organizational chart, an agency with a budget of $900 million in 2015 and employing three thousand people.

But in many ways, NIST is the little agency that could. Most importantly, it's an impressive and influential entity in the minds of every type of stakeholder who engages with the federal government.

It was the ideal entity to craft a cybersecurity strategy that would avoid the political pitfalls exposed in the recent Senate debate, while steering clear of traditional government–industry antagonisms. As the legislative effort began to crater in the summer of 2012, senators including Jay Rockefeller and Kay Bailey Hutchison suggested NIST might still play a key role here. By late fall of 2012, the administration officials working on the executive order, a poorly kept secret in government circles, had already decided on a major role for NIST.

NIST officially got things started in February 2013 by issuing a request for information on what it would take to develop a framework of cybersecurity standards reflecting industry's best practices. The request sought to establish a baseline for discussion by asking a series of questions about industry's current risk management practices, the existence and use of cybersecurity tools, and how various—and sensitive—privacy issues were currently being addressed. "We had a little bit of a runway to get started," an administration official recalled, saying the "RFI" was ready to go as part of a well-developed, "high-level" implementation plan.

The request was signed by Patrick Gallagher, NIST's director and the Commerce Department's undersecretary. Gallagher would leave NIST a year later, after five years at the helm, with the framework of cybersecurity standards as his crowning achievement. He was moving on to become chancellor of the University of Pittsburgh, where he earned a PhD in physics twenty-three years earlier.

But first, Gallagher would spend a year championing the framework to the public and Congress, and navigating the political shoals as everything from a government shutdown to the Edward Snowden affair threatened to push the process off course.

Gallagher was frequently the public face before Congress and in other high-visibility settings. Adam Sedgewick, NIST's senior technology policy adviser, was carrying the ball down on the field as the project lead for the framework effort. Sedgewick, a Princeton University graduate, joined NIST in 2012 after serving on an interagency information security council and for nine years as a staffer on the Senate Homeland Security Committee.

After college, Sedgewick found work, in the fall of 2001, as an intern in Sen. Joe Lieberman's office. On his third day, Sedgewick and many other staffers were sent home following the anthrax attack on congressional offices. With Lieberman's digs in the Hart Senate Office Building closed as hazmat teams scoured the building, Sedgewick and other staff were sent to temporary quarters in the offices of the Senate Governmental Affairs Committee, which Lieberman chaired. Sedgewick was able to make contacts and learn about the subject matter, and had an inside track when a staff position finally opened up on the governmental affairs panel, which would be renamed the Homeland Security and Governmental Affairs Committee in a post-9/11 reform.

E-government, information technology, transparency, and online security issues landed in Sedgewick's portfolio. It was heady stuff for a young staffer, but typical of how responsibility accumulates on the desks of twenty somethings in the nation's capital.

A decade later, Sedgewick, by then a senior NIST official, would be at the forefront of the showcase initiative within the Obama administration's cybersecurity strategy. His work at the Senate homeland security panel, where he was one of the few staffers who straddled both the security and the government affairs domains, would be invaluable in shepherding the cyber framework process. He "got" the security side, and he also understood how the governmental policy levers actually worked, and how to move around the political pitfalls.

Fast-forward to 2013. Just before the initial comment period closed, NIST would host the first "workshop" on the framework on April 3, 2013.

Over six hundred people filled the seats at the Commerce Department's ornate auditorium on Constitution Avenue in Washington, DC. Lobbyists and journalists leaned over seats to chat and try to figure out what this new process would be, and how they could get a piece of the action. Gallagher acted as a master of ceremonies, while officials from the White House, Department of Homeland Security, and NIST appeared on panels. Representatives from major corporations, trade groups, and critical infrastructure organizations made presentations.

It was a strategic device ingrained in the DNA of the Obama administration: Get the possible business-sector adversaries onstage—and on-board—for the program. In this case, the industry representatives' remarks would carry great weight throughout the process. Industry didn't

want a one-size-fits-all approach, or mandatory requirements. Cyber policies should be risk-based, outcome-based, and globally relevant. Companies needed liability protection.

As a full day of presentations progressed, NIST's Matthew Scholl had
a message for participants. "This is the last workshop where we talk *at*
you," Scholl quipped.

NIST didn't yet have a clear vision of what the framework would look
like, but it did have a pretty good idea of how the process should unfold.
Gallagher announced plans for three more workshops, which would be
true, roll-up-your-sleeves gatherings held on college campuses across the
country in the coming months.

"The framework will be drafted at these sessions," Gallagher told the
audience. This framework would address managing risks and cybersecurity metrics, and it would point to industry's own existing security standards. He sought to tamp down regulatory concerns expressed throughout
the day by some participants.

And he tried to give off a hint that the final product would be much
more powerful than just a collection of old standards. It needed to be a
meaningful tool that industry could embrace at a time when corporate
leaders were beginning to realize the need for action.

"When you go back to February 2013, one of the challenges was
administration-wide we knew there was a [cybersecurity] risk out there of
increasing complexity," NIST's Sedgewick explained to an audience two
years later. This risk was at long last setting off alarms within corporate
board rooms and even getting the attention of the general public.

Major U.S. banks were hit with a string of "distributed denial of service," or DDoS, attacks in the fall of 2012. "The volume of traffic sent to
these sites is frankly unprecedented," Dmitri Alperovitch, co-founder of-
CrowdStrike, told CNN *Money* at the time. The well-known security
analyst added, "It's 10 to 20 times the volume that we normally see, and
twice the previous record for a denial of service attack."

Around the same time, hackers got into an unclassified White House
network. Earlier in 2012, natural gas pipelines were the target. The threat
level was spiraling upward.

The government wasn't going to be able to tackle this growing threat
on its own.

"We at NIST were not developing the framework ourselves," Sedgewick continued during that 2015 appearance. "We were a convener in a

process that by its nature had to involve a lot of people. We thought industry could speak better to their needs than we could."

NIST had a century of experience in voluntary collaborations with industry to produce standards that would benefit companies, consumers, and the government. "We thought 'voluntary' broadened participation," Sedgewick said. "We didn't have to choose who was in and who was out."

The process of self-selection would begin immediately with the public comment period and that initial workshop at the Commerce Department. The language included in the first request for information represented "our best guess of what should be in the framework," Sedgewick told the crowd at the February 2013 workshop at the Commerce Department. But this was to be an industry work product, for and by the people who would use it in real life. Further, NIST—and the broader federal government— wanted this to be in the hands of critical infrastructure operators, not just the tech vendors who wanted to sell products to those industries.

Over 270 sets of comments flowed into NIST in April 2013. There were major trade associations representing great chunks of the U.S. economy. Universities and labs weighed in. Companies that had endured high-profile beaches—like Heartland Payment Systems—offered advice. Companies ranging from Microsoft to Verizon to small "mom-and-pop" shops had opinions and experiences to share, as did interests as varied as the Philadelphia city government, state regulators, and dozens of technology and security consultants.

It was a jumble of histories, suggestions, arguments, and offers. Fitting together the views of such disparate stakeholders was a daunting prospect. But Sedgewick and his colleagues at NIST saw the potential for strength in what could have been an indistinguishable roar of input.

What was taking shape before Sedgewick's eyes was a clearer picture of how each piece of the American economy leaned on the next piece, and so on, in a cybersecurity context.

"The interdependencies came up nonstop during the framework development," Sedgewick would recall in that May 2015 public discussion. "It threatened to be overwhelming but at the end of the day, bringing all the sectors together was very helpful."

And it led to an early determination that creating a common vocabulary around cybersecurity would be of immense value to industry stakeholders who were often confronting cyber challenges off in their own silos, generally unaware of their contemporaries' activities. Pulling each industry out of its silo and creating a cross-sector exchange would drive improvements across the economy, the NIST officials believed.

The comments began to tease out what industry wanted to see in a framework—flexibility, a global perspective, a grounding in risk management, and reliance on the numerous existing standards and best practices scattered across industry sectors.

There were gaps, too, chiefly in the areas of measuring success and ensuring the protection of privacy.

But what did all of this mean? The real-world applicability of a flexible approach or a risk-management strategy needed more work. And government and industry stakeholders would have to come to a consensus on what these terms and concepts really entailed.

In late May of 2013, NIST moved the cyber framework production to the campus of Carnegie Mellon University in Pittsburgh for the first of what would total four workshops on college campuses around the country during development of the framework. Carnegie Mellon approached NIST and offered to host the event, as would other schools in the coming months. But Carnegie Mellon was a fitting choice for the inaugural campus-based workshop: The university was home to the U.S. Computer Emergency Response Team, the granddaddy of integrated, government–private sector collaborations on cybersecurity. The campus teemed with veterans of the Y2K scare and many other, generally unknown cyber incidents and threats.

Over three hundred people gathered at the university's McConomy Auditorium for the first workshop on the road. Most were from the corporate chief information officer- or chief information and security officer-level. There was much talk about the need to get CEOs and business- and policy-side executives into the room.

NIST's Adam Sedgewick would later tell InsideCybersecurity.com that a key take-away from Pittsburgh was that risk management should be the underlying basis of the framework. "We got the message," he said. "Determining cost-effectiveness goes to the heart of risk management. But cost-effectiveness is very different for a large, multinational corporation and a small water utility."

Here NIST began sketching in basic elements of the framework, including the concept that it would be based on functions such as cataloguing assets and identifying threats. These would be supported by categories and subcategories of security standards developed by industry. There would be some method of identifying where a company stood in terms of cybersecurity maturity.

Rick Weber, who attended for InsideCybersecurity.com, said participants were nervous about DHS's role and concerned that this framework not conflict with their existing requirements. What incentives would exist for industry to adopt the framework, they wanted to know, and how would the government measure adoption? Could they be held legally liable if they didn't, somehow, adopt the framework?

There was plenty of room for industry anxiety around this government initiative, even if it was in the trusted hands of NIST. There was also plenty of anxiety on the government side.

The next stop for the NIST workshop road show was a three-day event beginning on July 10, 2013, at the University of California's beautiful, ocean-side San Diego campus. The University of California–San Diego was a powerhouse in computer sciences and engineering, and was pleased to donate time and space to the prestigious NIST initiative.

But the six weeks between Pittsburgh and San Diego were "the tightest of the entire process," one source recalled after the framework had been completed. In that stretch, NIST needed to put together the details for a productive conference even as it was developing the first draft of the framework. "It was a little nerve-wracking," the source said. "But San Diego was where the framework took shape and people started buying into it. We laid the foundation there."

The University of California–San Diego drafted an army of students to shepherd the five hundred technologists, consultants, security pros, industry lobbyists, and other stakeholders between classrooms overlooking manicured athletic fields and the Pacific Ocean. The energy, telecom, finance, technology, and defense sectors were heavily represented. Companies like Microsoft, Bank of America, Dow Chemical, Shell, and Raytheon had representatives on site. Students enrolled in summer classes might shoot a curious glance at the odd platoon of mostly middle-aged men in blazers and loafers strolling among them.

But the serene scene belied the urgency of the topic at hand. One security consultant, a California native clad in shorts, a beach shirt, and sandals, casually explained the high stakes to a reporter: A successful attack on the electric grid could kill 80 percent of the U.S. population.

The reporter laughed skeptically.

No, no, the consultant said, this threat is legitimate. He explained that the real-time delivery imperative of the modern U.S. economy meant that only days-worth of food and other essentials were available within reach of the population centers at any given time.

An electric grid knockdown would severely limit suppliers' ability to deliver food, medicine, and other goods. Water pumps would shut off, the transportation infrastructure would dissolve into gridlock. The all-encompassing Internet would be beyond reach.

It was hyperbolic, but it contained some truth.

Security pros of all stripes were deeply rattled a few months earlier, in April 2013, when someone fired bullets from a high-powered rifle into a Pacific Gas and Electric substation in Metcalf, California. Utility workers scrambled to contain the damage and valiantly prevented a disastrous blackout on the West Coast. It was a physical attack, but cybersecurity experts grasped the implications about the grid's vulnerabilities. Further, the gunman or gunmen were not apprehended, which only stirred up speculation that the attack was some kind of probing exercise that could be the precursor of something else entirely.

It was a dramatic reminder of the stakes. The actual content of the nation's cyber strategy, though, would be hammered out in a much more mundane way that reflected the often paper-dry process of creating policy.

Just days before the workshop, NIST posted what it called a draft outline of the "preliminary framework to reduce cyber risks to critical infrastructure." Reading through it had been the assigned homework for stakeholders, who now made up the audience sitting before an early morning panel of NIST officials. The officials opened the San Diego workshop with a first-ever walk-through of their vision for this still-nebulous framework.

After introductions by Dr. Charles Romine, the director of NIST's Information Technology Laboratory, and Sandra Brown, vice chancellor for research at the university, the show was handed over to the NIST officials who were actually running this process.

Sedgewick was the project manager, a star in government cybersecurity circles, who earned awards for his efforts. With him were Donna Dodson, Matthew Scholl, and Kevin Stine. Together with NIST's Jon Boyens, a telecom source observed, "You really had an alignment of the best people in government working on this."

Dodson was chief cybersecurity adviser and director of the National Cybersecurity Center of Excellence. By this time, she said she had been commuting to the NIST's Maryland campus from her home in Gettysburg, Pennsylvania, for twenty-six years.

She raked in awards for innovation and cybersecurity and was a walking representative of two important hallmarks of cybersecurity: The cyber profession had already become an economic ladder for many thousands of Americans, and cyber policy worked best when grounded in collaboration.

"Growing up in a modest household with parents who worked hard to support my sister and I, it never occurred to me that I would have the opportunity to work at a place like NIST," she wrote on a NIST Web site bio page.

> My father taught me to solve problems in a practical way and my mother always encouraged me to work hard in school. My parents grew up in West Virginia and had limited employment opportunities when they moved to DC. We would visit my extended family often and while we did not have much money I did not notice because we were just like everyone else in that community.
>
> When I first began my career at NIST in 1987, I was working on a master's degree in computer science. I did not have a background in computer security; however to the best of my knowledge, there were no courses or degrees in security.
>
> Miles Smid, head of the Security Technology Group in the NIST Computer Security Division hired me and was my first true mentor outside of my family. Miles would host discussion sessions every Wednesday where we would debate the fine points of cryptography. At that time, businesses were being transformed through information technology. However many business documents required a signature. Business applications were automated but when a signature was needed, a paper document was still required.
>
> We were able to apply cryptographic techniques to generate a replacement for the "wet" or hand written signatures. I worked with two federal agencies to demonstrate this capability and later helped them to create the first fully automated government business application using electronic signatures. While this is not the only time in my career that I helped to lead a team that started with a blank canvas and created a platform for innovation, it demonstrated to me the power of collaboration.

Scholl, another official who collected awards for his work, was the deputy division chief in the computer security division, and would rise to head the division in the coming years. Stine joined NIST in 2006 after four years as the chief information security officer at the Food and Drug Administration.

These four were lead carpenters who would help hammer together the framework. The audience of security experts, industry lobbyists, academics, privacy advocates, and other stakeholders were expected to produce the planks and the nails.

On the opening morning, the NIST team took the stage to explain the organizational structure they were considering for the framework. It was based on risk management, an important concept that NIST believed would put industry and government stakeholders on the same page in terms of approaching cybersecurity from an economically feasible perspective.

The NIST officials believed the framework should be broken into five core functions: know, prevent, detect, respond, and recover. These would be informed by categories and subcategories of specific actions entities should consider taking. It would also include three Framework Implementation Levels. There was a section addressed to senior executives and a user's guide.

This basic architecture would endure throughout the framework development process, but the wording and the specifics would evolve significantly as industry representatives got their hands on it. "Implementation levels" would spur a long-running debate and ultimately be refined into "tiers," something interpreted as less threatening, in a regulatory sense, to industry. The message to senior executives would vanish later in the process.

This workshop was about working, the NIST leaders emphasized, pointing to the 240-day deadline to produce a framework. "Welcome to day 148" since the president's executive order had launched the process, Scholl told the audience. "Ninety-two days left!"

After the opening panel, participants were assigned to eight teams and dispersed across the vast campus to classrooms otherwise quiet in mid-summer. Student volunteers lined the way, pointing the visitors to the right buildings and the right rooms. This was where the framework would be constructed, the central piece of President Obama's strategy to secure cyberspace.

"There seems to be a good practical hook to these discussions," Eggers said during a break. "It's much better than Pittsburgh, it seems productive. The process seems worthwhile so far."

Eggers had an idea on how it would be judged: "The key will be to get buy-in from a few big groups and companies," he said. "Then others will follow." The Obama administration was largely banking on the same concept.

The U.S. Chamber would be an instrumental player in determining whether to offer a blessing. Eggers was the Chamber's point person. He had a master's degree from George Mason University and an undergraduate degree from Indiana University—a polite, easy-going Midwesterner who liked to discuss the realities of cyber challenges outside the beltway with the Chamber's Main Street membership. For the average small-business owner, the cyber predicament was pretty straightforward: How do I find additional tools, resources, and time to deal with *this* problem? Eggers tried to bring the same sensibility to discussions with policymakers.

During one of the classroom sessions, he made clear what it would take to earn the Chamber's blessing: NIST had to produce a framework that precluded the need for dreaded regulation.

Officials from the Department of Homeland Security sat at the back of the classroom sessions, furiously scribbling notes on the discussions. They were an affable and earnest bunch, but their presence—actually, their department's prospective role in implementing the framework—caused much of the unease at San Diego and throughout the framework process.

One aspect in particular of the DHS role caused friction and nearly caught fire during the San Diego workshop: Section 7(D) of Executive Order 13636, which required DHS to establish "performance goals" on industry use of the framework. The meaning was murky and the implications were explosive. Industry representatives heard the words "performance goals" and conjured images of those DHS officials with clipboards rating their companies' cybersecurity activities, dictating what they should and shouldn't do, and penalizing them for alleged failures.

The question of metrics was also connected to the question of regulation, and always triggered intense exchanges.

"There is a tension in the feedback we're getting," a DHS official privately told a reporter after the first day of the workshop. "'Be specific but don't allude to regulations.' My view is the framework lays out a buffet of options. The goals encourage companies to develop their own metrics and measurements. But the worst-case scenario is companies find it more cost-effective to just absorb the risk."

The DHS source tried to emphasize the department had no intention of "dictating performance standards." A session on this topic the next day "will be very interesting," the source said.

That was a bit of an understatement. The issue caused a tempest the next day, with DHS officials getting an earful from a room full of industry representatives. The industry participants expressed bewilderment over the purpose of the goals and concern that these could become de facto standards. The concept of performance goals tapped into lingering industry uncertainty over DHS's precise role and lines of responsibility between government and industry.

With a large lecture hall in near-mutiny, Robert Kolasky, the director of DHS's integrated task force on cybersecurity, tried to explain that the performance goals were intended to "talk about what we've accomplished" at the national level and to "measure progress in managing risk."

They would not be used as a DHS metric for individual companies, he stressed. "We will make that clear" in the next iteration of the performance goals, Kolasky said. He said the goals should be "layered," and "not reliant on the federal government setting standards."

Another DHS official told InsideCybersecurity.com, "DHS has no intention of developing measures and targets for implementing the goals." On the other hand, the official said, the goals would help senior managers in the private sector justify investments in cybersecurity.

Encouraging senior-level executives to engage on cybersecurity policy was a common theme in San Diego and throughout the framework process. DHS officials said they wanted to craft "aspirational" language that fulfilled the performance goal requirement of the executive order but wasn't a harbinger of future regulation

One participant in San Diego with long experience working with DHS said the department "was kind of thrown under the bus in the executive order," because performance goals implied metrics and standards. Now that the department was handed the requirement to come up with the goals, the source said, it was trying to craft language that encouraged companies' cybersecurity efforts while steering clear of government-imposed mandates.

After the meeting, a DHS official told InsideCybersecurity.com the feedback in San Diego would lead to a "resetting discussion" with industry. "We won't dictate the performance goals," the official said. "The goals drive how you [the private sector] leverage the framework. What is an organization going to get out of the framework? If the goal is resiliency, what are the metrics I need to accomplish that?"

In the coming months, DHS would quietly set aside performance goals as a topic. Officials had clearly heard industry on this, and they were responding. It was a positive sign to business leaders, evidence that the Obama administration meant it when asserting that this process would be driven by industry.

The third stop for the NIST framework road show would be in Dallas, Texas, in September 2013. In the meantime the Obama administration tried to fill in some of the surrounding policy architecture that would accompany and support the framework. Michael Daniel, the White House cybersecurity coordinator, posted a blog in early August explaining the administration's latest thinking on incentives to encourage companies to use the framework and otherwise bolster cybersecurity.

The White House had collected reports from the departments of Treasury, Commerce, and Homeland Security with recommendations on incentives. Streamlined regulations and targeted liability relief were highlighted, as well as grants and preferences in the federal procurement process for companies with strong cybersecurity practices. The departments said they could help foster a market for cyber insurance. They also proposed soft incentives like a public recognition system to honor companies that stood up on cyber.

"Over the next few months, agencies will examine these options in detail to determine which ones to adopt and how, based substantially on input from critical infrastructure stakeholders," Daniel wrote. "We believe that sharing the findings and our plans for continued work will promote transparency and sustain a public conversation about the recommendations. Publishing these agency reports is therefore an interim step and does not indicate the Administration's final policy position on the recommended actions."

"This is a fairly dramatic change in direction by the administration," said the Internet Security Alliance's (ISA) Larry Clinton, perhaps industry's most vocal and persistent advocate for addressing the economics of cybersecurity. "This is a very clear departure from the position the administration took for several years."

Clinton said the administration's work on incentives bore a striking similarity with the recommendations for a voluntary, incentive-laden cyber strategy contained in the 2011 report by the House Republican task force on cybersecurity.

"There are reasons for real optimism on this," Clinton said. "The House Republican task force and the Obama administration are largely on the same page. Even in Congress, the strongest proponents of a mandatory approach—I'm thinking of Jay Rockefeller—have moved to a voluntary approach."

Others were equally impressed. Bill Erny, a senior director at the American Chemistry Council, said his group was "very encouraged" by the administration's offering on incentives. "We're pleased the administration is reaching back out to the private sector to come up with real answers," he said.

"Hopefully this is an indication" of an administration commitment to a voluntary approach, said Brian Raymond, the National Association of Manufacturers' director for technology and domestic policy. "It's a move in the right direction."

The administration was sticking to its commitment to a voluntary approach, but unfortunately for Clinton and the others in industry, the August report on incentives was something of a high-water mark on that topic. When the issue was sent back out to the various federal agencies, it languished.

In January 2014, five months after his blog triggered such a hopeful response, Daniel told InsideCybersecurity.com that little progress had been made on incentives. The White House was in "different stages of figuring out how to move forward on these" recommendations from the assorted departments, Daniel said. There would be no "big-bang announcement" on incentives in conjunction with the framework's upcoming release.

There was only so much the White House could do. An incentive such as the availability of cyber insurance was largely in the private sector's hands, while liability relief was an issue for Congress. Some type of "public recognition" benefit was an incentive the government could provide, Daniel repeated, despite the decided lack of enthusiasm from many in industry.

Incentives policy remained at a "very nascent stage," Daniel said. "It's not as developed as I would like. We are proceeding at a methodical pace." Over the next two years the effort to take concrete steps in the identified incentive areas would barely move ahead.

Not so for the cybersecurity framework itself.

In late August, NIST issued a "draft framework" building off the San Diego discussions and paving the way to Dallas, where four hundred stakeholders would gather, beginning on September 10, for four more days of intense talks on the campus of the University of Texas–Dallas. The draft was garnering plenty of positive feedback in the days leading up to Dallas, but industry stakeholders still had concerns and were beginning to feel the pressure of a ticking clock. NIST was under orders to produce a preliminary version for public comment in October, and the veteran government affairs executives participating in the process knew from long experience that opportunities for meaningful input would diminish as officials ran up against a deadline.

Sedgewick sought to assure his industry counterparts that this process was different.

"There is still room to make changes," Sedgewick said. "This is a stepwise progression and we're hoping for no surprises at any stage. We still have the capacity to make changes."

Sedgewick said NIST might even schedule an additional workshop after the preliminary framework was released in October. "We will continue to have stakeholder meetings . . . in some ways the engagement increases" after the proposed framework is published. "We're looking forward to hearing from people who couldn't attend the workshops."

"They're not quite there yet but the latest draft is one more step in the right direction," said Nathan Mitchell, the American Public Power Association's director of electric reliability standards and compliance. "They're listening to the various critical infrastructures and what we're saying about making it useful. It's getting closer but there's more work to be done."

But Larry Clinton of the Internet Security Alliance said the draft reinforced his concern that the framework was a technical manual that wouldn't be very useful in persuading upper management at companies to invest in cybersecurity. "The first question a senior manager will ask is, 'How much more secure will the framework make my company and how much more will it cost?'" Clinton said. Always eager to push, he said those issues weren't addressed, and that the document didn't spell out what it meant for a company to implement the framework.

"Presumably it will qualify you for incentives," he said hopefully. "Powerful incentives might make this a useful document," Clinton said.

Sedgewick responded to the worries by saying, "That's always one of the challenges in this space: How does a dollar invested get you a dollar of security?" Flexibility would make the framework cost-effective, he said, adding that "a lot of the questions in Dallas will be around does this provide what senior managers are looking for."

NIST officials announced a fifth workshop would be added to the calendar in early November, after release of the proposed framework and before the conclusion of a public comment period. NIST director Gallagher told the Dallas audience that the process was accelerating into the implementation phase. The agency heard the message in Dallas that companies need much more guidance on how to use the framework, and a proposed section on privacy protection was generating more and more heat.

Obama administration officials stressed repeatedly that the framework was not the basis for new regulations. But that message wasn't entirely taking hold among their audience. "No one thinks the voluntary framework will remain voluntary forever," one industry participant told Inside-Cybersecurity.com's Rick Weber. "And you heard that today."

NIST officials emerged from Dallas with less than a month to go before they would publish the preliminary framework. In addition to the mountain of work they faced in incorporating the running flow of input, there was one other hurdle: It seemed increasingly likely that a budget showdown between the White House and congressional Republicans would result in a partial government shutdown on October 1.

NIST was facing an October 10 deadline to release the preliminary version of the framework and had announced its plans for the November workshop in Raleigh, North Carolina. "The Administration strongly believes that a lapse in appropriations should not occur," the Commerce Department said in a statement. "There is enough time for Congress to prevent a lapse in appropriations. The Commerce Department is still in the process of updating our plans."

If a shutdown did occur, critical national security functions such as cyber monitoring activities at DHS would continue. NIST framework efforts would not. "Sadly, the framework is not critical," an industry source lamented.

NIST's Gallagher, at a Billington Security industry conference in late September, tried to project an air of calm. Work on the framework might be temporarily interrupted, he said. But the "secret" to the framework, he said, was that NIST managed to start the entire endeavor with no new budget authority or staff. "What made it work," he said, "is we turned it over to industry."

Stakeholder ownership was particularly important as the framework entered the implementation phase, Gallagher said, allowing companies to "bake it into" their operations, as well as providing for broader international acceptance.

"The adoptive phase begins now," Gallagher said. At this point, he said, companies should begin putting the framework into practice so that "it permeates all levels of an organization, particularly the C-level." The CEOs, CTOs, CISOs, and even the CFOs needed to know the framework and keep it at their fingertips.

Gallagher suggested that several companies were prepared to step forward as early adopters of the framework. "Ideally, some key organizations will step up and say we're going to adopt this," Gallagher said. "We hear through the grapevine a few companies are ready to do this."

At the same event, Michael Daniel delivered grim news from the White House: Staffers working on the framework would be furloughed. The administration announced that only six thousand of the Commerce Department's forty-six thousand employees would report to work during a shutdown; these were mostly physical security and safety workers, not the members of the NIST team working on the framework. The White House wanted industry audiences to know there were costs to this game of chicken with Congress—and to urge their Republican allies on Capitol Hill to back off. But Daniel agreed with Gallagher that the framework itself would not be materially affected. "Ultimately we will get there and we will get it published," he said.

As the calendar flipped over to October 1, work on the framework halted. NIST and DHS Web sites posted generic messages that work would resume once government operations resumed. But framework Web pages and resources were no longer available on the government sites. Government officials were no-shows at a variety of events promoting October as "Cybersecurity Awareness Month."

Impacts rippled across government cybersecurity efforts. Patrick Flynn, McAfee's director of homeland/national security programs, said the shutdown froze the procurement process for advanced continuous diagnostics and mitigation services that McAfee and other companies like Booz Allen Hamilton, IBM, and General Dynamics-IT were preparing to provide across the government.

"The shutdown essentially brings things to a halt," Flynn said. It was "disconcerting what this does to the [federal] cyber workforce. It's already hard for the government to hold onto these people with such special skills," he said.

There were practical security concerns as a reduced force of federal employees analyzed an ever-growing amount of data on possible cyber attacks.

The shutdown entered a second week and it was clear the October 10 release of the preliminary framework would be pushed back. But federal officials, those still on duty, emphasized over and over that the final version of the framework would be released on February 12, 2014, regardless of how long the shutdown endured.

Over the course of the year, business representatives praised the way NIST solicited industry input and ran the framework process. Now, some were expressing concern that this inclusiveness would be limited in the final lap. Stakeholders were "chomping at the bit" to get started again, a source said.

Another source who participated in the NIST process said federal officials "got an earful" in Dallas and were likely to get a very negative reaction if the preliminary framework didn't evolve beyond the late summer draft. This source pointed to industry concerns about the level of detail in the August draft, saying the agency still had to be moved away from such a prescriptive approach in the short time remaining before the February release.

Finally, after three weeks of political stalemate and forced holidays, on October 17 federal employees returned to work. The preliminary framework is "coming very soon," a NIST spokeswoman told InsideCybersecurity.com just hours after getting back to her office.

Less than a week later, on October 23, NIST released the preliminary framework for public review. A forty-five-day comment period would give industry and other stakeholders an unabridged opportunity to review the document and formulate proposed changes. The preliminary framework included revised language on levels of implementation, a tightened six-step process for establishing or improving a cybersecurity program, and discussion of privacy protections that went much further than a draft released over the summer.

Initial reactions from industry groups were generally positive, although sources said the document didn't resolve how a company would demonstrate adoption nor specify whether there was a size threshold for the type of entities that should be covered.

The new version largely tracked with the structure of NIST's August draft, with the adjustments in areas like implementation tiers and profiles, and more guidance for companies on getting started. The framework maintained the five-part "core" structure: identify, protect, detect, respond, and recover. It further explained how a "framework profile" could be used "to describe both the current state and the desired target state of specific cybersecurity activities."

The document now included implementation tiers one through four, jettisoning a "zero tier" contained in previous versions. A zero tier sounded too pejorative; landing there could cause big problems for business executives and their regulators alike. Many might choose not to use the framework at all, rather than risk earning a zero. However, NIST rejected calls to replace the tier system entirely. Business representatives remained concerned that the tier structure still provided too much of a metric for possible use by regulators.

An expansive privacy section still raised questions. Industry groups would be deeply concerned about the privacy language unless and until NIST killed the section entirely.

Among other nagging issues to industry, the overall framework still did not seem to speak to the vast majority of executives who weren't directly involved in developing the product. Executives, industry sources said, just wouldn't "get" the return on investment they could expect from using the framework. Worse yet, it still seemed to create a "standard of care" that implied legal liability for companies that ignored the framework.

NIST director Gallagher, speaking with reporters, said it was "not fair to look at implied liabilities" arising from the framework. "It's designed to be assistive," Gallagher said. "Liability discussions will be between industry and Congress." Gallagher was struggling to convince the business audience of the powerful, cumulative impact of the framework.

A week later, a group of industry honchos was sitting in the Oval Office; the president was making a personal pitch to come out publicly in favor of the framework, InsideCybersecurity.com reported. The participants included Steve Bennett of Symantec; Renee James of Intel; Wes Bush of Northrop Grumman; Marilyn Hewson from Lockheed Martin; Joe Rigby from Pepco; Brian Moynihan from Bank of America; MasterCard's Ajay Banja; and Visa's Charles Scharf. Some of them, including Rigby, would be on stage when the framework was released at the White House three months later.

The CEOs "expressed appreciation for the way the framework was developed in partnership with the private sector and support for the process moving forward," the White House said in a statement after the meeting. "The conversation focused on how to encourage its adoption."

They "discussed the need for framework adoption by both critical infrastructure and by their suppliers—and the difficulties involved in helping small and medium sized business to adopt best practices," according to the statement. "Both companies and government officials also expressed the strong desire to have Congress pass information sharing legislation that protects privacy and civil liberties."

InsideCybersecurity.com's Dan Dupont surveyed the companies and found two—Symantec and Lockheed Martin—were already willing to publicly embrace the framework. The others offered positive words but held back from embracing the "early adopter" label. They would get there in the end, and Pepco's Rigby would be one of the stars on stage at a White House ceremony to release the framework.

Other ideas were percolating in the private sector as well. Larry Clinton proposed a "beta testing" phase in which select companies would work out the framework. Clinton, who had a master's degree from the University of Maryland and a bachelor's degree from the University of Illinois at Urbana Champaign, had led the ISA since 2003 and was a vice president at the U.S. Telephone Association for twelve years before that.

Clinton brimmed with policy ideas that sought to push discussions in new directions. But when he alighted on an idea that he thought properly framed the question and provided an innovative, workable answer, Clinton was unrelenting in pushing his approach in public and private settings.

His proposal now would involve selecting companies in targeted critical infrastructure sectors to attempt to fully implement the framework, in the process generating a trove of data that would inform broader adoption. Under the plan, the selected companies would be granted the kinds of incentives that federal officials had discussed and, perhaps, receive some other form of compensation for carrying out the experiment.

"I'm suggesting that NIST or DHS do what any organization does when rolling out a new product and beta test it," Clinton said. "I'm talking about a funded project to test the framework with targeted audiences. NIST or DHS would work with the private sector to select companies in targeted areas, and could provide government assistance for them to implement it."

The beta testing would allow government and companies to assess the costs and quality of the framework and precisely determine the types of incentives that would encourage adoption. "We would do this if we were launching a new technology product," Clinton said. "Beta test it and use the data to perfect the product. . . . How difficult it is to implement and how costly it is to implement—we should know these things," Clinton said. "Then we would know the appropriate targeted incentives."

Clinton questioned the administration's emphasis on early adopters, saying a "scientific process is necessary to get the data," rather than a "self-selected sample" that could be signing up for a variety of political or other reasons. He said early adopters likely would be sophisticated companies that are already performing the activities spelled out in the framework, much like the industry leaders who visited the Oval Office days before.

NIST and administration officials politely promised to consider the idea, but they were well along their own path to pushing out the framework. They believed the relevant data would be produced by the process that was already underway. Early adopters—even if they were big, sophisticated companies—would encourage others to do the same. Clinton thought the government officials were missing a chance—and, by doing it their way, would fail to produce data and insight that could meaningfully guide future cybersecurity policy development. Clinton would keep pitching his idea, in North Carolina and beyond.

Next up, NIST as scheduled on November 14 convened the fourth and final stop on its national framework development tour, and the fifth workshop overall, this one on the campus of North Carolina State University in Raleigh. Another four hundred stakeholders would take part in this event, starting off with a welcoming ceremony at the modernistic Hunt Library.

Eggers would say there was "a growing appreciation of what NIST was trying to do" that congealed between the Pittsburgh and Dallas meetings. "By the fifth workshop, there was a feeling that this could be very good," Eggers said.

NC State Chancellor Randy Woodson welcomed the crowd and enthusiastically urged everyone to tour the high-tech library; through glass walls robots could be seen retrieving books from towering stacks of metallic cases. *Complex* magazine called it one of the "25 coolest libraries in the world." Dozens of companies paid the university to join its "Technology Incubator," for space on the campus, and just to be part of this tech-driven ecosystem.

NIST's Dr. Romine, at the opening session, said the remaining work on the framework shouldn't be "a heavy lift." Donna Dodson urged stakeholders to take the preliminary framework for a "test drive" before the final version was released in February. "Kick the tires?" she said. The audience wasn't entirely in hand: What did it mean to kick the tires? someone rose from the audience to ask. "Should companies try to implement it now, before it's released?" the participant asked.

Kicking the tires, Dodson explained, "begins with 'Do I have a risk management plan? Have I identified assets?' Organizations may have done this five or six years ago," she said. They should do it again.

"Look at the preliminary framework," Dodson beseeched the audience. "Are the appropriate standards in there? Are there gaps? These are things companies can do today."

It wasn't rocket science, but the message from NIST and the Obama administration in general was that dedicated attention, not rocket science, was the main ingredient at this point. NIST, and by extension the White House, DHS and the rest of an expectant government, were eager for "early adopters" to step forward and become champions of the framework and the philosophy behind it. Widespread failure to embrace it—after Congress's failure to adopt the alternative, mandatory approach to ginning up security—didn't seem to be an option.

Larry Clinton stood up to raise the concern that early adopters would be the big companies that were already doing the things described in the framework. This wasn't going to improve overall cybersecurity; it was more of a status quo strategy. "We need to get to the companies that are not doing it for cost reasons," Clinton told the audience, many of whom had heard his message repeatedly throughout the process.

Ola Sage, who owned a small technology consulting firm in suburban Maryland called eManagement, stood up to say she'd done just that. The crowd in the auditorium turned her way. Sage stood in an aisle by her seat and explained she walked through the framework's functions, categories, and subcategories over a couple of days. "It was not too onerous," she told InsideCybersecurity.com on the sidelines of the conference. "At least how we interpreted how to do it." But she called it an "eye-opener," even for the operations of her small business.

NIST might have summoned her from central casting to be a small-business ambassador for the framework, though of course they hadn't done anything like that. But Sage would go on to be a frequent small-business representative on industry panels to discuss cybersecurity. Tying her firm's services to the framework was good business, she would later decide.

However, Sage said her company would avoid the "early adopter" label, "because it's not clear what that means. But we are happy to take it out for a test drive."

It took "less than a day" to measure eManagement's practices against those contained in the framework, Sage said, but that was possible only because she participated in two NIST workshops and understood the context of the document. That level of attention from a closely engaged CEO and a chief information officer wasn't feasible for all small businesses.

"We absolutely found value in going through the process," Sage told InsideCybersecurity.com. "We've already implemented something based on the results. . . . Using the framework lets people know you're paying attention. It's like having an ADT sign outside your house."

Others shared the reluctance to publicly proclaim they had "adopted" the framework. Phil Agcaoili, a cyber strategist and practitioner at several major private-sector organizations, asserted: "The first company that says it's adopting gets hacked. How can we say we want to kick the tires without publicly saying we're adopting? We're looking for a private way to participate."

NIST and DHS officials jotted the thought in their notebooks. DHS officials stressed that the administration was not seeking "high-level attestation" that companies had "adopted" the framework. Samara Moore from the White House told the audience that senior administration officials were reaching out to regulatory agencies with the message that this shouldn't be seen as a tool for more regulation.

The Obama administration's top security officials were joining NIST in a high-energy pitch to industry: This is your framework; come on in, the water's warm!

Industry groups weren't the only ones with concerns as the sessions plowed ahead in Raleigh, just three months until the framework was due for release. For one thing, the privacy issue was unresolved.

The American Civil Liberties Union detected an unfolding retreat on privacy in the framework, while business groups warned that "excessive" privacy protections would be a "deal-killer" that would preclude companies from adopting the framework.

The ACLU's Michelle Richardson used language that was just as strong and full of implications: Cybersecurity, she said from the stage in Raleigh, could easily become "the new terrorism [scare] . . . used by government to collect more information from private Americans."

There was another way, she said: The NIST framework could incorporate long-standing principles on privacy, minimize the collection of personal data in the first place, and ensure the data that was collected would not be "repurposed" for surveillance activities. "It's not beyond your capability" to use the framework as a new standard-bearer for privacy, she argued, using the words NIST's own leaders employed when discussing the document. "The framework is aspirational. That's how privacy protection should be written as well. . . . It's important to build this in now or it won't happen."

But industry representatives warned the government appeared to be creating a new privacy standard. The privacy language alone could be a barrier to adopting the framework in the eyes of corporate attorneys. Industry attorney Harriet Pearson drafted an alternative, streamlined approach to privacy that business groups supported. The ACLU rejected Pearson's plan as "meaningless" and a step back from existing privacy protections.

NIST was caught in the middle. What to do? The team in Gaithersburg actually had an answer: Get out of this debate altogether. While the need for privacy protections would be emphasized throughout the framework, NIST jettisoned the appendix dedicated to the issue and decided it wasn't the agency's role to create a new standard on privacy. Instead, NIST included a general privacy "methodology" that had the support of industry and privacy advocates, and would begin an entirely separate initiative on "privacy engineering" in 2014.

It was a clever, effective way of defusing a problem that could've blown up the greater cyber framework enterprise. "The one thing that tied things up nicely was when they dropped the privacy methodology," Eggers would comment. "That was the one place where NIST over-reached and caused great concern."

Eggers said the episode showed that NIST and the White House were really listening to industry, which was a huge relief on the business side. "They were practical and accommodating," Eggers said. "Of course, the constraints of the [February 12] due date helped make people accommodating."

On February 12, 2014, the Obama administration formally released NIST's framework of cybersecurity standards with a ceremony in the Old Executive Office Building adjacent to the White House. Commerce Secretary Penny Pritzker, Homeland Security Secretary Jeh Johnson, White House cybersecurity coordinator Michael Daniel, and Chief of Staff Denis McDonough presented the framework, along with DHS, NIST, and other officials. They were accompanied on stage by CEOs from AT&T, Lockheed Martin, and Pepco. Dozens of other corporate and trade association executives jammed the auditorium.

"Today I was pleased to receive the Cybersecurity Framework, which reflects the good work of hundreds of companies, multiple federal agencies, and contributors from around the world," Obama said in a statement. "This voluntary Framework is a great example of how the private sector and government can, and should, work together to meet this shared challenge." The framework "marks a turning point," he said, but "much more work needs to be done" to secure critical infrastructure and the economy as a whole from cyber threats.

NIST included with the framework a "roadmap" of issues to consider going forward. These covered technical questions such as improving authentication, macro needs like bolstering the cybersecurity workforce, and essentially political questions such as who would "own" and manage the framework in the future. It discussed how NIST would engage with other agencies to promote the voluntary use of the framework and how NIST might get involved in such thorny areas as securing industry supply chains. And it noted the ongoing effort to grapple with privacy standards.

At the same time, the Department of Homeland Security formally presented its voluntary program to encourage framework adoption, re-dubbing the initiative as "C-Cubed," or C3, for Critical-Infrastructure Cyber Community. The Department of Energy unveiled new tools mapping the framework for the energy sector and for more general audiences. In sticking with the administration's theme of letting a thousand flowers blossom, the American Water Works Association released a guide mapping the framework for the nation's drinking water providers.

Obama administration officials stressed the voluntary nature of the framework and said the White House's message to federal agencies was to use the framework to streamline regulations and encourage voluntary cybersecurity improvements. "For the administration, the goal is not to expand regulation," a senior administration official said on a call for reporters prior to the ceremony. Agencies were due to report to the White House that day, February 12, on how their existing regulatory authority tracked with the framework. The agencies were "looking at what cybersecurity guidance they now have and how that stacks up with the framework," the official said, as well as "engaging in a normal process with stakeholders."

The administration was still working on incentives for framework adoption, the officials told reporters, adding that proposals would be "shared publicly over the next few months." They acknowledged the importance of incentives but also emphasized their belief that market-based decisions would drive companies to use the framework. That belief would prove to be an important pillar for the administration, because actual work on incentives would take much longer than "the next few months."

Pritzker, the Commerce Department chief, called the framework "a starting point" for a sustained dialogue between government and industry. "The government needs to stay aligned with industry and move at your speed," Pritzker told the industry panelists at the public event.

AT&T CEO Randall Stephenson said "fear" would be the best incentive for companies to adopt the framework. Lockheed Martin CEO Marillyn Hewson praised the document as a "risk-based" tool that "helps companies make business decisions," but she agreed that incentives would be important for smaller companies and suggested some form of tax break. Lockheed Martin was "already using the framework to work with the supply chain," she added, noting that her goal is to "make sure we're teamed up with them in managing risk."

Pepco's Rigby said he had to "own" cybersecurity on behalf of his customers and couldn't blame vendors if the lights went out, suggesting the company would explore ways to ensure cybersecurity throughout the supply chain.

The Internet Security Alliance issued a statement in support of the framework, although Larry Clinton couldn't hide his disappointment. He questioned how widely it would be adopted without accompanying incentives or a better analysis of its cost-effectiveness. The administration "did what they had to do today, it was a good event and a positive atmosphere," Clinton said. Even big companies would have trouble "keeping up" with quickly evolving threats, he said, noting that the elements of the DHS "C-Cubed" program were "exactly the same stuff" that had long existed at DHS and wouldn't do much to encourage use among a broader category of companies.

"They need to get moving on regulatory streamlining and acquisition advantages" for companies using the framework, Clinton said. "They should have workshops on adoption. They have to face very real problems candidly. . . . I absolutely disagree that all we have to do is tell people there's a cyber threat" and they will rush to use the framework. "That's just whistling past the graveyard. We already have awareness of the threat; what we don't have is an understanding of the nature of the threat."

Completion of the framework drew praise on Capitol Hill. Senate Commerce Chairman Rockefeller, whose committee passed a bill that would give NIST an ongoing role in managing the framework, put out a statement of support, as did Senate Homeland Security and Governmental Affairs Chairman Tom Carper (D-Delaware). Carper said he would continue to work to ensure "Congress steps up to the plate" with cyber legislation. House Intelligence Chairman Mike Rogers (R-Michigan) and ranking member Dutch Ruppersberger (D-Maryland) issued a joint statement praising the process.

The media reaction was lukewarm, at best. In fact, much of the coverage was simply dismissive of the entire exercise. "Security experts" were quoted left and right saying there was nothing to be seen in this much-hyped framework.

The *New York Times*, in its "Bits" technology column, asked whether the framework would change anyone's behavior and suggested it was largely a collection of retreads. "Security experts say the framework is not all that different from the checklists chief security officers regularly implement at their companies," the *Times* wrote.

"When I look at this framework with its beautifully colored boxes, my first thought is 'Isn't this obvious?'" the *Times* quoted Vincent Berk, chief executive of network security firm FlowTraq, as saying. Because the framework was voluntary, the security experts questioned whether critical infrastructure companies would implement the practices, the *Times* reported.

The *Wall Street Journal*, in its "Law Blog," agreed the framework wouldn't do much in the real world.

"Administration officials said the framework avoids specific requirements because different types of organizations face different threats and would therefore require different remedies," the *Journal* blogged. "But security experts say the administration has backed away from any meaningful requirements in the face of industry concerns over cost and potential liability. Alan Paller, director of research for SANS Institute, a cybersecurity research group, said the administration had wasted a year developing voluntary guidelines that will do little to improve security even for the companies that adopt the recommendations."

The SANS Institute was comprised of vendors of cybersecurity products as well as researchers, and promoted its own "20 critical security controls." The NIST framework could be seen as a rival product, a point unmentioned by the *Journal*.

Politico damned the NIST framework under a headline reading, "Cybersecurity in slow lane one year after Obama order."

"Nearly a year after President Barack Obama issued an executive order to improve the cybersecurity of the nation's vital assets, the administration doesn't have much to show: The government is about to produce only some basic standards, with little incentive for the private sector to participate," the flashy and frequently quick-to-judge news site declared.

"The program's early weaknesses are a sign that—even as high-profile breaches at Target and other retailers compromise the data of millions of consumers—the White House and Congress have made minimal progress on the potentially more serious issue of protecting power plants, oil pipelines, and major banks from a crippling cyberattack."

It was a checklist, *Politico* decided, nothing more.

A week after the release, Daniel tried again to shape expectations with a post on the White House blog.

"The Framework is exactly that—a framework," Daniel wrote. "It provides a common language and systematic methodology for managing cyber risk. It does not tell a company how much cyber risk is tolerable, nor does it claim to provide 'the one and only' formula for cybersecurity."

Once more he asked organizations to "kick the tires" and offer feedback. "In short, we need your continued engagement. The Framework is intended to be a living document. We need your collective experience and knowledge to make it better over time."

The overall significance of the framework was being missed: Its individual elements might be the equivalent of hammers, wrenches, and screwdrivers already lying around in business's garages and storerooms. But put together in one place and wrapped in a unifying message of risk management, the framework in total was a powerful tool that could drive companies' decisions and efforts on cybersecurity in a completely new and unique way.

Larry Clinton, despite his pointed critique, recognized a remarkable accomplishment when he saw one.

"It does take some time to effectuate these changes, and that is frustrating," Clinton said. "We were calling for this kind of partnership in 2008 and 2009 and 2010 and 2011, and we were rewarded with Lieberman-Collins, which was the polar opposite of what we wanted."

Clinton and others kept at it. The reward was the 2013 executive order, the NIST framework, and the other policy elements that flowed from the order.

"They embraced our approach," Clinton said with some satisfaction. He was well aware this was just a step that needed plenty of support in other areas. But this one step by a small agency based in the Maryland suburbs was truly a landmark in the development of a critical policy; it represented formal government adoption of a philosophy that insightful industry leaders had been pushing for years.

Eight months after its unveiling at the White House ceremony, NIST convened another workshop, this one in Tampa, Florida, to discuss the early experiences with the framework. Some stakeholders griped that this was much too soon for a meaningful assessment. But putting the band back together—the core of a couple of hundred stakeholders who had traveled around the country as the framework was built—had its own value and revealed lingering tensions as well as successes.

At a two-day event in late October hosted by the University of South Florida's Florida Center for Cybersecurity, technology, communications, and energy companies explained they had customized the framework to meet their own needs.

Matthew Scholl of NIST said "several themes" emerged from the panel discussions on "use of the framework," including customization, development of new tools, and how to assess relative risk. Scholl described the framework as "an organizing superstructure" and stressed that "the decision on how to use it is a risk-based decision" unique to each organization. The industry input didn't suggest the need for fundamental changes, Scholl said.

Tim Casey of Intel said his company would release a paper on its uses of the framework. He approvingly called it a "lightweight, easily applied process" that consumed less than 150 work hours so far. He also stressed that it was not being used as a "checklist." NIST, in keeping with the mantra that the framework belonged to the business entities that were using it, would post the Intel white paper on its Web site as an important "how-to" guide.

Jeff England of the small, Wyoming-based telecom provider Silverstar, said he created a one-page executive summary to enable discussions between operational offices and senior management. He also said he created his own system for assigning value to relative risk. But "the framework gave us purpose and direction," England said.

NIST officials also took on lingering concerns that the very concept of "conformity" with the framework would be a bridge to regulation. "I want to move the conversation away from conformity assessment to confidence," NIST's Lisa Carnahan told a classroom full of industry representatives in Tampa. "It's about confidence that you're managing risk appropriately. This is about [a company's] internal use of risk management."

Carnahan said conformity had become "a lightning rod" in the framework process, even though officials meant to make language on the topic "as benign and industry-friendly as possible. I guess I missed the mark." She added: "NIST has no intention of developing a certification program" related to the framework. "There is no need for one," she said. Further, "industry should develop any conformity assessment if you need one."

Industry participants reacted positively, if cautiously. Larry Clinton noted that the concern wasn't with NIST at all, but with what other federal agencies might do with the framework. "It's about the [Securities and Exchange Commission] adopting elements of the framework and going out with particular regulations and threatening enforcement actions," Clinton said.

Subsequent conversations with government and industry leaders eighteen months after its release provided an even more informed view of how the framework was surviving out in the real cybersecurity ecosystem. These discussions suggested the framework of cybersecurity standards was holding up well and continued to be a chief organizing tool for industry and government alike. "Industry is farther along than I thought they'd be eighteen months ago," NIST's Adam Sedgewick said in July 2015. "We don't have to ask them for use cases—they reach out to us and show us how they're using the framework."

In July 2015, Sedgewick and Matthew Barrett, who had been named framework program manager, discussed the framework's evolution since its release in an exclusive interview with InsideCybersecurity.com. The agency was making a concerted effort to show where the framework was at this stage and how it could help. They wanted to make sure it didn't gather dust as so many government policy manifestos tended to do after a year or two.

"The proposed value of the Framework has been validated through a large volume and breadth of interactions between NIST and industry," NIST said in an update posted on July 1, 2015.

> One of the most frequently cited benefits of the Framework is a common cyber risk management language, so that more efficient and precise discussions can be held up, down, and across a company's management structure, with auditors, and with supply chain partners. The Framework is now being used as a basis for security-oriented discussions and decision-making in corporate boardrooms, the C-Suite, and among line managers and staff with cyber responsibilities.

The NIST officials said they were spending an extensive amount of time speaking with colleagues in government about the purpose of the framework and its voluntary nature. Concerns about an eventual regulatory outcome often permeated discussions at the six public workshops NIST held on the framework. "A lot of our message to government folks—whether they are regulators or not—is that making something mandatory actually moves it out of security operations and into the compliance mode," Barrett said. "It causes a shift from dynamic risk management decisioning to compliance decisioning."

Barrett added, "So we're trying to get agencies to think about the downstream impacts and we do spend a lot of time working with regulators so they understand the purpose of the framework."

"From the very first meeting, people wrapped themselves around the axle about the regulatory threat," commented a source from the energy sector. "That wasn't the intent and it didn't happen."

Many in industry agreed that the NIST framework effectively structured the government–private sector dialogue on cybersecurity and provided valuable tools such as a common lexicon around the issue.

"I think it will continue to play the chief organizing role," said one trade association lobbyist. "The framework embodies the key business security risk management principle. It's probably the best thing government has done in this space. And we're only going to be successful in this space if business is enthusiastic about it."

Karl Schimmeck of the Securities Industry and Financial Markets Association said financial firms were "actively using the framework as a communications mechanism and are starting to align their internal controls to it and use it externally with partners." The framework was proving quite valuable in assessing and addressing vendor risk, he said, which was one of the goals NIST laid out early in the process.

The energy industry source said: "I don't know if the framework was intended to be the end-all for the nation on cybersecurity, but it has served the purpose of bringing people together, creating a dialogue, walking through the process and talking through issues."

The source added: "That's more important than 'using' the framework. My member companies don't talk about 'using' the framework for the most part, but they are more focused on cybersecurity and the framework allows that dialogue."

The energy industry source suggested NIST hold annual workshops, such as the Tampa check-in, to foster a running dialogue on cybersecurity issues large and small. "The workshops were tremendously helpful," the source said. "They should bring that group of stakeholders together every year."

"Someone needs to own it and keep it a living document," the tech sector source added. "NIST has done a good job but we will need a strategy on how to keep improving it."

However, a tech industry source said more work needed to be done to demonstrate the framework's effectiveness, a theme that would reemerge consistently.

"The metrics are unclear on who's implementing the framework or how it's being implemented," the tech source said. "I'm not sure we've determined what success looks like. Is it the number of companies 'adopting' the framework? Is it the companies that are 'aware' of the framework? Or is it improved cybersecurity? That's much harder to prove."

The tech source said government and industry need to work together on metrics. "At eighteen months, maybe it's too early to evaluate how successful it's been," the source said. "But the community hasn't even begun the discussion on what success means."

"Metrics are always on our minds," Barrett replied. But the issue was extremely complex. "A modern computer security enterprise has so many different parts," he said. "Implementing the framework or following up on a self-assessment are just among the many things that happen within an enterprise. It's hard to isolate the framework's impact."

The question NIST asks, Barrett said, is "has this helped you improve risk management and security? In conversations with industry we keep it conversational and qualitative."

Metrics was a complex issue with many sides. As an agency based on weights and measurements, NIST would always seek ways to quantify and assess progress. Stakeholders like Larry Clinton and the tech industry source were seeking metrics as a basis for business decisions and investments in costly cybersecurity defenses. As Clinton would say repeatedly, cybersecurity was primarily an economic issue and companies wouldn't invest in it unless it made business sense.

Something quite different happens when politicians and government officials begin to demand metrics. The NIST framework would continue to be the most important manifestation of the government–industry collaboration on cybersecurity. But perception—on Capitol Hill, within industry, and in the media—would be critical to maintaining support for its voluntary, flexible, and innovation-driven spirit.

The Tampa conference—and industry responses to a request for information released shortly beforehand—served a tangible purpose as some in Congress began looking for evidence that the framework was working. Rep. James Langevin (D-Rhode Island) added an amendment to a congressional spending bill demanding a formal survey of companies. That set off alarm bells throughout business circles. It was much too early to begin tabulating "adopters," whatever that meant. If companies gave the wrong answer to the question of whether they were using the framework, industry feared, the next logical step might be onerous regulation.

Langevin indicated that the NIST survey and subsequent conference would meet his objectives, for the time being.

Going forward, NIST would focus on ensuring there was an adequate "feedback mechanism" to ensure the framework was kept fresh. "Don't let it be static," Sedgewick explained. "It must be useful to executives. Sharing use cases and guidances helps keep it relevant."

The business decision made by "security practitioners" to build products around the framework kept it relevant.

And taking "a long view" would keep it relevant, Sedgewick explained. "There's a rich vein of experience in our work on standards and best practices," he said. "We end up taking a longer view of where the market and technology are going, instead of going for an immediate 'security' solution that may be short-sighted."

He noted the time NIST officials spent on Capitol Hill explaining the value of the framework. He noted the efforts of House and Senate staffers to attend the NIST workshops.

The integrity of the little agency that could was intact. NIST would continue to drive the government's cybersecurity strategy, if it could keep the risk-management based strategy front-of-mind. And help make sure it worked.

By the end of 2015, another industry-based initiative was taking shape to ensure positive answers to those questions. Leaders of the communications, energy, water, IT, and other critical infrastructure sectors decided to invest in a high-profile effort that would serve as a second-round awareness and reminder campaign for the framework. But this would be an enduring structure, a cross-company entity with resources and a defined mission to ensure the voluntary framework remained the basis for government–industry policy on cybersecurity.

Robert Mayer of U.S. Telecom, Larry Clinton of the Internet Security Alliance, and representatives of the water works and energy trade associations were behind the effort. Significantly, most hailed from sectors that routinely faced heavy regulation. They were determined to keep the voluntary, industry-led approach to cyber policy on course.

The initiative came as some in industry were beginning to whisper about "drift" in the program and flagging attention in the private sector. But that happened in every policy area, not just cyber. The fact that industry leaders recognized it—and responded with their own answers— was exactly the kind of initiative NIST was hoping to see. It was especially important as the Department of Homeland Security frequently appeared to be stumbling in its designated role as an industry liaison and evangelist on the framework.

NIST itself was prepared to invest in supporting the industry move with another request for information in late 2015. This was the government's preferred device for sparking a dialogue with industry. The agency would go straight to the stakeholders for advice on reinvigorating the substance of the framework and ensuring it was being used. NIST and the business group leaders agreed the new effort would focus on industry's role, gaps left open by the framework, and the ever-present question of measuring effectiveness.

It all suggested the spirit of the framework was intact too.

5

THE DEPARTMENT OF INSECURITY

This is not necessarily a technology discussion. It doesn't even have much to do with technology providers. This is about how does business protect themselves and how does the government—what you can do is help incentivize that, and that will actually foster creative innovation for new and better and less expensive methods.

—Phyllis Schneck, soon-to-be-named deputy undersecretary for
cybersecurity and communications,
Department of Homeland Security, July 23, 2013

In the spring of 2013, a new kind of cyber threat was discovered, adding to the ever-growing list of things American consumers needed to worry about. In this case, the U.S. Computer Emergency Response Team, or CERT, had detected cyber vulnerabilities in medical devices. Yes, your pacemaker could be hacked. Someone tapping away on a laptop could reach into your chest and kill you.

U.S. CERT was a Department of Homeland Security-affiliated entity; its job was to uncover such threats, and overall it was a positive example of the Department of Homeland Security (DHS) collaboration with the private sector. But that, unfortunately, was something of an anomaly as the massive department struggled to define its place in the cybersecurity world.

Phyllis Schneck, in a congressional appearance while she was still in the private sector, spelled out a Department of Homeland Security role on cybersecurity that most industry representatives would applaud. It would be based on collaboration and supporting industry's creativity and self-interest in securing cyberspace. But whether DHS could pull this off was a big question mark for lobbyists. Most thought the answer was no.

If the National Institute of Standards and Technology (NIST) came into the cybersecurity framework process as the little agency that could, DHS was at risk of becoming the big agency that couldn't. The department had structural problems, its employees headed for the exits with alarming frequency, and it suffered a trust deficit in both the business community and on Capitol Hill that was a kind of death spiral virtually impossible to reverse.

But as the Obama administration moved through its first and into its second term, the DHS leadership saw cybersecurity as a potential success story for the department. First-term Secretary Janet Napolitano, the former Democratic governor of Arizona, early on said she wanted to hire an army of one thousand cybersecurity experts at the department.

"I hope to recruit some of your smartest people to join the government, so watch out," Napolitano said at a cybersecurity conference in August 2009. Reuters reported that "Napolitano also acknowledged that because DHS was a new department, it was not well organized initially to deal with cybersecurity issues when she came on board at the start of the year but that the agency was beginning to mature to address the evolving threats."

It was a subtle swipe at the previous administration—and a rather blatant attempt to position the new regime as the cyber champions—but the Napolitano team was strongly attracted to cyber policy.

Napolitano moved to centralize functions and in October 2009 opened the National Cybersecurity and Communications Integration Center (NCCIC), consolidating DHS cyber and telecom system monitoring activities. The next year, National Security Agency (NSA) analysts were embedded in the NCCIC.

She brought white-hat hackers, who understood where the vulnerabilities really were, into the department's advisory council process. She started the push to get enhanced hiring authority so the department could go out to get those cyber professionals she wanted to hire.

And she bemused friends and foes alike by saying she didn't use e-mail or online services. Going back to typewriters would be safer too, some wags suggested, but it didn't really practically address the problem.

Cybersecurity, in the end, would be a little-noted part of Napolitano's legacy at DHS. The department's effectiveness would remain a much-debated point, but there was no disputing that she had energetically positioned DHS at the forefront of cyber policy development.

After four years as a lightning rod and target for Republicans in Congress, Napolitano in July 2013 announced her decision to resign as DHS secretary to become president of the University of California system. Despite working to raise DHS's profile on cybersecurity, she didn't dwell on it during a farewell speech at the National Press Club that was largely given over to the ongoing battle with Congress over immigration, the *Washington Post* reported. But she did leave her audience with a warning: "Our country will, at some point, face a major cybersecurity event that will have a serious effect on our lives, our economy and the everyday functioning of our society. More must be done, and quickly."

Napolitano's resignation followed the April departure of Deputy Secretary Jane Holl Lute, who often represented the department on cybersecurity matters on Capitol Hill. Lute was also a fervent believer that mandatory cybersecurity regulations would be needed in the future, so her departure wasn't much lamented on K Street. But the undersecretary for cybersecurity, Mark Weatherford, had resigned in March and his position remained vacant into the summer.

Bruce McConnell, who was now serving as acting undersecretary, told participants at the July NIST workshop in San Diego: "Other countries are having the same challenge of figuring out who's in charge of cyber. We're doing as well or better than anyone."

But even as the department fine-tuned a vanguard role for itself on cybersecurity, the departures were causing alarm on Capitol Hill. Senate Homeland Security and Governmental Affairs Chairman Tom Carper (D-Delaware) said the senior management level at DHS was beginning to resemble Swiss cheese. "At DHS alone, I believe there are fifteen senior leadership positions that are, or will be, vacant in the very near future," Carper said in July 2013. He could've added that dozens of cybersecurity positions—as many as seventy-five—at DHS were political appointments. That could bring in fresh talent on a regular basis, but it also meant proven talent was constantly exiting the building more quickly than it could be replaced.

McConnell followed the others out the door in August 2013, leaving to take over the global cyber program at the East/West Institute in New York City.

The roster gradually would be refilled, as the Obama administration moved to create a DHS cyber team that seemed likely to surpass its predecessors' records on durability if not performance. Suzanne Spaulding took over as undersecretary for the National Protection and Programs Directorate, a dismally named bureaucratic construction that had a key piece of cybersecurity policy. Spaulding had law and undergraduate degrees from the University of Virginia, worked for both the House and Senate Intelligence committees, and spent six years at the CIA.

The directorate's mission included providing for both the cyber and physical security of the nation's infrastructure. On the cyber side, Phyllis Schneck was tapped to serve as deputy undersecretary, Spaulding's top assistant on cybersecurity.

Schneck, with a PhD from Georgia Tech, was a fresh face, full of energy and catchy phrases, and she quickly won fans among the mostly middle-aged men who filled the middle and upper ranks of industry's cybersecurity teams. Schneck liked to call them "rock stars" in a new, rapidly changing security environment, and many were flattered. She would laugh at the name of her directorate and roll her eyes; the times demanded something sexier and sleeker. It wasn't entirely clear what she meant but audiences ate it up.

Before joining DHS, Schneck was vice president and chief technology officer for the public sector at the security firm McAfee, and chairwoman of the board of directors of the government–private sector National Cyber Forensics and Training Alliance. Schneck also chaired the FBI's "Infragard" board of directors for eight years, an information-sharing venue between the government and private sector on cyber attacks and crime. Further, she chaired a working group that helped produce the influential Center for Strategic and International Studies (CSIS) report for the forty-fourth presidency. She was the proud holder of three patents "in high-performance and adaptive information security," Napolitano said in announcing her selection.

Her journey from the private sector into government was a frequent theme of her speeches and the underlying message was clear: The government folks doing cybersecurity are much smarter and harder working than was popularly imagined, but government must learn and draw inspiration from tech leaders and the business world. On the surface, business leaders were reassured that the department's cyber portfolio was in the hands of someone who wasn't bent on regulating. But they weren't quite sure of how much clout she would actually have.

Dr. Andy Ozment, an affable Georgia Tech graduate with a doctorate in computer sciences from Cambridge, was named as DHS's assistant secretary of cybersecurity and communications. Ozment helped write Executive Order 13636 as a White House aide.

But the big hire came in the fall of 2013, when Obama nominated Jeh Johnson to become the fourth secretary of the department and the first who didn't come from a political position or a federal judgeship. Johnson's first name was pronounced "Jay," he would explain to inquisitive senators. He would also be the first African American to serve in the role.

Jeh Johnson was practically unknown in cybersecurity circles, but he was well-known and trusted within Obama's White House. He would provide a steadying influence at the Department of Homeland Security that was vitally important in the coming months.

He was born in 1957 in New York City, graduated from Morehouse College and Columbia Law School, and served as a prosecutor, a corporate attorney, and a Democratic Party activist.

Johnson supported Obama's presidential bid from the early days, and was appointed general counsel of the Department of Defense in January 2009. From drone strikes to repealing the ban on gays serving openly in the military, Johnson was a central player in the deliberations as the top lawyer at the Pentagon during Obama's first term. The *Daily Beast,* which first reported plans to nominate Johnson for the DHS post, noted the challenges ahead for the new secretary: "Still experiencing considerable growing pains, running DHS will require someone with a forceful personality and a sharp set of bureaucratic skills," the news site said. "Johnson has never managed an entire government agency, but he has overseen one of the largest law firms in the world: Ten thousand civilian and military lawyers work for the Department of Defense all over the world."

The site went on:

> Johnson was a familiar face at high-level White House meetings and has a good personal relationship with Obama dating back to the 2008 presidential campaign. On national security matters he is known as a pragmatist who for the most part stoutly represented the institutional interests of the military, and was often hawkish on the use of military force during internal administration debates.

Still, he could be relied on to advance the White House's legal agenda within DOD; he'd often refer to himself as "the president's man" at the Pentagon.

At his confirmation hearing in mid-November, Johnson touched on cyber issues in a generalized way and offered assurances that he knew the beleaguered department needed to get its own house in order. He offered one tantalizing hint that he did in fact get some of the underlying nuances of cyber policymaking, noting that government and industry had different ways of calculating risk and each should be respected.

In Washington, DC's, coded language on cybersecurity, that implied a willingness on the government side to allow industry to define its own appropriate cybersecurity best practices and priorities.

The committee approved Johnson's nomination by voice vote, though Sen. John McCain (R-Arizona) voted no over immigration issues and Rand Paul (R-Kentucky) voted no in absentia without explanation. Other senators including Lindsey Graham (R-South Carolina) wouldn't allow the floor vote to proceed until late December in running disputes between congressional Republicans and the White House. It was yet another example of cybersecurity priorities—in this case, filling the government's top cybersecurity leadership ranks—being subjugated to unrelated and often far less important political imperatives.

When the Senate finally cleared Johnson's nomination and the new secretary was sworn in before Christmas 2013, cybersecurity was just one area that needed immediate attention at the huge, awkward Department of Homeland Security. And there were a multitude of issues within the cybersecurity matrix that he needed to address. To name a few, an industry source said, "There's an astounding lack of clarity on the voluntary program. There is a lack of action on incentives [for adopting the NIST framework], and there's a lack of prioritization and attention to cost-effectiveness in the framework."

Sen. Tom Carper would recall that he and Tom Coburn, the top Republican on the Senate Homeland Security Panel, approached the new secretary and asked what he needed in order to empower DHS. "Hiring people on cyber," Johnson told Carper and Coburn. "They had the same problem that the government as a whole had on IT," Carper said. One answer was enhanced hiring authority.

Johnson also said the department needed clear authority to secure the federal government itself from cyber attacks. Under the system in place in 2013, Carper said, the White House Office of Management and Budget had much responsibility for the government's own cybersecurity but few resources. DHS had a full bureaucracy but little authority to mandate improvements. "Sen. Coburn and I thought that made no sense," Carper said.

"What we had in place was the equivalent of taking a picture once a year and then doing a bunch of paperwork," according to Carper. "We knew we had to give DHS authority to say to other agencies, 'What you're doing is wrong.'"

And, Johnson and the two senators agreed, the department needed to turn the DHS cyber information-sharing center—the National Cybersecurity and Communications Integration Center—into a real functioning asset. "The NCCIC existed as kind of a fiction," Carper recalled. "It wasn't authorized" in law and "it didn't have adequate resources."

Improvements on personnel, legal authority, and sufficient resources devoted to its information-sharing center together would help make DHS "a prime-time player," Carper, Coburn, and Secretary Johnson all believed.

Strictly in the policy realm, there were three areas where DHS might find success if it was going to seize onto the cyber issue: running a so-called voluntary program to spread awareness and use of the popular NIST framework; as the civilian government's hub for information sharing; and securing the civilian government's own computer networks.

In September 2013, DHS launched the Voluntary Program Working Group as mandated under Obama's Executive Order 13636. DHS said in a document circulated to working group participants that it would adopt a "formal," catchier name and described the mission as spreading the word about the voluntary framework even before its scheduled release in February 2014. The new working group would "develop sector-specific strategies" on promoting framework adoption, reinforce the framework within "critical risk management planning efforts," and support outreach efforts, according to the document.

"The working group will figure out how to go out and encourage adoption" of the framework, a DHS source told InsideCybersecurity.com. "It's a more formalized approach to encouraging adoption. This is a good example of the transition from drafting the framework to 'now, go do it.'"

Unfortunately, this mission wasn't necessarily compatible with DHS's skill set.

As sort of a run-up to the voluntary program, which wouldn't begin to unfold in earnest until the framework was actually released in February 2014, DHS was trying to push out a new "National Infrastructure Protection Plan," or NIPP, in the summer and fall of 2013. This was the first revision of the NIPP since 2009 and that earlier effort—and the unfortunate acronym—were largely the work of the George W. Bush administration.

The process of developing the plan, and how well DHS did in promoting a collaborative process with its industry partners, was as important as the substance in the ultimate document. It was intended to be a blueprint for government and critical infrastructure sectors on planning for both cyber and physical risks. Earlier versions earned praise from industry groups; the initial efforts under Obama's DHS were viewed with concern.

A draft was circulated to 1,100 stakeholders in the summer of 2013 and a public meeting was scheduled for late September. The whole thing was due at the White House by October 10, but once more a government shutdown would imperil that schedule.

The early reviews of the draft weren't good. Industry groups expected more collaboration on revising the NIPP, "but that hasn't happened," one source said at the time. The proposed NIPP didn't lay out a process for joint planning or ways to measure outcomes, key industry objectives. "It's a document, it's not a plan." There were "significant gaps" between government and industry on cost-effectiveness and risk management. "I'm going to remain optimistic but there are huge disconnects here," the source said.

"It's too long, it's too wordy and it doesn't have a clearly defined core," said Internet Security Alliance president Larry Clinton. "They should streamline it and make it more usable. Explain the value proposition for industry to work with government. And explain how [industry] will interact with government." Industry was comfortable with the existing 2009 NIPP, Clinton said, although "updating it is probably a worthwhile exercise. But if they just keep the current draft, that would be problematic."

Voices were raised at increasingly tense DHS-industry meetings. Department officials seemed to have already written the plan, industry sources believed, and were merely going through the motions of collaboration. Once again, the dread prospect of regulation was hanging over an Obama administration cyber initiative. The DHS officials bristled in response and tried to stress that the work product belonged to the critical infrastructure operators who would have to use it.

Was this the precursor of a doomed DHS voluntary program to promote the framework?

In the end, the industry side believed that DHS partially responded to the concerns and revised the NIPP document, which was finalized in December, somewhat to their satisfaction. The problem was that work on the NIPP took place in a closed circuit, regardless of DHS's emphasis on the 1,100 participants in the process. These were mostly familiar faces who had engaged with DHS before.

The voluntary program, carrying some of the high hopes for the NIST framework, was a different matter entirely. DHS would need to reach a new audience and help persuade business owners from far outside the beltway to participate in an ambitious plan to shore up cybersecurity.

"DHS just doesn't collaborate well," an industry source said. "Sometimes the White House has to intervene. But in general, DHS has the power in its relationship with us and they will plow ahead regardless of our view. DHS is the unequal partner."

As usual, the department's efforts on the voluntary program got off to a bumpy start. At an opening meeting of the working group in September 2013, DHS came prepared with a series of questions on industry expectations and instead were peppered with questions about what, exactly, the government expected this "voluntary program" process to deliver.

"There is still a lot of conversation that needs to take place on the goals for this group," said an industry source. "What is the goal and what is the time frame when this working group will be operating?"

The anxiety was palpable around the initiative. Questions tumbled over questions and the government side had little chance of catching up.

Another source said, "Industry people are still struggling with how much we have to do" under the framework. "The government hasn't whittled down who has to participate, they haven't defined the benefits of participating. What's the government's take on this—and what is DHS going to require from us?"

The perception that the government in general and DHS in particular would "require" something of industry in the framework process was stubbornly enduring.

The White House had released the proposed incentives developed by DHS but still hadn't answered questions about the "sequencing" of industry efforts to use the framework. DHS was encouraging along the insurance industry in the development of a cyber insurance market, but other possible incentives were in limbo.

Spaulding, in a November 2013 appearance at the Brookings Institution, said DHS was analyzing further incentives for adoption of the framework, noting that grants and expedited security clearances for those trying to implement the framework could be near-term incentives, while insurance was probably a longer term incentive.

The message from the voluntary program, Spaulding said, was: "How can we help? How can you look at this framework and translate it into a program to reduce risk?" The department would make the private sector aware of "all of the assistance that's available now" on cybersecurity including information-sharing arrangements and a program called "Enhanced Cybersecurity Services." She told the audience, "These are all critical parts of the voluntary program."

But the message wasn't being disseminated broadly enough, and as incentives languished, DHS didn't have much to offer companies.

DHS's Thad Odderstol, speaking at NIST's fifth workshop on the framework at North Carolina State University, acknowledged that the department could offer few incentives to companies as the voluntary program got started. Odderstol said the "very limited incentives" available could include technical assistance, continued engagement with the insurance industry, and engagement with the Defense Department and the General Services Administration on procurement issues.

He attempted to leaven that message with assurances that DHS intended to assist companies with the framework rather than impose demands. And, he said, the DHS-led interagency task force on cybersecurity would be a "centralized place" to continue examining incentives, while the department would play a leading role in advocating for regulatory "harmonization" across government—an industry priority—and would not include onerous requirements to prove adoption of the framework.

DHS "recognizes different methods and approaches to adoption," he said, adding, "Industry will drive how it wants to be recognized."

Following the delay due to the government shutdown, the Voluntary Program Working Group held its second meeting in early December 2013 amid industry questions about what role this new body would play.

Working groups were proliferating; stakeholders on the industry side were unconvinced that their government partners knew how the pieces fit together or the time demands they were imposing on private-sector representatives who had day jobs, after all.

The second meeting drew at least one hundred attendees, plus more who participated by conference call. Officials offered a glimpse at their proposed definition of cybersecurity framework adoption, said they would take a three-phased approach to the voluntary program, and that monthly meetings would be held going forward.

The phases included promoting and enabling early adoption of the framework in the first phase; a more industry-specific focus to encourage adoption across critical infrastructure sectors in phase two; and moving toward future versions of the framework in phase three. DHS officials indicated that phase one of the voluntary program would cover the next twelve to eighteen months, sources said, and would focus on "establishing momentum across the critical infrastructure community."

DHS officials showed participants a proposed draft definition of framework adoption, "inviting feedback on what adoption means," in the words of one attendee. "The draft statement on defining framework adoption was very vague," said an industry source. It appeared that "in order to say you've adopted, you just have to say you've reviewed your cybersecurity program and this is where you stand. Anybody could say they've adopted."

A utility industry source said: "DHS was very disorganized in their approach to requesting comments on the proposed definition of 'adoption' and the examples given in the presentation. We also need further clarification on the timeline for the rollout of the three phases of the [voluntary] program. . . . So, still a lot of questions that need to be addressed."

The view wasn't unanimous. A technology sector source said there was a "useful discussion" of how to move from "participation" to "adoption," and how that was to be measured, as well as talk of whether adoption was even the right word. Another industry source said DHS provided helpful scenarios and that officials got the point that it was essential to better define adoption. "The adoption language is still a bit muddy but the intent is good," this source said. "We can live with it, though it still isn't what I would put in front of my CEO."

By the start of 2014, the department faced growing pressure to spell out how the voluntary program to encourage adoption of the framework of cybersecurity standards would actually work. Stakeholders said DHS should be prepared to offer specifics at the third working group meeting on January 17. It may have been wishful thinking and the department was busy trying to temper expectations and pitch the question back to industry on what it should try to accomplish.

DHS's Jenny Menna, who would leave the department in the coming summer, cautioned at a public meeting that there was "no additional funding or authorities" for "phase one" of the voluntary program. Speaking before the Information Security and Privacy Advisory Board, Menna said the initial phase of the program would involve making existing resources available to the private sector, such as cybersecurity best practices developed for the government. DHS was also developing a Web site that would serve as a repository of information on the program, although Menna declined to offer a launch date. "We're looking at this to be an industry-led activity," she said, and officials hoped to "gather more industry input" at the January meeting.

That message didn't resonate with representatives of various industry sectors. Uncertainty over the voluntary program was creating reluctance among companies to become "early adopters" of the framework, which was due out the next month. "We shouldn't have to wait until January 17 to get their vision," one industry source said of DHS's plans. "There's a high level of frustration over both the product and the level of maturity of thinking about this program."

Another source said DHS appeared to be "holding its nose" as it implemented the program, adding, "They don't want the job and are executing accordingly."

One industry source said DHS could provide much more than a catalogue of existing best practices, even without additional funding. This source said DHS should be prepared to offer specific information on what activities qualified as adoption of the framework, how companies could prioritize cybersecurity efforts, and how critical infrastructure sectors should measure success, along with providing a "structure of available resources."

These were elementary steps, but they weren't being executed.

In early 2014, DHS also needed to do a better job reaching out to the private sector on incentives, even if that simply meant greater communication and dialogue as the department analyzed what incentives might work best for various sectors. Instead, DHS's work was happening behind thick walls.

Industry representatives unfavorably compared the voluntary program with NIST's development of the framework, saying NIST was much more transparent and collaborative. But NIST officials were consummate team players and pushed back on that characterization.

"NIST will continue to partner with DHS on the voluntary program, just as DHS partnered with NIST on the workshops and the overall development of the framework itself," NIST's Sedgewick told InsideCybersecurity .com. "I think many of the comments talked about additional implementation needs—including sector specific ones—and DHS has capabilities and existing programs to work in those areas and ensure effective use of the framework."

Sedgewick added, "I thought the [privacy board] presentation highlighted all of those things very well—and you could see that in the board's response." Board members expressed a great deal of interest in— and some skepticism about—DHS's efforts to help expand the insurance market for cybersecurity, as well as support for efforts to extend the availability of cybersecurity tools throughout critical infrastructure sectors.

"This is a very important period of activity and [I] can tell you that we are committed to 'getting this right' and ensuring that we have a successful launch of the program and framework and that we keep our partners involved in the process," a DHS official told InsideCybersecurity.com. "We have a lot of good ideas that we'll be discussing on the 17th and we are going to be asking for feedback from a lot of our key partners."

Mindful of the comparisons to the NIST process, DHS announced it would add a second day to the meeting and pledged plenty of opportunities for industry engagement.

At the second meeting, DHS officials met some of the targets. They offered assurances that they would align an unwieldy assortment of cyber policy initiatives to avoid duplication and excessive demands on the department's business-sector partners. Schneck said DHS would be flexible in defining adoption of the framework, drawing praise from industry participants in the working group. But she also said there was still a ways to go in developing metrics for measuring success and for helping companies prioritize activities under the framework. She called for more input from private-sector stakeholders on these and other issues. An industry representative at the meeting called for metrics that are "objective, comparable, and focused on self-assessment."

But overall, industry sources expressed disappointment that DHS didn't offer more detail at the meeting on how the voluntary program would function going forward.

"It was a significantly better show" than the first two working group meetings, said one industry source. "They were able to explain the resources they have for the program and they emphasized the role of the private sector, which was good. Now the question is what's their ability to execute?"

DHS officials stressed that they would promote their Cybersecurity Resilience Review as a tool companies could begin using immediately, this source noted, but they did not make clear what resources would be available to promote widespread use. "Do they have the resources to support it? Is it scalable?" the source asked.

Sources also noted that DHS had little new to offer on incentives for adopting the framework. DHS officials did say the incentives program would focus initially on six "lifeline" areas of critical infrastructure including energy, water, communications, finance, health care, and transportation.

"I'm most disappointed that the framework is ready to go out in a few weeks and we still need some way to get at the target companies," another industry source said. "They said nothing new that would motivate a company that isn't already following the best practices in the framework." This source said DHS failed to provide clarity on what framework adoption meant and offered only limited information on incentives. "Technical assistance seems to be the only incentive that will be available at the beginning, but it's unclear what that will be or who will qualify," the source said.

Schneck told meeting participants that the department was taking a very flexible approach to defining adoption. DHS "provided a lot more information on where they're going on incentives and a lot of thought is going into this," said a third source. "But the incentives are years away. Businesses shouldn't get hung up on this."

The source said DHS was "on the right path" with its plans for outreach and educational efforts throughout the country, and on helping companies get started with their cybersecurity programs through use of the resiliency tool and a soon-to-be-unveiled Web site. "It was heartening that they really committed to working with the private sector," the source said. "And we're very happy with their broad interpretation of adoption."

That was good news to another source, who said concerns about legal liability would make framework adoption essentially mandatory, even if regulators don't do so explicitly. "Once this is in ink, some attorney is going to ask 'why didn't you adopt the framework?'" the source said. "People will simply have to adopt it."

Overall, the voluntary program "is going to move slowly," commented another participant. "It all depends on the resources. The technical assistance they're talking about is already existing resources matched to the framework, and that's good, because a lot of the [critical infrastructure] community doesn't know they're there."

It moved more slowly than these sources imagined. There would be a new name: the Critical Infrastructure Cyber Community Voluntary Program, to be known as C-Cubed. That was, perhaps, sexier and sleeker. But there wouldn't be much more in terms of tangible assistance to industry.

In February DHS held an invitation-only teleconference in which it revealed the new branding and again tried to explain how the "voluntary program" would actually help industry use the new framework. Some industry sources said the purpose and the usefulness of the DHS-managed voluntary program were coming into focus; others called C-Cubed the same old wine in a new bottle. There were fewer than 250 participants on the February C-Cubed conference call.

C-Cubed consisted of three pieces: converging resources, connecting stakeholders, and coordinating efforts. A slide presentation touched on next steps, promising "sector by sector events" and, "potentially," regional workshops and requests for information to encourage "broad public engagement."

Joining the program was "as simple as visiting the Web site," a senior administration official said. "And there's no magic—you don't have to sign up, you don't ever have to let us know even that you've been to the website. But if you would like to avail yourself of some of those resources, again, we're going to make it very easy for you to know how to do that and how to interact with the folks in the government who might be able to provide varying degrees of assistance in this option of the framework."

"This has been hard for DHS," said McAfee's Kent Landfield, "but I do see a good deal of evolution. They are starting to get a handle on the messaging and building a community."

Landfield said outreach—in particular, efforts to draw in companies that hadn't engaged on cybersecurity—was the essential goal for the DHS program, and suggested that DHS understood this challenge.

"I don't see any downside to participating," commented Kevin Morley of the American Water Works Association. "I'm cautiously optimistic." It "seems like they are seeking a pretty open and collaborative 'community,'" Morley added. "I think anything that elevates awareness and makes the issue actionable by management is critical—that is the underlying objective of our effort."

Other industry observers also saw benefits in C-Cubed.

"The C3 Voluntary Program will assist stakeholders with understanding the use of the Framework and other cyber risk management efforts, and support development of general and sector-specific guidance for Framework implementation," the American Gas Association's Kimberly Denbow said in a statement to InsideCybersecurity.com. Denbow noted that AGA was working with the Department of Energy on implementation guidance.

Questions persisted on whether the DHS resources would be particularly valuable, and how they related to other programs such as the "C2M2" maturity model developed by the Energy Department to help companies measure their cyber readiness. One industry source who was closely involved in developing the framework said the department's Cyber Resilience Review tool was helpful, but added that industry groups were already moving beyond what DHS had to offer.

That wasn't necessarily a bad thing: Perhaps the DHS offerings provided a baseline that could, in fact, be of significant value to less cyber-mature companies. More advanced approaches could proliferate through the private sector. Perhaps, but that would be a very modest take on the mission at hand; industry was seeking more from the department at this stage of cybersecurity policy development.

"There's nothing new here," said another industry source. "DHS is putting together existing resources and programs and bundling them under a new name. Questions remain as to what will drive industry to 'participate' in this voluntary program, what 'participation' means, and what the incentive is to participate."

This source added: "DHS has said in the past that each sector will develop their own 'voluntary program' through the sector coordinating councils. I don't know how that reconciles with this national C3 program."

By the winter of 2014, DHS had offered about all it had to offer on the voluntary program. Meetings would appear and disappear, like an announced session focused on the financial sector in New York that was never actually discussed with financial-sector representatives and mysteriously vanished from the calendar. A DHS inquiry on cyber solutions for small businesses prompted concerns that the department was looking to shape the market and pricing for cybersecurity products, forcing DHS officials to hastily clarify what they were looking for.

DHS pitched the NIST framework at a June 2014 C-Cubed event in Boston, in what the department promised would be the first part of an extensive road show. About 150 people participated. Considering the thousands and thousands of companies that needed to be reached, observers questioned whether DHS was getting much bang for its buck.

Why not a national advertising campaign like the old "Smokey Bear" forest fire messages? asked Danielle Kriz of the Information Technology Industry Council. Surely that would be more cost-effective. Kriz had a master's from Georgetown, a bachelor's from Ithaca College and was a veteran of both Silicon Valley and the Commerce Department. She understood the audience that had to be reached.

October was already "Cyber Month," with DHS promoting various activities. Why not launch "a national educational campaign every day?" asked Juniper Networks' Robert Dix, leveraging public service announcements, government relationships with various organizations, and the multitude of contact points between government and citizens.

Dix, a Virginia Tech graduate, had spent over a decade working on software and Internet security issues in the private sector, after doing his spell as a subcommittee staff director in the House. But he'd also learned how to carry a message out to the front porch and the neighborhood sidewalk, serving on town councils and county boards in suburban Virginia. He coached kids' athletic teams and knew a bit about messaging.

"It's a little disappointing," Dix said. "National Cybersecurity Awareness Month seemed a natural place to launch a comprehensive public awareness campaign."

Such an effort could be relatively inexpensive and packaged in fun ways, he said, with a heavy emphasis on outreach to students. Every congressional home page could have a link to cybersecurity information. The platforms available to government to put the cybersecurity issue in front of people were practically endless.

Couple this with sustained campaigns from major industry groups—Dix mentioned the U.S. Chamber of Commerce grassroots effort as an example—and cybersecurity would become a front-of-mind topic pretty quickly. "The NIST framework is a nice toolbox but it can't reach its full potential unless people are better educated," Dix argued.

DHS wasn't much interested, and it didn't seem much interested in its roadshow either, as subsequent sessions failed to materialize for many months. When the DHS roadshow landed in Houston in November 2014, forty people showed up.

A U.S. Chamber of Commerce roadshow would hit more cities, reach larger audiences, and gradually, if only partially, supplant the DHS effort. Communication wasn't DHS's forte—a shortcoming department officials like Schneck were willing to acknowledge—and the voluntary program was all about communication.

But C-Cubed was a mandated responsibility and DHS kept trying. By the fall of 2015 the department put together events aimed at state governments, small businesses, and promoting enterprise-wide approaches to cybersecurity. It would be a bit more manageable and, perhaps, effective to tackle the outreach responsibilities in smaller pieces. This was the modest, lightly promoted start to phase two of the DHS plan for its C-Cubed program.

The information-sharing function was, perhaps, a different and happier story for DHS. Schneck would tell audiences that the DHS National Cybersecurity and Communications Integration Center was "one of the jewels of the department."

Schneck's top priority, she said, was to build trust between the government and the private sector on information sharing and to spur the development of real-time, automated sharing of cyber threat indicators.

A "utopian" vision of success for the department would include "perfect information sharing," Suzanne Spaulding said at a Brookings Institution event in November 2013. It would include deepening the understanding of what resources government and private-sector entities could bring to bear in an information-sharing arrangement. The system would include "sensors to detect perturbations and the ability to communicate perfectly," she said, along with the capacity to shift quickly and innovate.

Larry Zelvin, then the National Cybersecurity and Communications Integration Center chief, testified in 2014 that the NCCIC received 350,000 reports of cyber incidents between October 2013 and July 2014, up from 230,000 in all of fiscal year 2013. The NCCIC could drill down into these incidents. Terrorists were targeting U.S. Web sites and networks, often deploying relatively low-grade directed denial of service attacks. Faith-based groups were a rising target, Zelvin said.

Predictably, the finance, energy, telecommunications, information technology, and transportation sectors were the most frequent targets of cyber attacks of all kinds, Zelvin said, but he added that other sectors were being attacked and perhaps didn't know it. Many of these sectors were under no legal requirement to report attacks or breaches, Zelvin said, highlighting the NCCIC's success in fostering a collaborative atmosphere in the absence of mandates.

Here's how it worked, as explained in messages to Congress by top DHS officials:

The NCCIC, as codified by the National Cybersecurity Protection Act of 2014, serves as a central hub for cybersecurity information sharing between federal agencies, the private sector, law enforcement, and the intelligence community. Through a watch floor that operates twenty-four hours a day, seven days a week, the NCCIC provides a forum for real-time collaboration to understand and gain situational awareness of cybersecurity incidents and risks.

Currently, representatives of several federal agencies (U.S. Northern Command, U.S. Cyber Command, National Security Agency, U.S. Secret Service, U.S. Immigration and Customs Enforcement, U.S. Department of the Treasury, the Department of Justice's Federal Bureau of Investigation, and the U.S. Department of Energy) and four Information Sharing and Analysis Centers, which represent the financial, aviation, and energy sectors as well as state, local, tribal, and territorial governments, have dedicated liaisons on the NCCIC watch floor.

Further, 114 private sector companies have as-needed access to the NCCIC through their participation in CISCP.

Federal agencies with cleared personnel maintain similar as-needed access.

The NCCIC enjoyed broad support on Capitol Hill. Sen. Ron Wyden (D-Oregon), Congress's most vocal critic of government surveillance activities and its collection of personal data, pointed to the NCCIC process as an appropriate model for collecting and sharing cyber threat indicators.

"This watch center receives cyber security threat information from around the Federal Government and from private companies, and this watch center sends out alerts and bulletins to security professionals to provide them with technical information about cyber security threats," Wyden said on the Senate floor during debate over cybersecurity information-sharing legislation in August 2015.

> In fiscal year 2014, this watch center sent out nearly 12,000 of these alerts to more than 100,000 recipients. That happens today, with lots of companies participating.
>
> The system that is in place today includes rules to protect the privacy of law-abiding Americans.

President Obama delivered a speech at the NCCIC headquarters in Arlington, Virginia, in January 2015 to unveil his plans on cyber information sharing. It was a salute to the work going on at the center, as well as a call on Congress for greater authority for NCCIC to do its job.

The NCCIC process showed great promise, though DHS and industry representatives alike warned it wouldn't reach its full potential until companies were give some level of legal immunity in exchange for their participation.

There were also structural issues. Dix of Juniper Networks noted in the spring of 2015 that only three of the fully functioning industry information sharing and analysis centers were represented in the NCCIC. "One reason is resources," Dix said. Further, he said, it was time to review whether the NCCIC was structured appropriately considering the evolving threat environment. "There is value being delivered every day by the NCCIC, they are trying, but the current architecture doesn't reflect the need of the current threat environment," he said.

NCCIC was too slow, another source said. By the time private companies got the information, it was hopelessly dated.

As DHS faced another shutdown in the winter of 2015, part of the seemingly endless skirmish with Congress over immigration policy, Ozment testified before the House Homeland Security Panel that 140 NCCIC employees would be sent home. The volume of threat information shared with companies would be reduced and would not be as timely. DHS would be unable to bring on new companies as partners and unable to begin planning next generation information-sharing capabilities for real-time and automated sharing.

The message to lawmakers was that DHS had a program that was providing real value for the private sector as well as improving the nation's security. The NCCIC—and DHS's information-sharing role—had friends on Capitol Hill and showed much promise. But it still needed tending. It would be a mistake to think of this DHS function as a success story; it was a work in progress.

The third area—how well DHS was doing in securing the government's computer systems—would remain an open and exasperating question for years to come. DHS saw its "continuous diagnostics and monitoring" system, designed to detect anomalies on federal computer networks, and other programs like "EINSTEIN" as uniquely effective and even as models for the private sector. But revelations about the breaches of the government's own sensitive databases didn't help.

In August 2014, DHS revealed that USIS, a private contractor that performed the department's employee background checks, had been breached. It was embarrassing, but far worse was still to come.

Andy Ozment frequently took on the job of testifying before Congress on DHS's role and how the system was intended to provide cyber tools throughout the federal government.

He explained the process as such during one appearance: "Although agencies must take the lead in their own cybersecurity . . . DHS helps federal agencies protect their systems using two programs: (1) EINSTEIN, a perimeter protection program that detects and blocks threats attempting to access agencies' unclassified networks, and (2) Continuous Diagnostics and Mitigation (CDM), a DHS program that provides federal civilian agencies with tools to monitor agencies' internal networks."

Ozment used a simple illustration:

> Like a fence around a physical building, EINSTEIN protects agencies' unclassified networks at the perimeter of each agency. Furthermore, EINSTEIN provides situational awareness across the government, as threats detected in one agency are shared with all others so they can take appropriate protective action. The U.S. Government could not achieve such situational awareness through individual agency efforts alone.

There was a next step:

> The first two versions of EINSTEIN—EINSTEIN 1 and 2—identify abnormal network traffic patterns and detect known malicious traffic. This capability is fully deployed and screening all federal civilian traffic that is routed through a Trusted Internet Connection (a secure gateway between each agency's internal network and the Internet). EINSTEIN 3 Accelerated (EINSTEIN 3A), which actively blocks known malicious traffic, is currently being deployed through the primary Internet Service Providers serving the Federal Government. EINSTEIN 1 and 2 use only unclassified information, while EINSTEIN 3A uses classified information. Using classified indicators allows EINSTEIN 3A to detect and block many of the most significant cybersecurity threats.

The department was also providing agencies with another tool, continuous diagnostics and mitigation, to provide a real-time view of what was happening on their networks and the ability to respond.

But this all took time to implement and the system was coming into question, most spectacularly in the spring of 2015.

The Department of Homeland Security detected "malicious activities" on the Office of Personnel Management (OPM) networks in April 2015 and determined in May that the system had been compromised. Federal employees were notified on June 4 that sensitive personal data had been breached.

That notification letter triggered a media firestorm and a ferocious reaction on Capitol Hill. Just what was DHS doing with its billions of dollars in budget authority to protect the government itself?

In the days that followed, the government would acknowledge many more federal employees were affected by the breach—perhaps 14 million current and former employees. And, though officials wouldn't publicly say it, China was tagged as the perpetrator. The *Washington Post*'s Ellen Nakashima, who was exceptionally well-wired into the intelligence and security communities, reported "that a database holding sensitive security clearance information on millions of federal employees and contractors also was compromised."

The hackers were going after specific pieces of data, deeply personal information on government employees and their foreign contacts, that would provide a treasure trove of information to a foreign intelligence service.

Ozment was hauled to Capitol Hill to testify on a panel that included the OPM director, the agency's chief information officer, and its assistant inspector general.

House Oversight and Government Reform Chairman Jason Chaffetz (R-Utah) and committee members of both parties lambasted officials from OPM, the Office of Management and Budget, the Interior Department, and DHS. Chaffetz told reporters later that OPM Director Katherine Archuleta and Chief Information Officer Donna Seymour should resign.

As her boss sat ashen-faced beside her, Seymour heatedly responded that she and Archuleta had had been hired to fix these very problems. "These were years in the making," she stressed. "We're not going to solve this in one or two years."

"That's where I disagree," responded Rep. Will Hurd (R-Texas). Hurd was a newcomer to Capitol Hill but he had a special cachet as a former CIA officer and had been awarded the chairmanship of an Oversight subcommittee on information technology as well as a seat on the Homeland Security Committee. "We don't have one or two years," he warned the witness.

There was far more heat than light at this hearing, as Democrats and Republicans took turns tossing the word "failure" at the witnesses.

"You made a conscious decision to leave this system vulnerable," Chaffetz said to Archuleta.

"This has been going on for a long time," Chaffetz said. "And yet when I read the testimony it's 'We're doing a great job.' You're not!" The federal government spent $80 billion on information technology in 2014, Chaffetz said, "and it stinks!"

Oversight ranking member Elijah Cummings (D-Maryland) tried to put the OPM breach in the context of large-scale, sophisticated attacks affecting all industries and aspects of the U.S. economy. "We have to remember who the bad guys are," Cummings said. These federal officials were not the enemy. On the other hand, Cummings too said the government failed to honor the trust it was given by employees.

Archuleta had been political director for Obama's 2012 re-election campaign, though she wasn't particularly well-known nationally as a political operative. She had been chief of staff to the secretary of labor in

Obama's first term and the top staffer to the secretary of transportation in the Bill Clinton administration. She was active on Hispanic issues in Colorado and had worked as a top adviser to Denver Mayor John Hickenlooper. She was brought in to run OPM as a human resources manager who could imagine ways to improve and diversify the federal workforce. Archuleta was well-versed in the demands of the bureaucracy and she discussed cybersecurity priorities during her confirmation process.

But she wasn't hired to be a cybersecurity professional. It was unclear whether the critics on the congressional panels thought a cyber professional should run the Office of Personnel Management, but it was becoming clearer that something was missing: Was it the lines of authority, the availability of tools, or the recurring tendency among both elected and nonelected officials to put other priorities ahead of cybersecurity?

DHS's Ozment sat largely out of the direct line of fire. But when Chaffetz said the EINSTEIN system was "completely useless" in the OPM hack, Ozment responded eagerly. This was the department's prized baby, after all.

OPM was leveraging tools provided by DHS when it first identified the breach, Ozment explained. OPM then notified DHS's NCCIC, which in turn used its EINSTEIN 2 system to search for similar threats across government, identifying a second intrusion at OPM. Then the next line of government defense, EINSTEIN 3, was deployed to block similar intrusions. These efforts may have headed off yet another attack of "severe consequence," Ozment told the committee.

He had another message: Both the government and the private sector were desperately trying to make up for "twenty years of under-investment" in cybersecurity.

It wasn't particularly well received. "Hasn't the private sector already moved past EINSTEIN?" Rep. Mark Walker (R-North Carolina) demanded.

"EINSTEIN is absolutely necessary but it's not sufficient," Ozment said. "EINSTEIN 3A will be a significant step forward . . . but no one tool will solve all our problems."

It was an accurate, if nuanced, response, but members of the Oversight Committee had no time for nuances.

Homeland Security Chairman McCaul had a different take. That wasn't surprising: McCaul sharply criticized DHS on occasion but his job was to try to make the department work as effectively as possible. The

Oversight Committee was just that, a perch from which lawmakers could toss partisan bombs at an administration of the other party, without much responsibility to do anything about shortfalls, real and imagined.

McCaul shook his head as a reporter recounted the criticisms tossed about during that day's House Oversight Committee hearing. The evidence suggested EINSTEIN 2 and 3 had worked, McCaul said in a brief hallway interview with InsideCybersecurity.com. His own committee—and the Senate homeland panel—would be looking at the OPM breach the following week. But they would look at the mechanics of the DHS efforts to detect and respond, not searching for scapegoats.

Ozment testified before the House Homeland Security Committee that DHS had no "stick" to compel agencies to improve cybersecurity.

Ozment did confirm before the homeland security panels that EINSTEIN 3 had yet to be installed at OPM, but cited the important role played by earlier versions that were in place. "OPM detected the intrusion because we've been rolling out these capabilities," he testified before the Senate Homeland Security and Governmental Affairs Committee on June 25. "OPM's upgrades are why we detected the attack." In addition, he said, EINSTEIN 3A was deployed to prevent the same kind of hack on other federal systems.

But the EINSTEIN 3 system was in place at less than half of all federal agencies.

"I've heard enough about EINSTEIN 3 in the last few weeks to think that's something we ought to do," Carper, the top Democratic senator on homeland security, told his colleagues. He promised a legislative push to ensure DHS had the tools to get this deployed.

In response to the breach, the Obama administration launched a thirty-day "sprint" to quickly drive up cybersecurity capacities within government using existing authorities. Tony Scott, the federal government's chief information officer, and Michael Daniel were able to point to some positive results with DHS and agencies using the powers they had. By the end of the sprint on July 29, fifteen of twenty-five agencies met a key metric for measuring security practices. That was up from four agencies in April and passed for progress. By late September 2015, DHS reported that CDM tools were finally available to 97 percent of the civilian government.

The OPM breach did more than force Ozment and Archuleta to march from congressional hearing room to hearing room over a sweltering two-week stretch in June 2015: It threw into relief some of the problems inherent in DHS's position.

On one hand, there was a congressional oversight structure that was often at cross-purposes—or no purpose at all. Sen. McCain, who served on the Homeland Security Committee and was chairman of the Armed Services Committee, demanded that Archuleta answer whether China was behind the breach. How would she possibly know? On the same day, Director of National Intelligence James Clapper finally stated publicly that China was the "leading suspect."

Clapper, of course, would be the right person to address this question. That an astute, experienced senator like McCain would berate Archuleta for an answer to an intelligence question was just more evidence that Congress didn't know what it wanted on cybersecurity or how to organize itself to address the issue.

On the other hand, DHS's precise authority was often in question.

"Do we have a government-wide plan?" Sen. Jon Tester (D-Montana) asked Ozment, certainly a softball question.

Ozment paused. There were a variety of documents, he said. "In aggregate they lay out a plan."

Tester was a burly, straightforward, and low-key farmer who asked direct questions.

"Is that effective?" he probed.

Ozment gamely said the department was focused on implementing new security programs, which was a better investment of time and energy than preparing reports. But toward the end of the hearing he would try to regroup and reassure Tester and his colleagues that the government did, in fact, have a comprehensive plan to protect its cyber assets.

"We have a skeleton of a path forward," he asserted. "We want to flesh out the skeleton."

That wasn't exactly a declaration that the government was marching into cyber-battle with a clear-cut strategy.

Ozment remained at Archuleta's shoulder as officials tried to stem the criticism and put in place an effective response plan. But the bottom fell out when OPM revealed on July 9 that 21.5 million current and former federal employees had been affected. "If an individual underwent a background investigation through OPM in 2000 or afterwards . . . it is highly likely that the individual is impacted by this cyber breach," OPM said in a statement. "If an individual underwent a background investigation prior to 2000, that individual still may be impacted, but it is less likely."

Archuleta, Ozment, and White House cybersecurity coordinator Michael Daniel led a conference call with reporters that day to discuss the recovery plan. Ozment said OPM used the government's cybersecurity tools appropriately. "This incident unfortunately is not without precedent," Daniel said.

Daniel said the event highlighted three policy needs that permeated both the public and private sector. Government and industry alike, he said, needed to raise their game on cybersecurity. New policies—and laws—were needed to deter adversaries from mounting these attacks in the first place. And everyone needed to improve their capacity to respond and recover from attacks, because they simply weren't going to stop coming.

Archuleta responded the same way to two reporters who asked if she would resign: The answer was no, and she was leading the charge to fix the problems.

But a growing chorus of lawmakers were demanding her head. And many cybersecurity professionals and business advocates said the hacks—and the response—may have diminished the Obama administration's ability to lead on policy in the cyber arena. "If it were private industry, someone would've been fired," commented an industry leader on cybersecurity issues. "That's not to say I'm not sympathetic, they have huge responsibilities on their shoulders, but when the government asks us to live up to a standard they're not living up to, that's a broken system."

On July 10, as anger swelled across Capitol Hill, Archuleta resigned.

DHS didn't take the direct hit, but once again the department was on its heels and seen as part of the problem rather than an enabler of solutions. Even the department's successes, like growing its capacities on information sharing, were qualified and sandwiched between failures. The NCCIC, a jewel in the crown, went years without a leader.

But the department had a leader in Johnson. Whether a strong, smart secretary with a true vision for the department could cure its ailments was questionable. But Johnson served notice in the aftermath of the OPM breach that he was in it for the duration.

"Cybersecurity is a top priority for me, for the President, and for this Administration," Johnson said in a speech at the Center for Strategic and International Studies. "It is my personal mission, before I leave office, to significantly enhance the Department of Homeland Security's role in the cybersecurity of this Nation."

There would never be perfect cybersecurity, Johnson said, and achieving any level of security would involve trade-offs.

"I will begin this speech like I end most of them," Johnson said.

> I tell audiences that homeland security is a balance—a balance between basic physical security and the freedoms we expect as Americans. As I have said many times, I can build you a perfectly safe city, but it will look like a prison. We can build more walls, install more invasive screening, interrogate more people and make everyone suspicious of each other, but not at the cost of who we are as a Nation of people who cherish privacy, value the freedom to travel and associate, and celebrate our diversity.
>
> The same is true of cybersecurity. Cybersecurity involves striking a balance. I can build you a perfectly safe e-mail system, but your contact will be limited to about ten people, and you would be disconnected entirely from the Internet and the outside world. This, too, would be like a prison.
>
> The reality is we live in an interconnected, networked world. Cybersecurity must also be a balance between the basic security of online information and the ability to communicate with and benefit from the networked world.

The department was aggressively using the authorities it had—on EINSTEIN and information sharing—and was eager for more authority from Congress, Johnson said. Lawmakers needed to do their part and incentivize companies to share more information with the NCCIC, for instance.

"But, my message today is we have increased, and will continue to increase, the instances in which attempted intrusions are either stopped at the gate, or rooted out from inside the system before they cause damage," Johnson said. "We are taking action. We are aggressively strengthening our defenses. We are accelerating the deployment of the tools we have, and working to bring new ones online. Thank you."

Johnson combined personal credibility with a defined vision for his department, which was a good start, but perhaps it was coming much too late in the life of DHS.

"DHS is not up to the task," Melissa Hathaway said bluntly in late 2015. The department was being asked to develop cybersecurity policy, build relationships with industry and across government, and have an operational role collecting and sharing cyber threat information. "It's doing all three poorly," she said.

The department's skill sets simply didn't match up and there was a critical lack of leadership in each area, Hathaway asserted. "We've spread them like peanut butter in three directions."

Asked what the department could do best, Hathaway agreed the operational information-sharing role through the NCCIC was probably the best bet for success. "If they can get good at one function," she suggested, "maybe they can improve in other areas."

But it wouldn't come easily. Hathaway and various industry observers firmly believed that the Obama administration would once again undermine DHS even in its strongest area—information-sharing—by creating the Cyber Threat Intelligence and Integration Center in 2015.

Secretary Johnson understood the tensions—and possibilities—and moved to ensure the NCCIC's place in the hierarchy.

"Given the central importance of the NCCIC to the DHS cybersecurity mission, I have determined that we must elevate the NCCIC within our Department's structure, with an incident reporting line directly to me as Secretary," Johnson announced on August 10, 2015. "Equally as important, I have also directed the National Protection and Programs Directorate to develop a reorganization plan that will ensure the NCCIC is focused on strengthening our operational capabilities for mitigating and responding to cyber incidents."

Johnson put John Felker in charge of the operational side of the NCCIC, after the long gap following Zelvin's departure. Felker had a thirty-year career at the Coast Guard and had worked in the private sector.

And, Johnson announced, Andy Ozment would take on direct responsibility for the NCCIC. Ozment had contributed to the key executive orders on cybersecurity, diligently represented DHS on Capitol Hill in the bad moments, and now he would be in charge of the department's most important cybersecurity operational responsibility.

"They keep reorganizing and reorganizing," commented Scott Algeier, who ran his own cybersecurity consulting firm and was executive director of the IT sector's information sharing and analysis center. "Until the NCCIC and U.S. CERT get more authority over federal network security, there won't be any improvement. It's a mess."

The reorganization moves also drew fire from Capitol Hill, where key lawmakers felt left out of the loop by the department's leadership. "We share your desire to ensure the Department is optimally organized to achieve its vital mission and appreciate the responsiveness of your staff on some aspects of this effort," the bipartisan leadership of the House Homeland Security Committee and its various subcommittees wrote in a September 15 letter to Secretary Johnson.

There was a substantial "but" coming.

"However, we are concerned with the lack of transparency on the proposed reorganization of the National Protection and Programs Directorate (NPPD). Despite multiple media reports . . . and numerous requests for information from our staff, we have yet to receive any specific details from the Department."

The committee staff, in fact, had been tipped off by a reporter, who heard about the reorganization plans from a lobbyist. That lobbyist learned of the moves in a casual conversation with a DHS official. It wasn't an ideal process or demonstration of transparency.

Cybersecurity subcommittee chairman John Ratcliffe (R-Texas) issued a sharply worded statement saying:

> DHS has been less than forthcoming about its NPPD reorganization effort. The Department has persisted in its "go it alone" mentality and has ignored Congress's requests for information—despite a record that demonstrates its need for oversight and accountability. I'd certainly like to see DHS enhance and prioritize NPPD's cyber mission. But I hope DHS will recognize that NPPD's mission is critical and that partnering with Congress, rather than obstruction, will produce a stronger, more effective outcome.

It was the kind of unforced error DHS was known for; worse yet, it strained relationships with the department's best, if not only, friends in Congress.

6

THE TELECOM CHALLENGE

The communications sector is at a critical juncture. We know there are threats to the communications networks upon which we all rely. We know those threats are growing. And we have agreed that industry-based solutions are the right approach. The question is: Will this approach work? We are not Pollyannas. We will implement this approach and measure results. It is those results that will tell us what, if any, next steps must be taken.

—Thomas Wheeler, chairman,
Federal Communications Commission, June 12, 2014

The telecommunications industry has confronted hacks since the dawn of the cyber age. In the mid-1980s, local Chicago TV stations and even the Playboy channel were targeted by activists with murky purposes. Telephone service was an even juicier target, from both a criminal and national security standpoint. The Federal Communications Commission (FCC) had responsibility for ensuring the safety of the broadcasting system, cable and satellite services, old-fashioned "landline" phones, and mobile devices. The commission had a new, controversial leader at the beginning of 2014.

Thomas Wheeler was a venture capitalist and former communications industry leader, who might be expected to become a certain type of chairman at the Federal Communications Commission. Instead, Wheeler seized the reins at the FCC and quickly became a populist live wire who frequently kept the executives in his own former industry off balance.

Wheeler's Internet "neutrality" plan would trigger one of the great regulatory and legal conflicts of the Obama years.

By contrast, his approach to cybersecurity would be grounded in collaboration between the FCC and industry. But as was often the case in both Wheeler's administration and the Obama administration's interactions with private industry, there would always be a catch.

Wheeler was sixty-seven years old when he was sworn in as FCC chairman, in November 2013, after his nomination had stalled for months in the Senate. Some Republicans feared Wheeler would use the position to advance President Obama's campaign finance reform agenda, perhaps by forcing disclosure of the donors behind certain political advertisements. That, of course, would be the least of the Republicans' worries as Wheeler's term progressed.

Wheeler did raise hundreds of thousands of dollars for Obama's 2008 presidential campaign; he and his wife, Carole Wheeler, moved to Iowa to support then-Senator Obama in the run-up to the critical Iowa caucuses that year. Sen. Ted Cruz of Texas and other Republicans worried that Wheeler's nomination was a Trojan Horse, carrying a secret plan to enact campaign finance restrictions that couldn't get through Congress. Across the aisle, some Democrats and liberal groups feared the ex-lobbyist for the wireless and cable industries might turn out to be an industry shill.

"Wheeler's nomination presents a conundrum for public interest groups," *Time* reported in May 2013. "On the one hand, Wheeler is a consummate D.C. insider who ran two major industry groups and raised hundreds of thousands of dollars for Obama. These facts . . . reinforce the stereotype that D.C.'s most desirable jobs tend to go to those with the best industry and administration connections."

But *Time* added that Wheeler was well-known and liked in the technology community.

Cybersecurity wasn't one of the issues flagged by either supporters or critics of Wheeler's nomination in 2013. Surely his term would be dominated by more familiar issues such as net neutrality and spectrum auctions.

Wheeler, like Obama, saw cybersecurity as a foundational issue and a challenge that needed to be taken on sooner rather than later. But the path he would select for cybersecurity in the communications sector was far from clear when Wheeler took office.

Plenty of voices were calling for straightforward regulation to bolster the sector's cybersecurity. Melissa Hathaway, Bush's former cybersecurity adviser, in an October 2013 speech, said the FCC should be "empowered" to regulate industry's cybersecurity efforts. She dismissed the National Institute of Standards and Technology's (NIST) nascent framework as "a lot of paper."

But within weeks of Hathaway's speech, Wheeler took the FCC effort in a different direction. FCC officials announced at the November 2013 NIST workshop in Raleigh, North Carolina, that they would develop a cybersecurity strategy based on the framework of standards, with industry in the lead. The communications sector would be the first to embrace the framework, which had yet to be released, as its guiding light on cybersecurity.

The FCC's public safety chief at the time, David Turetsky, quietly approached the major telecom trade associations in early 2013 about launching a process to update the sector's cyber best practices. Industry officials responded by pointing out their commitment to the NIST framework process, which would be a massive undertaking. The FCC leadership agreed to hold off until the framework was completed in February 2014, although Turetsky and other officials made clear that the commission was determined to address cybersecurity policy.

"This was a major turning point, in that [the new approach at the FCC] shifted attention away from the previous focus on technology practices that would certainly be required to be updated on a regular basis, to a risk-management approach where processes could be embedded within enterprises to enhance their ability to manage a constantly evolving ecosystem and cyber-attacks," said U.S. Telecom's Robert Mayer.

"Furthermore," Mayer said, "the timing was such that we would be in a position to take a framework that we would be working on for a year and turn around and adapt that multi-sector framework to the five segments in the communications sector. This approach addressed a key concern that industry had been expressing for several years which was the importance of avoiding simultaneous and duplicative activities in multiple government venues."

In March 2014, Wheeler formally put the challenge to a security advisory committee that had served as a forum for industry–government collaboration for over twenty years. The Communications Security, Reliability, and Interoperability Council (CSRIC) emerged a few years after the breakup of the Bell telephone system to help the different companies and services collaborate on important security issues. Wheeler in late 2013 ordered the creation of a new cybersecurity working group within the council. After the pause to allow NIST to finish its work on the cybersecurity framework, Wheeler, on March 20, gave "working group 4" its orders and one year to produce results.

"Because the project began a year late, we faced significant pressure to meet a CSRIC-imposed deadline of March 2015," Mayer recalled. "To meet this aggressive timeline, we knew we needed to assemble a group of highly motivated professionals who would have to accomplish the task at hand while also performing their regular 'day jobs.'"

Wheeler was also putting the personnel pieces in place. In November 2013 Wheeler named retired Rear Admiral David Simpson as chief of the Public Safety and Homeland Security Bureau, replacing Turetsky who was a familiar, comfortable presence for the industry side. Simpson graduated from the U.S. Naval Academy in 1982 and earned a PhD in systems technology at the Naval Post-Graduate School. He served in Baghdad for two years as the director for communications services and information technology for American forces and worked on building up the Iraqi government's IT capacities and the country's telecom system.

The admiral, clearly, had experience in difficult stakeholder environments. He was a career Navy man. His approach was to push hard, constantly, and it would be interesting to see how this unfolded with civilian interlocutors who could simply walk away from the table.

In January 2014, Wheeler pulled Clete Johnson from the Senate Intelligence Committee staff to work on cybersecurity issues. Johnson was a starting defensive back on the Harvard football team in the mid-1990s even as he went through the ROTC program. He served overseas in the Army and earned a law degree at the University of Georgia before a stint on K Street and on Capitol Hill. In addition to working on the Intelligence Committee staff, he addressed cyber and other issues as a staffer in Sen. Jay Rockefeller's office.

The Georgia native and son of a one-term congressman was gung-ho and relentlessly positive.

He was also something of a contrast to Simpson in his approach to engaging with the telecom industry: Johnson never came off as telling the industry representatives what they had to do, and seemed to understand viscerally that this was their process and their product.

With Simpson—as with Wheeler—the industry folks were never quite sure. Wheeler seemed to delight in the fearsome reputation he was earning. Simpson, on the other hand, felt the FCC leadership got a bad rap at times from its industry partners. The commission was truly committed to the industry-led process, he felt, but actually securing the nation's communications systems simply had to be achieved. Simpson didn't necessarily dispense with the niceties, but the Navy man would insist on achieving the objective.

Mayer of U.S. Telecom and Brian Allen of Time Warner Cable were named co-chairmen of working group 4. Samara Moore was assigned as a liaison from the White House, signaling interest from the highest levels of the Obama administration, and Donna Dodson would provide NIST's perspective. The working group enlisted over one hundred participants from five segments of the telecom sector: wireless, wireline, broadcast, cable, and satellite. Their work would be bolstered by subgroups addressing issues particular to small business and barriers to implementation.

"We're talking about building a new regulatory paradigm," Chairman Wheeler said at the inaugural session in the FCC hearing room. "If this works—when this works, this must work—it will prove over-regulation is not necessary. . . . This is a new model, for this building, for this government. But we have to make it work. The alternatives are not attractive."

Simpson told InsideCybersecurity.com: "I'm really excited about the response from industry. There's a national security imperative and they're taking on the challenge."

"We have hit the ground running and are making sure our process is both directed and inclusive," Mayer told InsideCybersecurity.com a few weeks later. "Our goal is to look at the [NIST] framework and create an adaptation for our segments," Mayer said. "The change here is we're moving from a standards-and-controls-based construct to a risk-management construct." This shift, or evolution, had been embraced by the different industry segments and by the FCC, Mayer said.

Quick-witted and personable, Mayer would be the glue that held the entire process together. Mayer earned an MBA from Boston University's School of Management in 1979 and his law degree from New York Law School a decade later. Mayer did his time as a regulator on telecom issues in New York State and served as chairman of the communications sector's security policy coordinating council. Beginning in 2007, he was a leading voice on security issues for the telecom sector as a vice president at the U.S. Telecom Association.

Over the coming year, as messages from FCC headquarters seemed to vacillate between regulatory warnings and enthusiastic encouragement of the industry group, Mayer tempered the agitation on his side of the table and cajoled and nudged FCC officials to firmly and completely embrace the collaborative approach. Mayer understood the bureaucratic imperatives from the FCC side—to do something measurable on a critical, high-profile issue—and he knew where industry's leverage resided.

The FCC wanted industry on board; in essence, the commission was eager for industry to carry the heaviest share of the workload. Industry had the expertise and it had the motivation, commission leaders and staff knew. But securing the telecom system from cyber attacks was also a national imperative. The process was one of voluntary engagement and collaboration, but the commission's leadership made clear there was nothing voluntary about the FCC's responsibility to ensure security.

The industry representatives had a hole card too: If they felt the voluntary process was a charade, they could demand the FCC pursue its goals through a full-blown regulatory process. That could drag on for years and give industry all kinds of appeals options and access to court rooms. That was the last thing Wheeler wanted to see. The telecom sector could also turn to allies on Capitol Hill, who would take a dark view of any FCC regulatory initiative.

But the industry side wasn't looking for this outcome, either.

"We needed participation across all five segments and we needed a leadership structure that could manage a diverse group of cybersecurity professionals," Mayer observed. "In addition, we knew we would have to reach consensus on a broad set of findings, conclusions, and recommendations before we could submit the final report to the CSRIC Council members for their consideration."

To make it work, "We had to be very well organized and efficient in our work."

By May, working group 4 had settled on five "foundational objectives": conforming the NIST framework to the telecom sector; maintaining flexibility for companies; developing streamlined practices and common risk-management approaches; developing use cases; and offering guidance on how companies could use the framework.

As the process chugged along, absorbing hours and hours of participants' time every week, Wheeler in June 2014 explicitly spelled out his expectations in a speech before the American Enterprise Institute (AEI) in Washington, DC.

"The challenge is that this private sector-led effort must be more dynamic than traditional regulation and more measurably effective than blindly trusting the market or voluntary best practices to defend our country," Wheeler said. "The new paradigm for the communications sector must be real and meaningful. It has to work. The commission's commitment to market accountability will help ensure that it does work. And, while I am confident that it will work, we must be ready with alternatives if it doesn't."

A standing-room-only audience of lobbyists, lawyers, and journalists knew the alternative was mandatory rules, enforced by the FCC, with stiff financial penalties as the cost of noncompliance. Wheeler, Simpson, and Johnson all said that was an outcome they didn't want to see. But industry representatives heard an implicit threat, and weren't so sure.

"It is good that they aren't jumping the gun on regulation but they are leaving open the possibility," one industry source said. "The possibility is still there and it is concerning." The source added that the private sector would bear all of the costs under the FCC's approach.

Robert Mayer said he took away a more positive message.

"The message I heard is that if we demonstrate a commitment to the [National Institute of Standards and Technology's cybersecurity] framework, if we provide guidance to our members and encourage its use, we won't get to that point," Mayer said of possible regulation. The expectation, Mayer said, is that companies and trade groups will use the framework to communicate risk management strategies internally, as well as use it to speak to vendors, customers, and the public. "That reflects what we're going to do and what our plan is," Mayer said.

Privately, many in the telecom sector were appalled by the speech. Wheeler had implied there was little accountability for cybersecurity in the telecom sector. He'd warned explicitly that industry had to stand up or face regulation.

"That room at AEI was full for the speech because we were afraid," an industry source said. "It did work."

Within days of the speech, Rep. Mike Rogers (R-Michigan) sent a letter to Wheeler demanding to know the basis of the commission's view that it had any authority to regulate the telecom sector's cyber practices. Rogers was asserting his oversight role as a member of the House Energy and Commerce communications subcommittee, but he also carried great weight in the cybersecurity realm as chairman of the Intelligence Committee. By July, a House-passed funding bill that covered the FCC likewise raised concern that the commission was "overstepping its jurisdiction in the area of cybersecurity."

Industry lobbyists expressed unease about lawmakers' efforts to insert themselves into the FCC policy development process. But the lobbyists were clearly concerned, too; and their worries were stoked by a July 25 FCC public notice seeking comments on the effectiveness of previous voluntary efforts by industry to improve cybersecurity. An FCC official told InsideCybersecurity.com, on condition of anonymity, that the notice didn't indicate any kind of shift away from a commitment to an industry-led process.

Industry attorneys detected something else.

"Cybersecurity has been on the FCC's radar for some time, though with this Public Notice, the FCC may be to inching closer to a regulatory and oversight paradigm," attorneys Megan Brown and Caroline Rose Van Wie wrote in a "client alert" for their clients at the law firm Wiley Rein.

"Now the FCC is publicly entertaining a more muscular role, beginning with an apparent attempt to demand some accountability," the attorneys wrote. "This raises important questions about the FCC's goals, as well as its continued adherence to longstanding federal policy to leave the Internet and mobile ecosystems free to manage and develop technical and operational solutions."

Two other telecom industry attorneys, speaking on background to InsideCybersecurity.com, expressed concern that the entire working group 4 effort could blow up, seven months before its planned conclusion.

"That's a different tone, that's not the conversation we were having in the CSRIC process," said one attorney. "Turning CSRIC into an inquiry on 'are you implementing' isn't how the process was intended."

The second attorney summed up the fears that had been growing as industry leaders continued to mull the AEI speech.

"The FCC chairman, in the AEI speech, made an explicit threat that if industry didn't meet some unspecified level of activity, the FCC would rely on traditional regulatory mechanisms," the attorney said. "It's hard to see how an industry that's regulated by the FCC would feel comfortable writing what could be future rules in the CSRIC environment."

The source added: "That industry may be better served by going through a traditional rulemaking process with the opportunity for notice and comment, and the ability to establish a record for appeal that challenges FCC's jurisdiction in the Internet space."

The FCC, through the public notice, seemed to be "assuming responsibility over a much broader set of participants in the ecosystem. This is an area that falls more rightly under the scope of the Department of Homeland Security and Department of Commerce."

These attorneys were in the room and deeply involved in all of the working group 4 activities, not—as some at the FCC suspected—regulatory ambulance chasers seeking to stir up fears and clients.

An FCC official stressed that the public notice wasn't about "compliance" with regulations. "It is about finding out what is working and what's not working now that we're several years past the recommendations having been adopted. . . . Public safety relies on the availability of resilient communications; together, we need to make this new paradigm work."

Still, on the eve of an all-hands meeting of working group 4, Simpson warned in a speech that "if industry doesn't pull it together and do so in a way that is recognizable for those charged with determining the appropriate risk for consumers, for citizens, for the markets that we in fact regulate, that we may in fact have to go to the same kind of a—it's time for us to step in and to increase the level of accountability there."

FCC officials were generally enthusiastic publicly about working group 4's prospects, but industry representatives were often dismayed by parallel comments such as Simpson's—and Wheeler's in the June speech—in which the commission's leaders made clear that a regulatory cudgel was available if they decided to use it.

Simpson opened a meeting of the CSRIC days later with a hearty endorsement of working group 4's work so far, causing some lobbyists' heads to spin. "We don't want to define a checklist and enforce it," Simpson assured the CSRIC participants. "We want to orient our approach around owner/operator expertise. But we have to get at these cyber risks."

The FCC sought to amplify the message that industry owned this process as summer turned to fall and the deadline for a work product neared. Communications companies would develop their own methods of measuring the effectiveness of their cybersecurity efforts and determine how that should be communicated to the government, Clete Johnson said at an event sponsored by the law firm Pillsbury Winthrop Shaw Pittman and the International Energy Forum. "The companies themselves are the accountability mechanism and the [NIST] framework of cybersecurity standards is the common language."

"We're expecting big things from this group," Johnson said. The FCC was "asking the companies themselves to answer how they'll communicate their work to us. How do they measure risk internally and what elements do they need to communicate externally," including to the government. The FCC had not "pre-judged" the answer, Johnson stressed, and the industry was "in the driver's seat."

Industry representatives continued to hear regulatory threats in FCC leaders' words throughout the fall. As the holiday season approached, some began to suggest, very privately, that perhaps they wouldn't provide such a robust final report—not if regulators were merely going to use it against them in the future.

In fact, the hundred-plus working group 4 participants had put in far too much work to pull back now. By the holiday season in 2014, FCC officials believed they had at last turned a corner with their industry partners. On the FCC side, officials felt it took much of the year to convince industry representatives that the exercise wasn't about laying the groundwork for regulations. It was a different kind of process, and would lead to a different kind of product. Eventually, the FCC officials believed, each side learned to trust the other and that showed up in the final strategy.

In February 2015, almost exactly one year after the release of the framework of cybersecurity standards, working group 4 put finishing touches on the most direct and comprehensive effort to apply the National Institute of Standards and Technology's handiwork to a specific industry's cybersecurity needs.

"I am not aware of any other sector effort that's involved over one hundred people and twelve months of effort to incorporate the framework's risk management process," Mayer said in an interview with InsideCybersecurity.com. The working group and its component subgroups held over one hundred meetings including five all-hands sessions involving most of the one hundred participants.

"We're preparing to deliver a report that does more than we were asked to do," Mayer said. "We took framework version 1.0 and asked ourselves what can we do to develop a deeper understanding so we could provide enterprises with answers to both 'why this is valuable' and 'how to use it.' . . . We're confident that the FCC will recognize the substantial contribution our sector has made to critical infrastructure cybersecurity."

Of course, the glide path to completion of the process couldn't be entirely smooth.

Weeks before the FCC advisory council was scheduled to consider the working group plan, communications industry representatives scrambled to express support for their sector's proposed cybersecurity strategy after a leaked copy of the proposal prompted a highly critical article in one publication.

Industry sources said the article misrepresented both the industry-led effort and the content of the recommendations on cybersecurity, which were submitted to the CSRIC on February 20. Working group 4 members had agreed not to divulge the contents of the report prior to the CSRIC meeting, but the news service Politico obtained a leaked copy. Politico quoted former FCC Public Safety Chief Jamie Barnett as sharply criticizing the working group's report. Barnett, a retired rear admiral, left the FCC in 2012 and was not part of the working group 4 process. Barnett's comments were the only negative assessment of the working group 4 product contained in the article, which said "critics" saw the proposal as "a cop-out."

The FCC wouldn't comment on the substance of the working group 4 report in advance of the March 18 meeting. "We are encouraged by the unprecedented effort that over one hundred industry experts are putting into developing this plan for future action," a spokeswoman did say.

Based on Barnett's comments, the article proclaimed that working group 4 had failed to produce a "new paradigm" around cybersecurity, as mandated by Wheeler. "FCC's 'new paradigm' for cybersecurity will have to wait," according to *Politico*'s headline. It wasn't surprising, perhaps, since *Politico* had trashed the NIST framework a year earlier.

Working group 4 members were incensed. "I think the 'comms' sector did a first rate job of developing a sector-specific implementation of the new paradigm first outlined in the president's executive order and further defined by the NIST framework," said Larry Clinton, who led a working group 4 "feeder" group on barriers to implementation.

"What is new about this model is that it departs from the traditional set of mandates and metrics," Clinton said. "Instead, what the president, and NIST, and presumably the FCC are looking for is a new approach which focuses on identifying and managing a set of rapidly changing risks and adapting best practices and standards as appropriate to the unique risk and attacks an individual entity might be facing."

Clinton added:

> The criticism seems to be that the new paradigm doesn't follow the model of the old paradigm such as prescribing a set of universal metrics that all entities would be expected to follow, but the point of a new paradigm is not simply to mimic the old one—that would not be new, or effective. . . . I would think it would be extremely disheartening if, after an extensive and fully open partnership process, the report is rejected because the new approach they outlined doesn't look like the old model.

Another industry source added: "The 'new paradigm' is about industry taking responsibility for improving cybersecurity across all segments. . . . We demonstrated exactly what [Chairman Wheeler] was expecting with regard to a new paradigm and to say the FCC 'has to wait for it' is frankly insulting."

The article produced sparks but did nothing to illuminate the sector's efforts to device the new paradigm.

With snarky articles receding in the rear-view mirror, the FCC's security council on March 18, 2015, approved the plan to create a post-regulatory "new paradigm" around cybersecurity.

The plan called on the FCC to "adopt availability of the critical communications infrastructure as the meaningful indicator of cybersecurity risk management." It was designed to be flexible enough for use by telecom companies of all sizes and levels of maturity to guide cybersecurity risk management strategies and practices. NIST officials said it faithfully adapted the framework to the telecom sector's unique needs.

The report provided tools for identifying an organization's current cyber practices, its desired state of cybersecurity and for measuring results. It included specific guidance for small- and mid-sized companies, or SMBs, along with "use cases" from the different segments "to illustrate steps taken" by SMBs to use the NIST framework. It prioritized the NIST framework elements for a small-business audience. The need for such prioritization was a common refrain at NIST workshops over the past two years where the framework was drafted.

The working group 4 report offered ten recommendations for the FCC, including using "availability" as the "meaningful indicator" of cyber risk management. The report urged the FCC "to promote an industry threat intelligence handling model" and to encourage information sharing. In addition, the commission should further examine issues specific to SMBs.

It called on the commission to promote voluntary use of the framework; encourage dissemination of the framework and the working group report across the sector; and to "coordinate and rationalize Framework related federal/state government initiatives to ensure efficient use of critical and scarce cybersecurity resources." Finally, the working group provided specific reports from each of the telecom sector segments.

"This is a fundamental product," Simpson approvingly told InsideCybersecurity.com. "It's up to the companies themselves to personalize this for their own [enterprises]," Simpson said. "We'll be there with them to facilitate" the process.

A month later, Wheeler offered his most extensive comments on the final product at the annual RSA Security conference in San Francisco. Some in the industry were holding their breath. If he offered praise, they fully expected to find a hook somewhere beneath the positive words.

"For more than a year, the commission and key stakeholders have been working together to develop a strategy to enhance the security of our wired and wireless broadband networks," Wheeler said. "Last month, we all agreed on that plan. Now our focus shifts to implementation."

Wheeler said: "Those that build, own, and operate these networks, and those that innovate at the edge of the networks, must work proactively and cooperatively to address shared risks. Companies need to 'own' their cyber readiness. This is the thinking behind the FCC's approach to cybersecurity."

Wheeler said the new paradigm must be "proactive and accountable self-governance within mutually agreed parameters. This isn't an ideological matter, but simply a logical conclusion. Things change so fast in the cyber world that prescriptive regulations could never hope to keep pace."

The NIST framework was "the essential starting point" for industry–government collaboration on cybersecurity, Wheeler said, adding,

"We see the FCC's role as building on the NIST Framework in the context of our responsibility to promote the reliability and resiliency of the communications networks themselves."

The working group's "most vital work" involved ensuring accountability, he said, and it "developed a range of activities intended to provide transparent assurances to the FCC, to DHS, to industry, and to consumers. These visible assurances should provide confidence that companies throughout the sector are actually taking effective steps to manage cyber risk."

According to Wheeler, the "core proposal is that members of the communications sector volunteer to participate in individualized, face-to-face meetings with the FCC to discuss each company's cyber risk management priorities, methods to address them, and the effectiveness of these methods. These meetings would be guided by the NIST Framework and occur at periodic intervals."

These would not be depositions, he stressed, and details must still be worked out.

"So just what is our expectation for these meetings?" Wheeler asked.

The answer is that we expect a thorough demonstration that a company's cyber risk management program is effective. Using the risk framework drives companies to consider their readiness not just in stopping attacks, but in each of the identify, protect, detect, respond, and recover phases critical to minimizing the impact of a malicious attack. The risk framework doesn't stand alone, companies need to have threat intelligence, they need to address supply chain risk and insider threats among other areas, but the risk management framework provides a great foundation from which to see the gaps and organize effective mitigation.

Wheeler said:

When fully developed and properly implemented, I believe that CSRIC's assurance model will provide much-needed accountability for network security, while avoiding top-down prescriptive regulation of industry practices. A cooperative and collaborative approach is the FCC's preferred means of engagement. I have every reason to be confident the industry will live up to its commitments and deliver meaningful action. But the hard work has only begun and our review of these next steps will be guided by the fact that cybersecurity is a national imperative.

Plenty of questions remained, such as how these assurance meetings would actually be accomplished, and how confidential industry data would be protected in the process. But the industry and FCC somehow had managed to clear a major hurdle without knocking one another into a ditch.

The five segments of the telecom industry wasted no time initiating activities to prove they were implementing the overall strategy. They quickly moved into extensive awareness and outreach campaigns, and were paying close attention to how they would demonstrate that an industry-led cyber approach actually worked.

There were plenty of common themes in the different segments' approaches. The trade associations "distilled" the working group 4 report for their specific industries, and prioritized the elements of the framework of cybersecurity standards. The groups—and NIST—developed "use cases" that could be of particular benefit for small- and mid-sized companies. "We've been focused on raising awareness but also on collecting use cases and sending them back out," said NIST's Sedgewick. NIST saw the working group 4 report itself as a use case that was helpful to companies in other sectors.

"Use cases help our members understand how to walk in these shoes," said John Marinho, vice president for technology and cybersecurity at CTIA—the Wireless Association.

The trade groups were well-aware that the FCC would insist on robust assurances that the process actually improved cybersecurity in the sector. One part of the effort on assurances would come in the Communications Sector Coordinating Council's annual report. "Cybersecurity is a journey, not a destination," Marinho said, "and the report is a milestone in the journey."

Capturing metrics in this report was "a big ask" of industry, according to Matt Tooley, vice president of broadband technology at the National Cable and Telecommunications Association.

"The big ask is you're trying to measure availability, but everyone is a little different," Tooley said. "You need to normalize it and make sure you're not asking for proprietary information."

There were critics, beyond those located by *Politico*.

"Lazlo," a technologist who insisted on anonymity but had worked with the communications sector, suggested it was a standard piece of work by a large committee, meaning it was compromised from the start and lacked imagination or ingenuity.

"Not so earth shattering," Lazlo said. "It's predictable. The communications sector took the path of least resistance and easiest to obtain."

The plan had its high points. "I agree that it sets a path for the small and midsized communications companies, so that's good," Lazlo said. But a technologist could see the seams in the strategy document, he claimed.

"If they wanted to go for it and make a difference, they should have incorporated not only DNS security, but from the other existing working groups on botnets and DDOS protection. CPNI enhancements would begin to address better customer information protection."

In English, that meant the report focused on the Domain Name System, or DNS, but didn't tackle the rampant problem of botnets or distributed denial of service attacks. Likewise, it didn't go deeply enough into "customer proprietary network information," CPNI, the data that telecom companies collect about their customers' activities.

The report, Lazlo said, represented "baby steps."

Lazlo chuckled and took a parting shot. "I'm glad that I'm no longer in that sector. Financial services, for instance, cares a lot about cybersecurity comparatively and is light years ahead of the communications sector in every aspect of maturity and application of sound security practices—basic cyber hygiene—and then some to keep their customers safe."

A camel, the old saying goes, is a horse built by committee. But in the world of government–industry collaboration, with scores of stakeholders clinging tightly to their own self-interest, creating a camel may represent victory. Cybersecurity is a journey, as Marinho put it, and camels come in handy on long, arduous treks.

Sedgewick, several months after the working group 4 report was released, offered the ultimate compliment from NIST's perspective. The CSRIC product "is the most robust response we've seen of a sector taking up the framework. We hope to share the lessons of CSRIC."

"Just as WG4 was getting underway, FCC Chairman Wheeler characterized the WG4 effort as part of a 'new paradigm' where industry would provide the FCC and the public with so-called assurances' that the appropriate cyber risk management activities were being undertaken by sector enterprises," recalled Mayer of U.S. Telecom. "The construct he proposed retained the voluntary nature of the NIST framework and recognized that one-size solutions and regulatory mandates were ill-suited to this emerging threat in cyberspace."

Now, Mayer said,

> After over a year of effort, WG4 produced a final report with over four hundred pages of analysis and guidance that is now serving as the basis for solidifying the public–private partnership model. The fact that industry in conjunction with our regulator could agree on a set of assurances and a path forward speaks to the success of the framework in facilitating a new conversation about shared responsibilities across a broad stakeholder ecosystem.

7

THE FTC,
"PROTECTING AMERICA'S CONSUMERS"

"But I wanted to start here, at the FTC, because every day you take the lead in making sure that Americans, their hard-earned money, and their privacy are protected, especially when they go online. And these days, that's pretty much for everything: managing our bank accounts, paying our bills, handling everything from medical records to movie tickets, controlling our homes—smart houses, from smart phones.
—President Obama, speech at the Federal Trade Commission,
January 12, 2015

If American consumers needed further evidence of the risks they faced in cyberspace, the Christmas 2014 attack on the Sony PlayStation Network probably crushed any remaining sense of security. Virtually every product or service that had a digital component was vulnerable to cyber attack. Some were for political reasons, like the 2014 attack that crippled computers at the Las Vegas Sands casino—motivated by the casino owner's support for Israel—and some were for straightforward theft. Regardless, the attack surface stretched across America's culture and economy, and responsibility for ensuring security was spread broadly across the government and within the private sector.

While the Federal Communications Commission (FCC) played a high-profile role in cybersecurity, largely collaborative efforts were blossoming across other departments and regulatory and independent agencies within the federal government. For instance, the U.S. Environmental Protection Agency (EPA) deferred to the water industry trade group, the

American Water Works Association (AWWA), to develop a cybersecurity plan. Entrusted with this responsibility, the AWWA would become an energetic promoter of the National Institute of Standards and Technology (NIST) framework and industry-led cybersecurity initiatives in general.

The Department of Energy churned out cyber tools for the gas and electric sectors, and did the painstaking work of mapping the NIST's cybersecurity framework to those industries' specific needs. Trade groups like the American Gas Association helped their member companies make use—and make sense—of the tools. The Department of Homeland Security (DHS) gave the green light for the chemical manufacturing sector to follow a plan developed by the American Chemical Council trade association.

On the law enforcement side, the Department of Justice rolled out new weapons to fight cyber crime and the Obama administration sought new legal powers. In January 2015 the administration called for legislation "that would allow for the prosecution [for] sale of botnets, would criminalize the overseas sale of stolen U.S. financial information like credit card and bank account numbers, would expand federal law enforcement authority to deter the sale of spyware used to stalk or commit ID theft, and would give courts the authority to shut down botnets engaged in distributed denial of service attacks and other criminal activity." The proposal would update both the Computer Fraud and Abuse Act and the Racketeer Influenced and Corrupt Organizations Act.

"We're tremendously supportive of modernizing the relevant statutes, both on increasing the penalties for hacking and apprehending bad actors," an industry source observed. Clarity was needed on how to indict individuals overseas as well as on issues such as seizing equipment used in a botnet action, for example, the source said. "We don't want different interpretations by different courts," the source added.

Here was a government initiative industry leaders could get behind because it addressed their long-held complaint that federal authorities were too busy blaming one of the victims—companies themselves—in cyber attacks. Instead, much more attention should be paid to getting the bad guys.

Elsewhere in what some called the civilian government, the NIST framework provided structure, but regulatory and independent agencies were largely on their own to craft cyber policy responses. The Securities and Exchange Commission (SEC) issued guidances—and warnings—on cybersecurity responsibilities in the financial sector. The Federal Energy Regulatory Commission updated mandatory cyber rules that affected the largest electricity providers. The Nuclear Regulatory Commission (NRC), which generally enjoyed a close collaborative relationship with nuclear operators on cyber issues, looked to streamline its regulations using the NIST framework as a guidepost. The NRC also initiated an interagency forum that would allow regulators to share insights and experiences on cybersecurity. The SEC was a founding member of that initiative.

But one of the most closely watched agencies was the independent Federal Trade Commission (FTC). President Obama chose to unveil his 2015 cybersecurity priorities in a speech at the FTC's headquarters—noting that he was the first president since Franklin Delano Roosevelt to visit a building on Pennsylvania Avenue just blocks from the White House. "I mean, you'd think like one of the presidents would just come here by accident," he said to laughter from an appreciative audience of career public servants and political appointees. "Anyway, I figured it was time to correct that."

Despite its name, the FTC wasn't about trade in the global sense; it was about business practices. The commission engaged in an often acrimonious relationship with industry as it sought to implement a mandate to protect consumers. It was often shunned when a Republican was in the White House.

Obama wanted to further bolster the FTC's authority to punish companies that failed to adequately protect consumers' data. "First," Obama said in his FTC speech,

> we're introducing new legislation to create a single, strong national standard so Americans know when their information has been stolen or misused. Right now, almost every state has a different law on this, and it's confusing for consumers and it's confusing for companies—and it's costly, too, to have to comply to this patchwork of laws. Sometimes, folks don't even find out their credit card information has been stolen until they see charges on their bill, and then it's too late. So under the new standard that we're proposing, companies would have to notify consumers of a breach within thirty days.

The new law, if passed by Congress, would be enforced by the FTC. Sen. Bill Nelson of Florida, the top Democrat on the Commerce Committee, introduced Obama's proposal but Republicans weren't interested in the president's approach, and weren't quite sure if they wanted to touch the issue at all.

The FTC, as the business sector knew, already had real power when it came to cybersecurity. The commission could—and did—drag companies into court for alleged cybersecurity shortcomings. About a mile south, across the National Mall, another alphabet soup agency—the Federal Communications Commission (FCC)—decided to start levying enforcement actions against telecom companies for allegedly poor consumer data protection in 2014. But this had been the FTC's space for quite a while before that.

Edith Ramirez, the FTC chairwoman, told the *Washington Post* in a June 2015 interview that she "absolutely" saw the commission as "the key cop on the beat" when it came to consumer data security, with broad reach across industry sectors. The FCC saw itself in that role for the telecoms. The SEC also saw itself as the "cop on the beat" for the financial sector. But the securities commission was more of a Sheriff Andy Taylor: often positive, encouraging, and turning to force as a last resort on cyber issues. To industry, the FTC under Ramirez was all Eliot Ness, stern and punishing.

The Federal Trade Commission claimed to derive its authority on cybersecurity from Section 5 of the 1914 Federal Trade Commission Act, which authorized action against unfair and deceptive practices. Claiming or implying that a service was cybersecure would constitute such a deceptive practice, the commission held.

That assertion was challenged in court by industry groups and questioned on Capitol Hill. A U.S. court of appeals upheld the commission's authority in a landmark 2015 decision in a case involving Wyndham Worldwide. The hotel resort operator's computer systems were breached three times, affecting 619,000 accounts and resulting in over $10 million in losses. The FTC swooped in with proposed fines and the company responded by challenging the commission's authority to exercise such power.

Industry groups lined up behind Wyndham; consumer rights organizations rallied behind the FTC. It may have been a curious choice of cases, from industry's perspective, for a pitched-battle over the commission's authority: The company claimed the FTC was assuming intrusive powers that could extend to penalizing a grocery store over a banana peel on the floor. The court of appeals observed, acidly, that any store that allowed 619,000 customers to slip on banana peels should expect to face enforcement action.

The closely watched case ended up affirming the FTC's power to regulate cybersecurity practices and fine companies that failed to adequately protect consumer information.

The "cop" could brandish a pretty big nightstick as it tried to influence corporate behavior. But it wasn't entirely clear to businesses when the cop would reach for the club. "[S]ince there are no set federal rules for protecting user data, fining a company for not following rules that don't exist doesn't make any sense," Malwarebytes Labs' Adam Kujawa said after the 2015 court ruling. "It's up to the government now to work with security experts and companies and identify a good solid baseline for the security of customer data."

It was a case of "excessive" regulation and "ad hoc litigation," according to industry groups. It was a perfect example of "blaming the victim," the U.S. Chamber of Commerce (Chamber), the nation's leading business organization, charged. The Chamber didn't say so, in this statement, but the sentiment was clear: When the government itself was hacked, it was a malicious, unavoidable act of violence; businesses, on the other hand, were just inviting the attacks against their own systems.

"American businesses—and our own government—are frequent victims of cyberattacks from foreign adversaries and businesses have every incentive to defend against these attacks," said Steven Lehotsky, vice president and chief counsel for regulatory litigation at the U.S. Chamber Litigation Center.

Lehotsky added: "However, excessive enforcement by agencies relying on decades-old laws that were not meant to address cybersecurity is not the solution to that national security problem. We are concerned that [the Wyndham] decision will exacerbate the unfortunate trend over the last ten years of ad hoc litigation and overregulation when it comes to cybersecurity."

Consumer rights groups like the Center for Democracy and Technology said the industry side was being deliberately obtuse to obvious, appropriate levels of care.

"Wyndham claimed that the plain language of the FTC Act . . . didn't allow for the agency to regulate data security," according to the Center for Democracy and Technology. "Wyndham argued that the FTC Act's prohibition on unfair practices was too vague and broad here. However, because the FTC Act contains a balancing test for unfairness claims, it's not surprising that the court didn't buy this argument."

Ramirez did try to spell out the standards throughout her tenure, though ideas discussed in an interview aren't the same as a detailed rule.

"In terms of the deception principle, it's really very simple," Ramirez told the *Washington Post*: "We expect companies that make promises to actually fulfill those promises. If a company makes a particular promise in their privacy policy or through some other mechanism, we expect them to comply."

Ramirez said it came down to this: "We think a company's failure to provide reasonable data protections constitutes an unfair practice, because we think it's a reasonable expectation for a consumer. If a company is making use of personal financial information, they ought to have appropriate protections in place to make sure that information isn't compromised."

Ramirez was born in California, the daughter of Mexican immigrants, and went on to obtain a bachelor's degree and a law degree from Harvard. She was a partner in a major Los Angeles law firm before Obama appointed her to the FTC in 2010, "specializing in intellectual property and complex business litigation matters," according to a BloombergBusiness profile.

By 2013, the FTC was already moving aggressively to fill a perceived vacuum in cybersecurity protections for consumers—and looking creatively and expansively at areas for potential action. In November 2013, the FTC held a first-of-its-kind government workshop on privacy and security issues related to the emerging "Internet of Things."

Ramirez boldly proclaimed that she saw the FTC as "the enforcer," even as she urged Congress to give the commission even more explicit authority to address data breaches.

"The touchstone to data security is 'reasonableness,'" FTC Consumer Protection Chief Jessica Rich said at an event in January 2014. "Companies must invest in privacy and make it a key part of their business strategy," Rich said. She noted the breach at Target and said the impact of a failure to secure data can be "enormous" in terms of lost profit and corporate prestige, in addition to the damages suffered by consumers.

How the FTC would determine "reasonableness" was a matter of huge concern to business groups.

In January 2015, the FTC issued a report full of recommendations on "reasonable" steps industry could take to secure the Internet of Things, or IoT.

"The recommendations are broad enough—they're not a checklist to show that 'A, B, C' equals reasonable," Karen Jagielski of the FTC told InsideCybersecurity.com. "These are reasonable steps but they don't have the force of law." She did add though, "They are things we would look at when evaluating" a complaint or action against a company.

Jagielski commented after making a presentation to the Information Security and Privacy Advisory Board, which advised the National Institute of Standards and Technology. She told the board there was no strict definition of "reasonable," but said the recommendations urged companies to "bake security into" IoT devices, hire trained personnel to ensure security is a part of product development, oversee suppliers, have a "defense in depth" strategy, and monitor products through their life cycle.

She noted the FTC's authority to penalize companies for unfair or deceptive claims, which she defined as "material misrepresentation or omission" causing "substantial injury."

Asked by a board member whether the definition of "reasonable" efforts to secure data was evolving in light of the Sony Pictures and other major breaches, Jagielski said there was "no specific definition," but that the FTC was urging companies to consider "security by design."

(Not entirely coincidentally, the Federal Communications Commission also placed a claim on the "security by design" issue, making it one of the chief topics to be addressed by the "CSRIC V" process launched in the summer of 2015.)

The FTC was not imposing specific cybersecurity requirements. But "certain principles" like those reflected in the IoT recommendations "do make sense," Jagielski said. "We're not imposing anything," she stressed to the NIST advisory board. "We want to give consumers confidence to use these products."

Jagielski repeated the FTC position that it was too early to legislate on IoT security while calling for data security and breach notification legislation. The FTC had also called for "broad-based privacy legislation," she noted. Jagielski said the commission believed companies would find the IoT recommendations useful, adding, "We're trying to help the marketplace."

The breach at Target became a rallying cry for those seeking to strengthen the FTC's hand. Ramirez testified before the Senate Homeland Security and Governmental Affairs Committee on April 2, 2014, amid a flurry of congressional activity following the Target and Neiman Marcus hacks.

Ramirez was making the rounds on Capitol Hill urging lawmakers to establish a national data-breach notification standard and grant the FTC new regulatory power to enforce data protections. Her call for legislation focused on three areas: granting the commission authority to seek civil penalties for unlawful conduct; authority over nonprofit organizations; and rulemaking authority under the Administrative Procedure Act.

Ramirez argued that "enabling the FTC to bring cases against non-profits would help ensure that whenever personal information is collected from consumers, entities that maintain such data adequately protect it."

More significantly, the chairwoman's call for rulemaking authority was meant to allow the commission to revise requirements in response to changing technologies. "Rulemaking authority would allow the commission to ensure that as technology changes and the risks from the use of information evolve, companies would be required to give adequate protection to such data," Ramirez said.

A report on the Target breach prepared in March 2014 by the staff of Senate Commerce chairman Jay Rockefeller provided more evidence in support of the FTC's call for additional authority.

Rockefeller suggested at a hearing in late March that companies hadn't done enough to improve consumer data security and that he was eager to move ahead with legislation. But he didn't mention a timetable for moving on his or other cyber legislation despite broad—if superficial—support for a uniform federal breach notification law.

Rockefeller was in his final year in the Senate and he and ranking member John Thune (R-South Dakota) generally collaborated on cybersecurity issues. But the two senators had their own bills and there were differences in the details. Thune pledged to work together with Rockefeller and urged that lawmakers "not allow the perfect to become the enemy of the good" as they pursued legislation.

Rockefeller's report detailed missed steps that contributed to the Target breach affecting millions of consumers. "Industry's data security standards were not enough," Rockefeller said, adding that he was "increasingly frustrated" that companies were not sufficiently investing in cyber-security.

"There has been a lot anxiety lately about what kind of information the federal government may be collecting about American citizens, as part of the efforts to protect our country from the ongoing terrorist threat," Rockefeller said. He continued:

> But the truth is that private companies like Target hold vastly larger amounts of sensitive information about us than the government does. And they spend much less time and money protecting their sensitive data than the government does. We learned yesterday that Federal agents notified more than three thousand companies last year that their computer systems had been hacked. I am certain there are many more breaches we never hear about.

Rockefeller said his message to the business community was "come to the table and be willing to compromise." In turn, he said he was willing to compromise too, though not on core principles.

Ramirez called for legislation that would allow the commission to require "reasonable security practices," timely notification after breaches and the authority to seek civil penalties when companies allowed breaches through negligence. How to define negligence? The "touch-stone," Ramirez said, was "reasonableness." A breach does not mean a company was negligent, she said, and the government should not require "perfect security."

She said there should be "concurrent" enforcement authority with state attorneys general, and that the federal standard would prevail when it was more stringent. "Companies continue to under-invest in this area," Ramirez said.

Rockefeller replied that this highlighted the weakness of relying on self-regulation.

"It's not enough," Ramirez agreed.

Meanwhile, the Federal Trade Commission's 2014 annual report on consumer complaints showed identity theft at the top of the list for the fifteenth year in a row and underscored the need for a strong federal data security and breach notification law, according to consumer activists. The report, issued in February 2015, said the FTC, state agencies, and other law enforcement entities received over 332,000 complaints of identity theft, which was the number one category at 13 percent of all complaints.

"Identity theft, and the data breaches that fuel it, must be a top concern not only of regulators at the FTC, but policymakers throughout Washington and beyond," National Consumers League executive director Sally Greenberg said in a statement. "The message from 332,000 identity theft complaints to the FTC is clear: More needs to be done to protect consumers from this fraud."

Ramirez had called for similar legislation since the beginning of her term. Representatives of various industries testified repeatedly that they would support a federal notification standard, with the caveat that it must preempt often stronger state laws. There were also substantial differences of opinion between different industry sectors over the advisability or scope of related security standards.

It wasn't all spinach from the FTC. In April 2014 the commission and the Department of Justice issued a "joint statement" seeking to temper antitrust concerns related to cybersecurity information sharing. Among the industry "asks" for cybersecurity liability protection, a shield from antitrust actions was always near the top of the list. Industry groups feared the government could swoop in—if it chose to do so—with an antitrust charge if companies collaborated closely on cyber threat indicators.

"Cyber threats are becoming increasingly more common, more sophisticated, and more dangerous," the FTC and Justice Department (DOJ) wrote, continuing,

> One way that private entities may defend against cyber attacks is by sharing technical cyber threat information—such as threat signatures, indicators, and alerts—with each other. Today, much of this sharing is taking place. Some private entities may, however, be hesitant to share cyber threat information with others, especially competitors, because they believe such sharing may raise antitrust issues.

Threat data was technical in nature and not the type of information that would suggest collusion between two companies, the agencies wrote.

"[I]t remains the Agencies' current analysis that properly designed sharing of cybersecurity threat information is not likely to raise antitrust concerns," the DOJ and FTC said.

Ari Schwartz, who oversaw cybersecurity policy at the National Security Council, said the antitrust issue was "taken off the table" by the FTC–DOJ statement. Industry lawyers and lobbyists said the guidance reduced antitrust concerns from cybersecurity information sharing but was no substitute for writing the liability protection into law. Attorney Brian Finch of the Pillsbury, Winthrop, Shaw Pittman law firm commented: "Legislation or a court ruling is always best, but I would think DOJ guidance is very helpful."

"Until," Finch noted, "they decide to change their minds."

Some observers suggested the perception of potential antitrust vulnerability was greater than the reality. "I agree—generally speaking—that legislation should not be necessary to remove antitrust issues as a matter of concern when companies share information about cyber risks," said attorney Robert Cattanach of the law firm Dorsey and Whitney. "That said, antitrust lawyers may continue to counsel restraint on any information sharing among potential competitors in an abundance of caution." Cattanach said companies in general shouldn't be too worried about antitrust liability. "[A]bsent egregious conduct masquerading as information sharing about cyber threats, I see no realistic exposure to antitrust enforcement," he said.

"Further, keep in mind that any antitrust protection in potential cyber information sharing legislation is certainly not likely to be absolute or unconditional," Cattanach said. "Thus, even assuming legislation would be passed that includes some protection from antitrust enforcement, it would most likely not extend to the theoretical 'egregious conduct' circumstances that could trigger enforcement without legislation. With or without legislation bad actors will face exposure, and those acting in good faith should not fear enforcement overreach."

Industry's desire for legislation that would embed liability protection in the law and create a uniform approach to issues like data-breach notification was matched by the administration's desire for a law codifying the FTC's authority over data breaches and other cyber issues. While the FTC was assuming and exercising powers, the Obama White House was well aware that the next administration and the next FTC chair might not view the issue the same way. They wanted the FTC not only to be *permitted*, but to be *required* by law to be the enforcer of business standards in cyberspace.

That's where the legislation became stuck and in the starkly partisan environment of the Obama years, there wasn't much chance to split differences and strike a deal. The FTC, unsurprisingly, continued to play aggressive cop on the beat, a role that unsettled business groups and angered Republicans on Capitol Hill.

In July 2015, the FTC sent LifeLock's stock price plummeting when the commission asked a federal court to impose penalties on the company for allegedly failing to live up to an earlier legal settlement. The commission, in a filing at the federal district court in Arizona, said LifeLock continued to make false claims about its online identity protection and data-security services, even after a 2010 settlement with the FTC and thirty-five state attorneys general. In the hours after the FTC filing, the company's share price fell 50 percent to eight dollars per share.

Former Homeland Security secretary Tom Ridge served on the Life-Lock board of directors, and put out a statement strongly supportive of the company and its practices. The company itself rejected the allegations and said it had engaged in good-faith efforts to settle the case with the commission. LifeLock issued a statement saying:

> After more than eighteen months of cooperation and dialogue with the FTC, it became clear to us that we could not come to a satisfactory resolution of their issues outside a court of law. We disagree with the substance of the FTC's contentions and are prepared to take our case to court. . . . Importantly the FTC is not seeking any relief that would change LifeLock services and products going forward. The claims raised by the FTC are all related to the past, not to current business practices.

The company also said the "alerting claims raised by the FTC did not result in any known identity theft for LifeLock members," and that "we do not believe that anything the FTC is alleging has resulted in any member's data being taken."

The FTC claimed that LifeLock violated the 2010 settlement by "continuing to make deceptive claims about its identity theft protection services, and by failing to take steps required to protect its users' data," according to a commission statement. The FTC "asked the court to impose an order requiring LifeLock to provide full redress to all consumers affected by the company's order violations."

One of five FTC commissioners voted against proceeding with the filing.

"It is essential that companies live up to their obligations under orders obtained by the FTC," said Jessica Rich, director of the FTC's Bureau of

Consumer Protection. "If a company continues with practices that violate orders and harm consumers, we will act."

The FTC said:

> The 2010 settlement stemmed from previous FTC allegations that LifeLock used false claims to promote its identity theft protection services. The settlement barred the company and its principals from making any further deceptive claims; required LifeLock to take more stringent measures to safeguard the personal information it collects from customers; and required LifeLock to pay $12 million for consumer refunds.

The company violated the order, according to the FTC, "by: (1) failing to establish and maintain a comprehensive information security program to protect its users' sensitive personal data, including credit card, social security, and bank account numbers; (2) falsely advertising that it protected consumers' sensitive data with the same high-level safeguards as financial institutions; and (3) failing to meet the 2010 order's recordkeeping requirements."

Further, "The FTC also asserts that from at least January 2012 through December 2014, LifeLock falsely claimed it protected consumers' identity 24/7/365 by providing alerts 'as soon as' it received any indication there was a problem."

The FTC saw the 2010 LifeLock case as a classic example of how a cybersecurity company should *not* behave in cyberspace, boasting about the commission's enforcement action against the firm in a 2015 guide for businesses that offered lessons from fifty-four data security cases brought by the FTC.

This enforcement action hinged on the FTC's interpretation of "reasonable" efforts by a company as well as the commission's definition of deception, which was a malleable standard enforced in different ways by different commission leaders. The FTC would produce such guides for businesses to help them determine appropriate behavior and levels of responsibility, though these were not strict regulations that clearly needed to be followed. Without a political deal on the FTC's cybersecurity role, however, this kind of ambiguous government demand and action would continue at least until a new commission chair was in place under a new administration. It would be a blunt but effective tool for consumer advocates and a source of aggravation for the business community.

On June 30, 2015, the commission released "Start with Security: A Guide for Business." It included eleven pages of easy-to-read, common-sense recommendations and references to other resources. "Control access to data sensibly." "Require strong passwords and authentication." It went on: Protect data at rest and in transit; segment networks; build security into new products; make sure the supply chain uses safe practices.

It all made sense. Business executives could certainly use it as a cheat sheet to assess their internal cyber efforts. But business attorneys knew something else: FTC lawyers would be using it to guide the commission's enforcement actions against companies. This wasn't just a helpful hand from government. It was a warning.

One segment of industry was delighted as the FTC made clear its intention to hold companies legally responsible for cybersecurity: vendors of security products. After the commission's powers were legitimized by a U.S. court of appeals in 2015, the vendor community quickly spread the word to potential customers that there was no longer anything voluntary about cybersecurity.

Vendors crafted security services based on the NIST framework and other government offerings, which they could market on the increasingly certain knowledge that both the government's regulators and the nation's courts expected companies to do *something* on cybersecurity, even if the required "something" would not be spelled out.

The FTC, with its court-approved power to penalize and initiate court actions, would be a locus of an approach to cybersecurity that was as ambitious as it was ambiguous.

8

FEAR AND FAILURE, AGAIN, ON CAPITOL HILL

The most important thing we need is the ability to share information [between industry and government]. Right now, we can't see what's happening.

—Army Gen. Keith Alexander, commander of U.S. Cyber Command and director of the National Security Agency, September 25, 2013 (Alexander, in the same speech at a Billington security conference, lamented that Edward Snowden's leaks about NSA activities were stifling cybersecurity policy development in many unrelated areas.)

Twitter revealed in early 2013 that it had been hacked and that 250,000 of its users were affected. The *New York Times* and *Wall Street Journal* were hacked around the same time.

Congress surely didn't need any more evidence that it was time to act, but two other events would bend the arc of cyber policy development on Capitol Hill in 2013: President Obama's February executive order and ex-National Security Agency contractor Edward Snowden's leaks about government surveillance.

After the bitter fight over cybersecurity legislation in the previous Congress, the executive order was like a policy balm that had a soothing effect from K Street to the halls of Congress. On March 7, 2013, the Senate Commerce Committee and the chamber's Homeland Security and Governmental Affairs Committee held a rare joint session on cybersecurity in a cavernous hearing room on the ground floor of the Senate Dirksen Office Building. The choice of venue was fitting, because every folding chair in the room was filled and reporters sat elbow to elbow at press tables along one wall.

"We hope to avoid another stalemate," said Sen. John Thune of South Dakota, the new top Republican on the Commerce Committee. Thune was moving up the ranks of the Republican leadership and his interest in cyber policy was encouraging to industry lobbyists. He seemed a natural advocate for an industry-driven approach.

"The executive order may open the way to progress," Thune said. If, he warned, the Department of Homeland Security (DHS) was up to the task of implementing it.

Sen. Tom Carper had replaced the now-retired Joe Lieberman as the new chairman of the Homeland Security Committee. He noted that the executive order contained "carrots rather than sticks," and observed a changed atmosphere around cybersecurity from just a few months earlier.

Carper said he had no timetable for legislation, and suggested letting the National Institute of Standards and Technology (NIST) framework process unfold to build confidence among all the stakeholders. Legislation could come in one comprehensive swoop, he said, or in smaller, easily digestible pieces. "I want to do what works. . . . But I want to get it done this year."

Sen. Tom Coburn of Oklahoma, the new top Republican on the Homeland Security Committee and a strong conservative critic of many Obama administration initiatives, was effusive about the cyber executive order. "Sen. Carper and I got a presentation on Wednesday about the executive order. It was very impressive. . . . The president has shown real leadership with the executive order. We need to come up and support it."

There was one little problem, Coburn said, which Congress needed to address: immunity for industry from "frivolous" lawsuits. "We need to get past that one issue," he said.

NIST director Patrick Gallagher told the senators that he expected "an enormous in-surge" of participation from industry around the NIST framework. And as a point person for the Obama administration on the initiative, Gallagher took on Democrats' concerns about the effectiveness of a voluntary rather than regulatory process. "'Voluntary' sometimes feels soft, but when developed by a consensus process it can be very muscular," he told a somewhat skeptical Sen. Mark Warner (D-Virginia).

Homeland Security Secretary Janet Napolitano told the senators that the administration and its industry partners were embarked on a "grand experiment" in which a national security issue was being left to a voluntary process. "I think we can make it work," she said with confidence.

The Commerce and Homeland Security committees would begin developing bills in the coming months that addressed some of the nuts and bolts of how government addressed cybersecurity and interacted with the private sector, while avoiding the "on-high mandates" that wrecked legislative efforts in 2012. These were the manageable pieces Carper was hinting about, though it took the entirety of the 113th Congress to digest even these relatively easy bills. House Homeland Security chairman Michael McCaul was eyeing similar moves in the spring of 2013.

It was a studied, reasonable approach and it was relatively uncontroversial.

McCaul and many other lawmakers of both parties believed legislation was also needed to promote information sharing by providing companies with antitrust and other liability protection. That would be quite a bit more complicated and primarily the responsibility of the House and Senate intelligence committees.

The House Intelligence Committee quickly put together a new, revised version of its Cyber Intelligence Sharing and Protection Act (CISPA) information-sharing bill in early 2013, and got it to the floor. It passed in April with bipartisan support, 288 to 127, a better showing than a year earlier. The White House still didn't like it and issued another veto threat. CISPA was still poisonous when it came to privacy and civil liberties despite multiple tweaks and additions to shore up protections in those areas. At the same time, the House would also pass a bill to improve the defenses of the federal government's own cyber networks as well as a measure on cybersecurity research.

CISPA amended the 1947 National Security Act to address cybersecurity issues. Like the 2012 bill, it called on the director of national intelligence to create a process for information sharing between government and industry, and it provided liability protection for participating companies.

The online privacy community liked nothing about it and once more lumped it into other debates, such as the uproar over the so-called Stop Online Piracy Act (SOPA), as yet another government overreach on control of the Internet.

Reps. Mike Rogers and Dutch Ruppersberger thought they had incorporated extensive changes to meet privacy concerns. They were increasingly confident the retooled version would satisfy critics in the Senate. The lawmakers held frequent conference calls with reporters to scroll through all of the privacy enhancements they'd added to the bill. They were determined to get control of how this absolutely necessary policy— improving the government's ability to detect and assess cyber attacks— would be portrayed in the media.

And then everything changed around cybersecurity policy.

In May 2013, a disillusioned former contractor named Edward Snowden slipped out of the country to Hong Kong; in June his illegal leaks about classified, long-running National Security Agency electronic surveillance activities began appearing in the media. He would end up in Moscow and the leaks would continue dripping out over the next few years.

For one thing, the leaked documents revealed the NSA had "broken privacy rules or overstepped its legal authority thousands of times each year since Congress granted the agency broad new powers in 2008," the *Washington Post* reported. The news seemed designed to confirm the worst suspicions of the privacy community and would overshadow any congressional moves involving the government's acquisition and handling of data from the private sector.

The leaks even nicked the National Institute of Standards and Technology. Director Gallagher was forced to defend NIST against allegations that the agency weakened cryptographic standards issued in 2006 under pressure from the National Security Agency. NIST issued a statement saying it would not "deliberately weaken" any standard.

Lawmakers like McCaul grasped how Snowden had tilted the debate over cybersecurity. The Rogers–Ruppersberger bill had already cleared the House but was going nowhere in the Senate, where Intelligence Committee leaders were cautiously surveying the upended policy landscape. The leaders of the House and Senate homeland security panels thought they had a separate, more tightly focused legislative approach that skirted the damage caused by the Snowden leaks by largely avoiding anything that smacked of surveillance.

"We want to make sure the NSA [controversy] doesn't spill over into this legislation," McCaul said in late June. "The best strategy is oversight of the executive order and then legislation. Fall is a good time frame for cyber."

"McCaul gets the issue . . . leadership doesn't want anything on the floor in July that even touches on the NSA issue," Ralph Hellmann, a tech lobbyist and former House GOP leadership aide, said in June.

McCaul had his doubts about the administration's approach through the executive order, but was willing to give it a chance. "I don't think the [NIST] framework will be well-received by the private sector," he said bluntly.

He didn't know it at the time, but by the end of the 113th Congress in December 2014, NIST's framework would be a shield that protected and guided the advance of legislation produced by McCaul, Carper, Coburn, Rockefeller, and Thune.

"The ground is being prepared," Carper said in the summer of 2013. "We're hoping to be ready to harvest by the end of the year."

Other lawmakers were a bit more impatient, especially Rockefeller who was retiring at the end of the session. He had been a leading advocate of strong, mandatory cyber controls for industry. He had been willing to negotiate in 2012 on possible alternatives with Republicans like Kay Bailey Hutchison. Now, nearing the end of his congressional career, he wanted to accomplish *something* on cybersecurity and he was more than willing to recalibrate.

In mid-July 2013, around the time of the NIST workshop in San Diego, Rockefeller and Thune circulated a draft bill that would formalize portions of Obama's cybersecurity executive order while avoiding hot-button issues such as mandatory performance standards and expansive information-sharing and liability protections.

The Rockefeller–Thune bill recognized the NIST role in developing a "voluntary, industry-led set of standards" through a collaborative process with the private sector. It would mandate close and continuous coordination between NIST and owners of critical infrastructure and relevant private sector entities, while emphasizing the protection of individual privacy and civil liberties. The bill included sections on research and workforce training.

What about mandatory requirements on industry?

During a hearing in late July 2013, Rockefeller turned aside the suggestion of Sen. Edward Markey (D-Massachusetts) that the NIST approach was fine, but needed to be supported by the steel girders of regulation. "I understand the thrust of [your remarks] and I share some of that, but that's not our jurisdiction, that's [the] homeland security [committee]," Rockefeller said.

NIST's Chief Gallagher, testifying at the hearing, acknowledged the onus was on the administration to make a collaborative, market-based approach to cybersecurity work. "If we can't make it work," Gallagher said, "Congress will have to consider what to do, because there are national consequences."

In the meantime, legislation like Rockefeller–Thune would help validate the framework strategy.

Rockefeller announced the Commerce Committee would mark up the cyber bill prior to the 2013 August recess, jumping ahead of the Senate Homeland Security and Intelligence panels on the cyber issue. Rockefeller made clear that the Commerce Committee would stay in its own lane on cybersecurity and only address issues clearly under its jurisdiction, such as the NIST process, research, and job training. He said the Intelligence Committee, on which he also served, would have to address information sharing, while the Homeland Security and Governmental Affairs Committee could take up the Department of Homeland Security-related issues under its jurisdiction.

Around the same time, Senate Intelligence chairman Dianne Feinstein (D-California) told InsideCybersecurity.com that her committee was unlikely to release information-sharing legislation before the August break. She was working closely with ranking member Saxby Chambliss (R-Georgia), she said, but the timing wasn't quite right. "We're trying," she commented.

The Commerce Committee approved the Rockefeller–Thune bill by voice vote on July 30. It was noncontroversial, but it helped solidify policy aspects that were already advancing under a broad consensus. The bill did, however, contain a small element that was mostly overlooked by industry lobbyists: It required the U.S. Comptroller General to assess the implementation and effectiveness of the NIST framework. The provision would be largely forgotten by lobbyists until the bill was signed into law late the following year. At that point, business sources realized this forgotten line in a harmless bill could be the precursor of future regulation.

But in the summer of 2013, optimism was suddenly fashionable around cyber legislation. Even the White House was expressing optimism about the much more difficult information-sharing legislation.

"We got the ball rolling" with passage of S. 1353, Rockefeller said. "I feel good about it," he responded when asked if Senate floor action was likely in the fall. Thune expressed confidence too, while stressing that the bill should move in tandem with information-sharing legislation from the Intelligence Committee.

Thune saw the bills as a package and believed the Commerce Committee's popular, NIST-based measure could help advance the more politically complicated information-sharing bill. Along with many industry lobbyists, Thune believed information sharing was still too much of a political target to move on its own and needed to be combined with something the Obama administration and its Democratic allies on Capitol Hill really wanted. The Rockefeller–Thune bill, plus homeland security committee bills affirming the Department of Homeland Security's authority on cybersecurity, could be the ticket.

A month after expressing concern about the Snowden impact, McCaul concurred that the Senate Commerce Committee action created momentum for cybersecurity legislation and said he was looking to mark up his own bill on the DHS role in October.

"There is a readiness to move forward in the fall with subcommittee and full committee markups," added House Homeland Security cybersecurity subcommittee Chairman Patrick Meehan (R-Pennsylvania). "We will lobby leadership to bring it up on the floor."

But the fall would come and go without action on cyber legislation. Other policy issues and the partial government shutdown had intruded, a common refrain when it came to cybersecurity and Congress.

When House Majority Leader Eric Cantor (R-Virginia) circulated a memo on the 2013 fall floor agenda, cybersecurity legislation wasn't on it. McCaul said he was ready to mark up a couple of bills on training the cyber workforce and research, but held back on more consequential legislation.

Carper, at a hearing on the twelfth anniversary of 9/11, detailed what he called six "not-so-easy pieces" that should be included in cybersecurity legislation. "Enacting a comprehensive policy will not be easy, but hopefully we can get it across the finish line this year," he said. Legislation should address ways to better protect critical infrastructure; information sharing; protecting the federal government's computer networks; improving DHS's ability to attract and retain qualified cyber professionals; research and development; and data-breach disclosure.

Carper didn't have a timetable for action.

In October, McCaul began circulating a draft of his major cyber bill even as the government stumbled through a partial shutdown. This was the third draft of his plan and the Texan was gradually narrowing differences with online privacy advocates and with the business community. The measure would deal with the mechanics and jurisdiction of cyber information sharing.

At the end of October, McCaul's panel waved through the workforce and research bills, but there was still no sign of the broader measure.

By now, there was a growing consensus that NIST's framework should be allowed to go into effect early the next year before Congress attempted any heavy lifts on cybersecurity. That consensus emerged by default because broad legislative efforts were bogged down and the Senate had yet to offer an alternative to controversial, House-passed information-sharing legislation. House Intelligence chairman Rogers said a Senate breakthrough on information sharing would be the key to passing cyber legislation. But that wasn't happening.

Rockefeller tried to get his committee's bill added to a defense measure as 2013 came to a close, but that gambit was rejected.

McCaul finally introduced his bill in mid-December. The bipartisan language, cosponsored by committee ranking member Bennie Thompson (D-Mississippi), wouldn't move until sometime in the new year, but it was earning praise from industry groups like the Internet Security Alliance and Financial Services Roundtable, and from privacy and civil liberties groups such as the American Civil Liberties Union.

That odd-partners collection of supporters boded very well for the legislation, providing a dose of optimism as the year wrapped up. The Feinstein–Chambliss information-sharing bill, on the other hand, was still on ice at the end of 2013.

That condition persisted through much of 2014. McCaul passed his cyber bill through committee in early February. The measure would codify roles for NIST and for the Department of Homeland Security's National Cybersecurity and Communications Integration Center. Secretary of Homeland Security Jeh Johnson, in his first appearance on Capitol Hill since his confirmation, voiced support for the McCaul bill.

"I have studied H.R. 3696 reported out of this Committee on a bipartisan basis," Secretary Johnson told McCaul and other committee members. "We think this bill is a good step forward. We want to continue working with Congress on this and other legislation to improve the government and nation's overall cybersecurity posture."

The Senate Homeland Security and Governmental Affairs Committee passed a workforce measure in May and bills on the security of federal networks and codifying DHS's role in June. The House and Senate homeland security panels at the mid-year point of 2014 had passed an assortment of cyber bills that could match up nicely.

And then they would wait.

Already by mid-March 2014, Congress's election-year schedule was beginning to work against lawmakers interested in moving cybersecurity legislation. When the House returned from its Saint Patrick's Day recess, it would be in session for just seventeen weeks before breaking in early October for the elections. The Senate was on roughly the same schedule.

The House-passed information-sharing bill known as CISPA had gained no traction in the Senate. A senior Obama administration official told InsideCybersecurity.com in March 2014 that the administration was not reconsidering its veto threat against that measure.

On March 27, the National Security Council staff issued a statement affirming the president's support for information-sharing legislation that included "targeted liability protection," safeguards privacy and civil liberties, and preserves the "respective roles and missions of civil and intelligence agencies."

"Many sophisticated companies currently share cybersecurity information under existing laws," the statement read.

> However, the Administration has consistently stated that carefully updating laws to facilitate cybersecurity information sharing is one of several legislative changes essential to protect individuals' privacy and improve the nation's cybersecurity. While there is bipartisan consensus on the need for such legislation, it should adhere to the following priorities: (1) carefully safeguard privacy and civil liberties; (2) preserve the long-standing, respective roles and missions of civilian and intelligence agencies; and (3) provide for appropriate sharing with targeted liability protections.

The statement continued: "We welcome a further public discussion to define the scope of liability protection for cybersecurity information sharing that increases the scale of appropriate exchanges, without creating legal immunity for reckless, negligent, or harmful actions."

Feinstein and Chambliss would finally pass their information-sharing bill through the Senate Intelligence Committee in July 2014. And then that measure would wait; in the end, it would wait for quite a bit longer than the McCaul or Carper bills.

By the fall of 2014, the clock was winding down on the 113th Congress. It was also winding down on House Intelligence chairman Rogers's congressional career. He tried repeatedly to light a fire under his colleagues. In September, he warned his colleagues that cyber catastrophe was just around the corner.

"We had better get it done in the lame duck or we are going to have a major catastrophic event within eighteen months that we're all going to look back and go, 'My God, why couldn't we get our act together?'" Rogers warned.

The answer lay in a crowded agenda, the Snowden impact, and the need to move deliberately through the complexities of cyber policy questions. It lay in a partial government shutdown and an unparalleled, unending political standoff between the legislative and executive branches over issues like immigration, health care, and government spending. There were plenty of reasons, but they didn't add up to a valid justification for the ongoing inaction on an issue as vital as cybersecurity.

Suzanne Spaulding, DHS undersecretary for the National Protection and Programs Directorate, urged lawmakers to move cyber bills that had broad support. In a September 2014 appearance on Capitol Hill she called on Congress to pass the legislation to protect federal networks, "clarify existing operational responsibilities by authorizing the [National Cybersecurity and Communications Integration Center]," and help bolster the department's cyber workforce.

Spaulding said there had been "significant progress" in Congress on cyber issues and that there was "strong consensus" in those three areas. "While deliberations continue on other areas of cybersecurity, don't wait on areas where there is consensus," she said.

That didn't seem to include information sharing. Spaulding repeated the Obama administration's principles for information-sharing legislation: privacy safeguards, ensuring that newly authorized sharing of cyber threat information entered the government through a civilian agency, and carefully targeted liability protection.

The administration didn't offer a formal opinion on whether the Feinstein–Chambliss information-sharing bill met the mark, although an official said over the summer that there were problems with the privacy elements. Further, Spaulding and other officials consistently emphasized their desire for action on other bills, while leaving Feinstein–Chambliss off the list. "Information sharing is only one element of what is needed," Spaulding told lawmakers.

The noncontroversial bills on DHS and NIST were passed almost as an afterthought at the end of 2014. Obama signed them into law without much flourish. The 113th Congress could boast of year-end accomplishments on cybersecurity, and victories for the chairmen of the homeland security panels and the Senate Commerce Committee. But the intelligence panels' information-sharing legislation was still hung up.

Cybersecurity policy felt decidedly unsettled.

9

THE INFORMATION-SHARING MATRIX

No foreign nation, no hacker, should be able to shut down our networks, steal our trade secrets, or invade the privacy of American families, especially our kids. We are making sure our government integrates intelligence to combat cyber threats, just as we have done to combat terrorism.

—President Obama, January 20, 2015, State of the Union address

In early 2015, the health insurance provider Anthem revealed that its networks had been hacked. As many as 80 million customers were affected and the company acknowledged that Social Security numbers, employment information, and other highly personal data may have been stolen. If there was any bright side, it was that Anthem relatively quickly uncovered the penetration and swiftly reported it to the government and to its customers.

After hanging back in 2014, supporting only modest cyber legislation and never quite signing on for the big information-sharing bill, President Obama pushed his chips into the middle of the table in January 2015. The Sony Pictures hack was fresh in the minds of lawmakers, White House officials, and the public. Here was a chance for a legacy-building accomplishment for both the Republican majority in Congress and an increasingly lame-duck president.

"I've got a State of the Union next week," Obama said on January 13 as he sat down at the White House for the first time with the leadership of the new 114th Congress. "One of the things we're going to be talking about is cybersecurity," Obama told reporters.

Turning to House Speaker John Boehner (R-Ohio) and the new Senate majority leader, Mitch McConnell (R-Kentucky), Obama said, "I think we agreed that this is an area where we can work hard together, get some legislation done and make sure that we are much more effective in protecting the American people from these kinds of cyberattacks."

The administration rolled out draft legislation on information sharing, consumer data-breach notification and tougher penalties for cyber crooks. The White House was going all-in.

Republicans were gracious as well, but also took a dig at the White House.

"While it took an attack on Hollywood for the President to re-engage Congress on cybersecurity, I welcome him to the conversation," said House Homeland Security chairman Michael McCaul. "My committee is currently working on cybersecurity legislation to remove any unnecessary legal barriers for the private sector to share cyber threat information."

McCaul had been a key ally the previous fall. Another set of allies, the online privacy and civil liberties communities, was less thrilled with the latest turn from the administration.

"Although the administration's proposal includes some modest privacy improvements . . . it ultimately falls short when it comes to addressing the significant privacy and civil liberties concerns that come with companies' sharing more data with the government," said Robyn Greene, policy counsel at New America's Open Technology Institute.

Likewise, the privacy community rendered a split decision on the data-breach notification proposal. Despite the inclusion of long-sought enhancements to the Federal Trade Commission's (FTC) authority, some lamented that it would preempt even tougher pro-consumer laws in places like California.

Regardless, the president carried his proposals to the podium as he delivered his January 20 State of the Union address. "And tonight, I urge this Congress to finally pass the legislation we need to better meet the evolving threat of cyber-attacks, combat identity theft, and protect our children's information. If we don't act, we'll leave our nation and our economy vulnerable. If we do, we can continue to protect the technologies that have unleashed untold opportunities for people around the globe."

The details still had to be worked out, but industry groups were pleased that the administration seemed to finally embrace the need for liability protection.

"The fact that the administration included a degree of liability protection shows they're probably willing to discuss" the details, a financial sector representative said. "Hopefully they can work together."

The second bill in the package proposed new criminal penalties to raise the price for cyber criminals.

A White House fact sheet explained the proposal "would criminalize the overseas sale of stolen U.S. financial information like credit card and bank account numbers, would expand federal law enforcement authority to deter the sale of spyware used to stalk or commit ID theft, and would give courts the authority to shut down botnets engaged in distributed denial of service attacks and other criminal activity."

It would also modernize outdated laws on racketeering and computer fraud.

The Obama administration would follow up with an April 1, 2015, executive order that empowered the Treasury Department to impose economic sanctions against individuals, companies, and countries engaged in the cyber-theft of U.S. companies' intellectual property (IP). The president proclaimed "a national emergency" around such massive-scale criminal hacking.

"That's the degree of importance the administration applies to this economic theft," observed former assistant secretary of defense for homeland security Paul Stockton. "These are new tools and this is a big, big step to protect IP."

Absent this new approach, Stockton said, "It's free, there's no cost to stealing our IP. This begins to alter the equation." He noted approvingly that under the April executive order, sanctions could be tailored to inflict pain on foreign companies that were dependent on both international trade and the global banking system.

The third part of the president's 2015 legislative proposal would create a national data-breach notification standard to replace dozens of state laws. The proposal would require retailers, banks, and other companies to notify customers within thirty days of a breach. Business groups favored a uniform standard over the current jumble of state laws on the issue, while some online privacy groups were concerned that the proposal would undermine the tougher state laws.

The administration wanted to fortify, in law, the Federal Trade Commission's authority to enforce data-breach standards, but this was a nonstarter in the Republican-controlled Congress of 2015. Even setting a uniform data-breach notification standard faced long odds on Capitol Hill, because it almost certainly would pit business groups in the retail and financial sectors against one another.

Calling for data-breach legislation and actually getting Congress to engage on the issue were two different things—even if action to help the millions of hacked consumers seemed to be a no-brainer after the string of incidents in recent months.

But the administration wasn't leaving it all up to Congress. Just as it had done two years earlier, the White House issued an executive order in February 2015 at the cybersecurity summit at Stanford University in Palo Alto, California. The summit—and the executive order on cyber information sharing—were classic Obama White House productions. Industry leaders were lined up to publicly commit to enhanced cybersecurity efforts, while the new executive order sought to frame the policy discussion before Congress could get to it. Stanford also committed to holding a cyber "boot camp" for congressional staff each summer.

The centerpiece of the executive order was a call for creation of new "information sharing and analysis organizations."

A February 13, 2015, White House fact sheet explained "the Executive Order expands information sharing by encouraging the formation of communities that share information across a region or in response to a specific emerging cyber threat."

Information Sharing and Analysis Organizations (ISAOs) could be developed along flexible lines, covering regions, supply chains, the retail sector or even lawyers, while the Information Sharing and Analysis Centers (ISACs) covered specific industry sectors.

The order stressed the administration's commitment to privacy protections, a mantra repeated in almost every utterance on cybersecurity.

"The Executive Order ensures that information sharing enabled by this new framework will include strong protections for privacy and civil liberties," according to the White House fact sheet. "Private sector ISAOs will agree to abide by a common set of voluntary standards, which will include privacy protections, such as minimization, for ISAO operation and ISAO member participation."

And, in a nod to Congress, the White House said the executive order would help in "paving the way for future legislation." Here and in its legislative proposal the administration was spelling out what it would accept in terms of liability protection for companies that participated in cyber information sharing.

The industry reaction was generally positive, at least publicly.

"The Sony Pictures hack may indicate the need for the 'ISAO' structure," noted an industry source, who observed that ISACs were designed to protect critical infrastructure like power grids, not movie studios.

In May, the Department of Homeland Security (DHS) issued a solicitation for bids for a private-sector body to develop "best practices" and manage standards for the ISAOs, with industry standards-setting organizations, universities, and nonprofit groups among the expected bidders, along with private-sector entities established with just this opportunity in mind. The winning bid would receive an $11 million grant to run the body for five years.

The department held workshops in Cambridge, Massachusetts, and San Jose, California, to discuss the mechanics and governing structure of the new entities. Stakeholders reported productive discussions, even though fewer than seventy participants showed up in San Jose. DHS's outreach problems seeped into every area where it had to engage deeply with the private sector.

"Our hope is the ISAO structure is a complement to the traditional ISAC system," commented Joshua Magri of the Financial Services Roundtable said at the time. "To the extent that it stays complementary, I'm very supportive of the ISAOs."

The financial sector, through the leadership of groups such as the Financial Services Roundtable and Securities Industry and Financial Markets Association (SIFMA), years earlier had developed an information-sharing ISAC that represented the gold standard. "It wasn't an overnight success, it was fifteen years in the making," noted Karl Schimmeck of SIFMA.

But it enjoyed strong buy-in from companies and groups in the financial sector. The smallest firms paid just $250 a year to be members; the big entities willingly carried the financial load, paying up to $25,000 in annual dues.

Financial firms, for one thing, had regulators that strongly supported cyber information sharing. And, the many elements of the financial sector were pulled onto the same page by the distributed denial of service attacks in 2012 and 2013, allegedly directed from Iran. Thousands of computers were targeted simultaneously, causing systems to overload and shut down. Online transactions, part of the sector's life blood, were frozen. "The increasing frequency with which we have seen that has really increased our relationship with financial institutions," then DHS Secretary Napolitano said at the time.

Two years later, financial industry officials wanted to ensure their highly developed system of cyber information sharing wasn't eclipsed in any way by the president's new ISAO program. But they were also huge supporters of bringing more types of entities into the sharing process in order to create a complete real-time picture of the threat environment.

The business-based Internet Security Alliance (ISA) and Carnegie Mellon proposed just such a cross-cutting approach to information sharing nearly fifteen years earlier. But the ISA–Carnegie Mellon proposal for a cross-sector entity was rejected by the National Council of Information Sharing and Analysis Centers precisely because it wasn't tied to a specific industry sector, ISA president Larry Clinton said. "We were structured as an alternative to the original ISACs."

The ISAC concept itself went back even further: T-Mobile's Harold Salters at an event in Washington, DC, recalled that the seeds of the communications sector's ISAC were actually planted following the 1962 Cuban missile crisis, when President John F. Kennedy asked for a comprehensive examination of the nation's emergency communications capabilities.

The Internet Security Alliance was launched in 2000 and shortly thereafter presented its proposal to the ISAC council. "We were turned down because we didn't represent a specific sector," Clinton said. "But the soda straws that we used in the late '90s are outmoded, so we're very enthusiastic about the ISAO structure," Clinton added. "We need to reformat the process of information sharing specifically for these smaller entities. The economics, not the will, is the problem."

Clinton said he was looking for a simple, "elegant solution" to cyber information-sharing challenges. "Don't load up ISAOs with excessive rules and requirements," he said as the administration's process got underway. "Don't weigh it down with bells and whistles."

Others, including Robert Dix of Juniper Networks, saw the ISAO initiative as a distracting sideshow.

"I hope in the conversation around ISAOs we can step back and look at the model," Dix said, noting that the current ISAC system evolved from a 1998 presidential policy directive. "Does the model still work? Are there gaps and how can we fill them? Can these affinity groups [ISAOs] help? That's the conversation I'd like to see."

The question, Dix said, is "what do we need to do to raise the bar across the community?"

The White House had another answer to this question, but it wasn't what observers such as Dix had in mind. The administration followed up the information-sharing executive order with the announcement that it was forming a Cyber Threat Intelligence Integration Center, to be known as the CTIIC (pronounced "C-Tick" among the wonks). The center would be small, officials said, with a staff that wouldn't exceed fifty people. And it was intended as an inward-looking entity to help the government make sense of the intelligence it was receiving.

A "Cyber Armageddon" destroying the nation's infrastructure was unlikely, Director of National Intelligence James Clapper would tell lawmakers. But "an ongoing series of low-to-moderate level cyber attacks from a variety of sources over time . . . will impose cumulative costs on U.S. economic competitiveness and national security," he said.

That kind of threat highlighted the need for enhanced integration and analysis of intelligence, Clapper said, a role the new CTIIC was intended to play.

The proposal was met with alarm by lawmakers on the House and Senate homeland security panels. Just months before, they had sent legislation to the president making DHS's National Cybersecurity and Communications Integration Center the centerpiece of cyber information sharing and analysis. Was the administration downgrading or sidelining NCCIC so quickly, lawmakers and lobbyists wanted to know?

Outside observers including Dix clearly thought so, and key lawmakers on Capitol Hill wanted answers.

The administration didn't need this conflict with the homeland panels and quickly realized that officials had inadequately prepped lawmakers on the CTIIC plans. The timing was especially bad: Due to an ongoing struggle over Obama administration executive actions on immigration, DHS was operating on a short-term spending act that expired at the end of February 2015. Republicans and Democrats on the homeland security committees were among the department's few unwavering friends on Capitol Hill—and now they felt snubbed by the CTIIC move.

White House cybersecurity coordinator Michael Daniel scrambled to the Hill to give House Homeland Security members an hour-long private briefing on the new center. Daniel and others stressed it would be small and was not meant to interact with the private sector; that was the NCCIC's job, which the administration strongly supported, the officials stressed.

The contrition helped soothe tensions, as did a relatively quick conclusion to the latest budget crisis.

Other criticisms began to emerge as industry chewed over the administration's strategic thinking around cyber information sharing. Some in the industry believed the ISAO proposal, for instance, was addressing a situation that the marketplace was already taking care of: The retail sector as well as law firms were organizing their responses without a new government-driven information-sharing structure.

"That takes time and resources away from other efforts," said one industry source. "We've been talking to DHS about better ways to share, but a lot of that was ignored. Now we have to spend a lot of time on this ISAO concept."

The Obama administration's infatuation with the financial sector information sharing and analysis center as a model of efficiency and performance also rankled some. Not everyone or every sector was going to invest that heavily, or in that exact way. Likewise, other groups had created different contractual relationships around sharing and weren't thrilled to tear those up and rewrite their rules. There were real-world, practical issues that had to be considered; the White House, in some eyes, seemed to be whipping up strategies in a reality vacuum.

For instance, the administration was looking to involve "atypical organizations" in the information-sharing process by creating the ISAOs. But if that meant small- and mid-sized businesses, it would require financial and other assistance. Promised DHS money for that purpose hadn't materialized by the end of 2015 and it was unclear where it would come from. Smaller entities "need a 'managed services approach' or they're just not going to get involved," commented John Abeles, president and founder of System1, a Bethesda, Maryland, consulting firm.

The White House was offering a tool, but who would be able to use it?

On September 3, DHS made a somewhat "atypical" choice, announcing that the $11 million grant to set and maintain standards for ISAOs would go to the University of Texas at San Antonio. The university beat out bids by better-known entities such as a consortium that included the financial sector ISAC, former DHS official Jane Holl Lute's Center for Internet Security and SAE International.

"The University of Texas at San Antonio will work with existing information sharing organizations, owners and operators of critical infrastructure, federal agencies, and other public and private sector stakeholders to identify a common set of voluntary standards or guidelines for the creation and functioning of ISAOs," Andy Ozment said in a blog announcing the decision.

"The ISAO standards developed by the University of Texas at San Antonio will reflect the most effective and innovative ideas from the public and private sectors," Ozment said. "Through a public, open-ended engagement with business communities, civil society groups, and other stakeholders, the University of Texas at San Antonio will develop transparent best practices that align with the needs of all industry groups."

"I think it's a perfect fit that it went to a university rather than a private entity," said John DiMaria of the BSI Group, also known as the British Standards Institution. The setting provided "a great ecosystem" for the standards-setting body, which could "draw from great minds with a tremendous range of expertise."

DiMaria predicted the university's role would be "more a matter of developing a standard way of doing things rather than creating standards." He added, "I'm glad to see a university was chosen."

Christopher Blask, chairman of the Industrial Control Systems Information Sharing and Analysis Center, commented: "While I am not yet knowledgeable about the proposal the University of San Antonio provided, I think that the selection of a university is generally a good move. I am looking forward to talking with them."

Blask noted that his group, which was part of Webster University, also bid for the grant. "We think it was a good one, but knew there would be strong competition," Blask said. "There are very good arguments for an academic base for such a creature."

Larry Clinton, president of the Internet Security Alliance (ISA), remarked: "Obviously I congratulate them heartily and offer any assistance ISA may be able to provide. I don't know them personally but the first vice chairman of my board is CSO at USAA which is based in San Antonio, and he tells me they have a very strong group there and we certainly wish them well on a challenging but critical endeavor."

As always, a DHS move raised plenty of questions. Many sources in the cyber information-sharing ecosystem just were not familiar with the University of Texas at San Antonio's programs or expertise. DHS did not expound on the selection process or the unique attributes of the winning bidder. It didn't even say who else had bid for the grant.

"To be successful, it will be imperative that the standards organization utilize and incorporate the expertise of the people and organizations who have been doing information sharing and analysis successfully," commented one industry source. "There are many successful organizations, including [existing information sharing and analysis centers] who have a tremendous amount of knowledge. The goal of the standards organization should be to aggregate that knowledge into a suite of effective practices."

Asked what he knew about the university, one well-known source in the info-sharing community replied, "Only that their nickname is the Roadrunners."

"My biggest question is what type of experience they have with the subject matter," the source said. "I've been doing this for many years and don't recall ever coming across them."

But the university wasn't an entire mystery. The school ran an Institute for Cyber Security and a Center for Education and Research in Information and Infrastructure Assurance and Security. The Ponemon Institute in 2014 said the school had the best academic cybersecurity program in the nation. Its cyber center and research institution earned coveted certifications from both DHS and the National Security Agency. Gregory White, director of the research center, was known and highly acclaimed in the cyber community, with a long list of writing credits to his name.

Christopher J. Castelli of InsideCybersecurity.com interviewed White just after the selection, learning that the university had a sophisticated and well-developed plan for broad outreach to the cybersecurity community and for drafting the standards. Amid questions from the greater cybersecurity community, White's remarks suggested DHS officials might want to consider a more visible public role for the cybersecurity expert. His comments on the universities bona fides were much more convincing than anything DHS could roll out.

Still, the choice triggered unease among existing information-sharing centers; a more-familiar face setting the ISAO rules would've tempered concerns about conflicting approaches. But perhaps a new face, relatively speaking, would be beneficial in an area where the goal was to bring plenty of new faces into the information-sharing matrix.

Overall, the administration continued to emphasize the perceived need to drive the dialogue in directions of its own choosing. Executive orders framed relations with critical infrastructure operators and compelled certain approaches to information sharing, law enforcement, and other cyber issues.

The legislative process wasn't quite as easy to manipulate, in 2015 just as from 2009 to 2012. Obama did find sponsors for his cyber legislative proposals this time around. But on Capitol Hill, lawmakers had their own plans.

10

A NEW CONGRESS BRINGS A NEW
ENERGY TO CYBER DEBATE

Not since the dawn of the nuclear era have we witnessed such a leap in technology without a clear strategy for managing it. To establish order and defend America's interests in the digital domain, we must map out the rules of the road and clarify responsibilities inside and outside of government. We are not quite there. In fact, I would argue that we are in a pre-9/11 moment when it comes to cybersecurity.

—House Homeland Security chairman Michael McCaul (R-Texas),
March 17, 2015, speech at the Center
for Strategic and International Studies

Presidential legislative proposals on any topic often receive a polite smile on Capitol Hill, before being plopped onto a bookshelf in some committee back room. Staffers might flip through the hundreds of pages over a cup of coffee during a brief pause in writing their own proposals.

Lawmakers were deeply into their own efforts to craft bills, on information sharing in particular, by the time the Obama administration submitted its cybersecurity proposals in early 2015. The key takeaways from the White House decision to offer bills were that liability protection was clearly in play and, more broadly, that the president dearly wanted something to sign into law. Unlike the case in previous years, the administration had a clear stake in achieving a positive outcome on information-sharing legislation this time around.

Members of Congress always know when an issue has become a matter of legacy for a president. Cybersecurity was in that category as Obama entered the final two years of his term, and that gave lawmakers leverage and an opportunity.

Mike McCaul was a former federal prosecutor and fourth-generation Texan with a shock of iron-gray hair that was the envy of his colleagues on Capitol Hill. He had an undergraduate degree from Trinity University and a law degree from St. Mary's University, both in San Antonio, and went through Harvard's senior executive fellows program. McCaul was understated in manner, practical, and solutions-oriented, with a sly sense of humor. He fashioned productive relationships with liberal Democrats on his committee like Bennie Thompson of Mississippi and Sheila Jackson Lee of Texas, while maintaining the respect and support of conservatives in the House Republican Conference.

McCaul had also been working the cybersecurity issue from the law enforcement and policy angles for over fifteen years by the time the 114th Congress was seated in 2015. "When we decided to do a report on cybersecurity in 2007, I was told 'you have to talk to Mike McCaul,'" James Lewis of the Center for Strategic and International Studies (CSIS) recalled in the spring of 2015. That conversation would be a springboard for the report to the forty-fourth president.

McCaul's interest went back further and he liked to cite a portentous date in the evolution of his work on the issue.

"In 2001 we had an idea to do an event on terrorism and cybersecurity," McCaul said, sitting onstage with Lewis. "The date of that event was September 12. It got postponed, obviously, but we had a premonition."

Now, McCaul said in early 2015, "the issue finally has the attention of the American public."

It had the attention of McCaul's colleagues as well. At the House Intelligence Committee, Rep. Devin Nunes (R-California) had replaced the retired Mike Rogers as chairman and Rep. Adam Schiff of California replaced Dutch Ruppersberger of Maryland as the new top Democrat.

It was a generational and stylistic changing of the guard, and perhaps a substantive one as well. Nunes was born in 1973 and elected to Congress in 2002. His family ran a farm and he had bachelor's and master's degrees in agriculture from Cal Poly San Luis Obispo. Nunes was a son of the San Joaquin Valley's agricultural elite that still worked the land and exercised the most significant conservative influence on government in the Golden State.

He was a strong national-security type with limited patience for criticism of the National Security Administration (NSA), which he saw as a vanguard in the battle against terrorism. His relationship with Schiff, a member of Speaker Nancy Pelosi's (D-California) circle and a strong voice on civil liberties, would test the committee's typical comity—and unanimity—on cybersecurity.

"There will be no shortage of issues to come before Congress in this session, from addressing new threats of terrorism at home and around the world, to reforming our surveillance capabilities and oversight, as well as securing and reinforcing our nation's cybersecurity," Schiff said in a statement.

Schiff experienced a different part of the California culture than did Nunes. He was born in 1960 in Massachusetts and moved to Oakland, California, as a teenager. He graduated from Stanford University with a political science degree and returned East to earn a law degree at Harvard University. Schiff was a prosecutor and was elected to Congress in 2000, representing areas including Burbank and Pasadena. Redistricting in 2010 would put Hollywood in his territory.

And he was seen as more skeptical of NSA surveillance activities than was outgoing ranking member Ruppersberger, whose twelve-year term on the committee had expired. It was unclear how Schiff would approach the information-sharing issue in 2015. In 2013 Schiff voted against the Cyber Intelligence Sharing and Protection Act (CISPA) information-sharing bill by Rogers and Ruppersberger, an ominous sign for industry lobbyists.

In December 2014, Schiff called for a strong response to the breach at Sony Pictures, a company headquartered in his congressional district. This attack demanded a broad policy response, Schiff said.

"The Sony hack is also a wake-up call to America and the West, who have been far too complacent in the face of the demonstrated and growing cyber threat posed by Russia, China, and Iran, as well as North Korea," Schiff said at the time. "Our national security is not only dependent on physically safeguarding the American people, but also developing the means to prevent a rogue nation or a terrorist group from launching a cyberattack that results in hundreds of millions of dollars in damage or the loss of life."

Nunes needed to get his relationship with Schiff and the committee's plans together quickly, because McCaul was moving on the issue and threatening to seize the baton on information sharing. The Texan mentioned his work on an information-sharing bill in every forum possible.

"I'd like to welcome Representative Schiff as the new Ranking Member of the House Intelligence Committee," Nunes said. "His appointment is one that will benefit both the committee and United States national security. This committee has a strong record of bipartisanship, and based on my previous cooperation with Rep. Schiff on the committee and on other issues, I am confident this tradition will continue in the new Congress."

Dianne Feinstein, who was moving from chair to ranking member of the Senate Intelligence Committee in the new Republican-led Senate, also offered support.

"I'm pleased that Adam Schiff was named lead Democrat on the House Intelligence Committee. He and Congressman Devin Nunes will represent California and the country well as leaders of that important committee," Feinstein said. "In appointing Congressman Schiff as ranking member, Leader Pelosi chose someone who cares deeply about national security, is steadfast in the need to protect the homeland and is committed to meaningful intelligence oversight."

Feinstein added: "I had a close working relationship with Mike Rogers and Dutch Ruppersberger, who led the committee last year. I look forward to continuing that bipartisan cooperation with Chairman Nunes and Ranking Member Schiff on intelligence matters, foreign policy and more."

This time around, the Senate Intelligence Committee would move first, passing a revamped version of its earlier information-sharing bill on March 12, 2015, on a fourteen to one vote in another closed session. Sen. Ron Wyden (D-Oregon) voted no, then hurried out of the Hart Senate Office Building and past reporters without comment. Within the hour his office would release a statement denouncing the measure as a "surveillance bill."

The committee's leaders didn't seem very concerned about the lone defection.

"This has been a long road, this is the third [cyber] bill I've worked on," Feinstein told the cameras and a throng of reporters clustered outside the Senate Intelligence Committee's secure hearing room in the Hart Senate Office Building. A year earlier, the committee's closed-door markup of a cyber bill had been staked out by a couple of reporters; TV cameras were nowhere in sight back in 2014. Now, the issue was exploding.

"We've learned from" the earlier efforts, Feinstein said. "We've bent over backwards to provide things in this bill that were important," Feinstein said. "The only way to get this first step done is in a bipartisan way."

"This is a very good start," said the new Intelligence chairman, Sen. Richard Burr (R-North Carolina), while cautioning, "This is the first leg in a very long race."

The Senate measure earned praise from the White House, which was exceedingly rare at this stage of the legislative process.

"We commend the committee on taking up cybersecurity information sharing, and look forward to continuing work on this important issue," a senior administration official said in a statement.

"In January, the President submitted an updated cybersecurity legislative proposal that would improve cybersecurity by striking a careful balance between improving information sharing incentives and protecting privacy and civil liberties," the administration official said. "We are committed to working with Congress to craft legislation that reflects that balance, and can pass both houses. In that spirit, we thank the committee for working with us to address some of the administration's most significant concerns with the committee's bill, and look forward to reviewing the legislation and amendments considered by the committee."

Of course, the elements that pleased the White House caused unease in the business community. Industry sources were anxious to scrutinize provisions that seemed to predicate liability protection on companies sharing cyber threat indicators, or CTI, solely through the Department of Homeland Security's (DHS) National Cybersecurity and Communications Integration Center (NCCIC). "The information sharing portal is too narrow: DHS is designated as the sole portal for sharing CTI in an electronic format," said a source who represented an industry categorized by the government as critical infrastructure. "We think that is too narrow and would support language that also allows sharing CTI with sector-specific agencies . . . as well as law enforcement entities to also be covered by liability protections."

But the White House decision to issue a statement served a strategic purpose: It sent a message to House lawmakers, as they put the finishing touches on their bills, on what the administration would accept. It was a clever attempt to avoid the veto threats and fruitless negotiations that had marked the White House's relationship with the House of Representatives on the issue over the preceding years.

In late March, Schiff appeared on a C-SPAN weekend program and said privacy concerns had been adequately addressed in the draft House Intelligence Committee bill. Schiff said there had been "convergence" between Democrats and Republicans—and the House and Senate—on requiring threat indicator exchanges to go through a civilian portal and to require efforts to strip out personally identifiable information.

It was a major breakthrough—and a major relief to industry groups. Adding Schiff's name to the bill provided a strong rebuttal to the online privacy groups' arguments.

The House Intelligence bill, circulated on March 24, called on the president to select an appropriate civilian portal for sharing between the government and private sector. "We wanted any agency that wanted to provide a portal to be allowed to do so," a committee source said. "Some companies might be more comfortable sharing with their own regulatory agency. Some might not be comfortable sharing with DHS. The whole point is to encourage sharing, so we just didn't designate a portal."

But the Nunes–Schiff bill would not allow direct, electronic, private-sector sharing with the National Security Agency. Privacy groups questioned the value of that restriction since the bill called for real-time sharing from the civilian portal to other federal entities. "The instant sharing requirement makes it irrelevant that it first goes through a civilian entity," said Gregory Nojeim of the Center for Democracy and Technology. "The bill requires that any cyber threat information shared with the federal government be immediately shared with NSA. No privacy group will support that."

Edward Snowden was alive and apparently well in Moscow, and the specter of his leaks still hovered over the latest cyber developments. The Center for Democracy and Technology, the American Civil Liberties Union, and other civil rights and privacy groups were all calling for NSA reform prior to action on an information-sharing bill. Many giants of the technology industry joined online privacy advocates in urging action on NSA reform.

But Schiff—who saw himself as a privacy fanatic—and other lawmakers were determined to take a stand on information-sharing legislation before Congress got wrapped up in addressing the upcoming June expiration of USA Patriot Act provisions that guaranteed a spring-time debate on the NSA.

"I think their concern is overstated," an industry source said of the privacy groups' criticisms. "I understand they're set on pushing for NSA reform, but the issues shouldn't be conflated. . . . The hackers are the real threat to privacy, that's a point that shouldn't be overlooked."

On March 26, the House Intelligence Committee unanimously passed its information-sharing bill in closed session in a dimly lit and secure room down in the bowels of the Capitol Visitor Center. Nunes and Schiff told reporters afterward there had been a few tweaks to the language. They tightened wording to ensure threat indicators shared with the government are only used for limited purposes, trying to address the civil liberties community's worry that information sharing would create a plethora of information that law enforcement officials could rummage through at will.

But most importantly, Nunes and Schiff stressed that the bill did not provide legal immunity for companies to share information directly with the NSA.

Schiff said the committee had "done everything we can to meet the demands of the privacy community." He pointedly questioned the strategy of linking information sharing to the debate over NSA reform. "The two are unrelated," Schiff said. The information-sharing bill "is not a surveillance bill."

The online privacy groups were unconvinced.

"While the committee did a better job trying to include privacy protections, mechanically, it's likely to operate just like CISA [Cyber Information Sharing Act] in Senate intelligence (i.e., you'd have 'auto-sharing' without adequate privacy protections with the military, including NSA)," the American Civil Liberties Union's Gabriel Rottman said in an e-mail response to InsideCybersecurity.com that could've been cut and pasted from comments a year earlier. "It also continues to have the broad use authorizations, including for Espionage Act cases. [The bill] could still be used to go after national security leakers and reporters."

Rottman said the draft McCaul bill expected to move through the House Homeland Security Committee in the coming days was "more narrow in certain key places. It's better especially in terms of use authorizations, but there are still a few areas that need to be improved."

McCaul was up next. The Texan unveiled his bill on April 13, including a few changes to satisfy industry and a few to satisfy the White House and privacy advocates.

The measure included liability protection for sharing with the DHS NCCIC or "other private entities," assumed to be information-sharing organizations envisioned in Obama's February executive order. The bill said DHS must have a portal—the NCCIC—but it was silent on whether other agencies could create a portal. "That was the compromise we worked," said an Intelligence Committee source. McCaul could emphasize the DHS portal without precluding the possibility of creating other pathways to share with the government.

"We were in contact with the Homeland Security folks throughout," the Intelligence Committee source said. "It was handled at the chairman-level and didn't really require any intervention from leadership."

The McCaul bill allowed companies to monitor their own networks with liability coverage and to engage in defensive measures. It also provided protection from regulatory or antitrust action, and from disclosure under the Freedom of Information Act (FIA).

The revised language stressed that uses of shared data were limited to cybersecurity purposes and couldn't be used for law enforcement or surveillance.

The proposal required private entities to "scrub" data of personally identifiable information before sharing with DHS, and required the department to perform a "second scrub" before distributing the information. It required "reasonable" efforts to remove personally identifiable information known as PII, even though many in the business community favored the Senate Intelligence Committee's formulation stating that entities must remove data "known at the time of sharing" to be PII. It was a slight but significant legal distinction and the kind of thing that kept congressional staffers hunkered down in conference rooms for days trying to figure out.

McCaul and his cosponsor, cybersecurity subcommittee Chairman John Ratcliffe, stressed the privacy elements in a press release. "This pro-security, pro-privacy bill is the result of close collaboration with industry and privacy stakeholders and other committees in the House," according to the lawmakers.

The measure unanimously passed the House Homeland Security Committee on April 14, after a short but spirited debate over liability language that had been developed by the Judiciary Committee in a jurisdictional compromise engineered by the House Republican leadership. McCaul didn't much like it either. "We didn't get everything we wanted but we did get some," McCaul said. McCaul added, "This bill does not go forward" without a sign-off from Judiciary. "That's just a fact."

House leaders set up a floor debate for the following week on the two committee-passed information-sharing bills, with plans to merge them into one piece of legislation for purposes of conferencing with the Senate. A Statement of Administration Policy issued by the White House on April 21 praised the House Intelligence Committee for strengthening the bill as it tried to address the administration's concerns. There were still problems, however: The liability protection should be coupled with a stronger requirement to remove personal information; the bill allowed too much sharing through "numerous federal departments," not just DHS; and its language on "defensive" measures raised an assortment of legal and policy issues.

But most critically, the White House urged the House to pass the Nunes–Schiff bill.

On April 22 the House passed the Nunes bill, 307 to 116, after adding an amendment saying the whole thing would sunset in seven years, at which time it would have to be renewed by Congress or it would die. "What if we have the balancing act wrong?" asked amendment sponsor Rep. Mick Mulvaney (R-South Carolina). A perpetually busy Congress needed a hard trigger to come back and review legislation, he said, while calling seven years "a long time" before the review.

The McCaul bill passed the House the next day on a 355 to 63 vote, after being amended to include the seven-year sunset. The White House praised the McCaul bill for focusing on private-sector sharing with DHS while quibbling over a few other details.

Now, there were three cyber bills for industry to plow through, evaluate, and compare. The two House bills were merged into a single piece of legislation, but there were still contradictions in the measures that would have to be resolved. That was left for the final stage of the process, after the Senate managed to get its version into the mix.

There were plenty of issues to resolve, though there also appeared to be plenty of time in April 2015. The tech sector, mindful of overseas perceptions, wanted the most restrictive language on what kind of information could be shared. Debate would continue on which agencies could touch the data, and when in the process. Industry wanted to make sure it got the most liability protection possible. Industry groups were urging senators to take a stand and kill the sunset provision in the House version.

It was all teed up for final discussions and actions. But now, another wait would begin.

"The Senate leadership is absolutely committed to getting CISA done, but it seems more likely in June," an industry source said on May 1. Iran nuclear negotiations, the budget, and trade were all ahead of cyber in the Senate's legislative queue.

Lawmakers faced a June 1 deadline to address expiring surveillance provisions in the USA Patriot Act. Most industry groups active on information-sharing legislation steered clear of the Patriot Act debate, which was "fraught with baggage," as one source put it. But they were intensely interested in how the NSA debate affected the separate cyber legislation.

"Reining in the NSA prior to Senate consideration of CISA would help with that consideration because CISA would channel so much user information to the NSA," said Nojeim of the Center for Democracy and Technology, hinting that privacy groups just might not mount such a vigorous campaign against information sharing if NSA reform was taken care of.

The White House, in mid-May, dismissed the idea of a short-term extension of government surveillance programs. "Our strategy on these important security matters is to not kick the can down the road," White House spokesman Eric Schultz told reporters. "Congress has known of this impending deadline for months and months. The June 1st expiration should not be taking anyone by surprise."

Finally, on June 2, 2015, the biggest perceived obstacle to Senate action on the cyber bill—debate over National Security Agency authorities under the USA Patriot Act—was demolished when the "USA Freedom Act" cleared the Senate, sixty-seven to thirty-two, despite the vigorous opposition of Majority Leader Mitch McConnell (R-Kentucky) and the grandstanding floor tactics of Sen. Rand Paul (R-Kentucky).

The Senate, McConnell charged, was undermining U.S. security. Veteran members of the congressional press corps had seldom seen such passion from the typically owlish majority leader. In this case, the talons were out. The president couldn't be trusted with the nation's security, McConnell thundered at his colleagues, harkening back to Obama's 2009 Cairo speech as a "disavowal" of American exceptionalism. If the connection between the Cairo speech and the expiration of Patriot Act provisions was a tad oblique, McConnell would put it more directly: The proposed reforms would be a victory for the traitorous Edward Snowden.

Senators were unmoved and overwhelmingly rejected four amendments to the legislation proposed by McConnell and Intelligence Chairman Burr. The Senate approved the House-passed "USA Freedom Act" on a sixty-seven to thirty-two vote and Obama signed it into law hours later.

The White House, industry groups, and key members of Congress all breathed a huge sigh of relief that CISA was finally poised to get its moment on the Senate floor, perhaps within weeks.

"We are really optimistic," Ari Schwartz, cybersecurity director at the White House National Security Council, said after the USA Freedom Act had been signed.

There were lingering issues in the cyber legislation, Schwartz said, and the White House was well-aware of the ongoing concerns from the online privacy community. Wyden was busy denouncing CISA as a surveillance bill masquerading as cybersecurity. Schwartz himself was a former leader of the Center for Democracy and Technology (CDT), which was not assuaged by passage of the NSA reform.

"We're not supporters of CISA," CDT's Nojeim said immediately after Freedom Act passage, dropping his earlier suggestion that NSA reform could smooth the way for CISA. "Significant amendments would be required in order to gain our support. They aren't likely to be adopted."

But "great" discussions were already underway with lawmakers and congressional staff, Schwartz said, expressing strong confidence that the moment was fast approaching for this piece of cyber legislation.

Excitement was rippling through the lobbying community. "If we don't get it done by October, I will be surprised," commented Larry Clinton, president of the Internet Security Alliance (ISA).

"It looks like information sharing will be moving up," a financial industry source said with enthusiasm. "If Congress can pass that, it'll really be a feather in the cap."

This source said the outstanding issues with the House and Senate versions of the information-sharing bills were merely matters of wording, not of substance.

And, this source added, "The fact that the USA Freedom Act debate wasn't too bruising will help."

The debate was bruising for some, most notably Mitch McConnell, but it didn't leave legislative scars that would haunt action on cybersecurity. McConnell had already pegged cybersecurity as the type of bipartisan issue he wanted to bring to the floor as he sought to demonstrate that Republicans—and he himself—could actually govern after the legislative stalemate of recent years.

The pathway for cyber information-sharing legislation was unfolding nicely in the eyes of supporters. But cybersecurity policy didn't develop in a news vacuum, and Edward Snowden's impact on the debate would be felt again within days of final approval of the USA Freedom Act.

On Thursday, June 4, 2015, the *New York Times* published the latest installment in a series of articles emanating from Snowden's leaks to the newspaper and ProPublica. "Without public notice or debate, the Obama administration has expanded the National Security Agency's warrantless surveillance of Americans' international Internet traffic to search for evidence of malicious computer hacking, according to classified N.S.A. documents," read the lead to the *Times*'s story.

Lawmakers, lobbyists, and civil liberties groups quickly grasped the policy implications for cyber legislation.

"Those who have said that the cybersecurity bills are not about surveillance have been proven wrong. The new revelations show that the NSA sees surveillance as the flipside of cybersecurity," CDT's Nojeim said in a June 5 statement. "Being the victim of a cyber attack should not be a reason for the NSA to collect your communications and mine them for intelligence purposes."

The CDT in a posting sought to explain the connection between the NSA program and cyber issues:

> The leaked documents show that the NSA is using Section 702 of the Foreign Intelligence Surveillance Act (FISA) in a far broader manner than previously understood. Section 702 is supposed to be used to monitor foreign targets. However, by using Section 702 to collect information directly from main internet cables in the United States, the NSA is sweeping up communications of Americans, including those who have been victimized by cyber attacks.

Nojeim said the revelation should slam the door on the pending cyber bill. "The backdoor search loophole in Section 702 of FISA is a far bigger problem than we thought," he said. "Unlike the bulk collection of phone records under Section 215, collection under Section 702 gets the actual content of communications. The scope of this incidental collection of Americans' communications in the name of cybersecurity is just not acceptable," Nojeim said.

The cyber information-sharing legislation passed by the House and pending in the Senate would shuttle mountains of additional data to the NSA, albeit after a two-step process of scrubbing intended to protect privacy and eliminate personally identifiable information that was unrelated to a cyber threat.

The sponsors of the Senate cyber bill vehemently rejected the connection being drawn by Wyden, Nojeim, and others.

"Recent media reports have shed light on NSA efforts to identify, track and thwart cyber attacks originating in foreign countries," Feinstein said in a statement. "These programs are not intended to go after Americans or small-scale cyber theft. They are targeted at foreign governments, terrorist groups and overseas criminal syndicates that commit sweeping attacks on U.S. networks, stealing data from millions of Americans and costing our economy trillions of dollars."

Amid this threat, Feinstein said, passage of the CISA bill was critical.

Industry sources—positively ebullient about CISA's chances just two days earlier—were suddenly nervous. Hopes for a June Senate floor vote were imperiled. They knew McConnell would be loath to schedule a debate that could replay all the unpleasantness of the recent Patriot Act fight.

Cybersecurity policy development was frequently a frustrating, one-step forward, one-step back process. By the spring of 2015, Snowden's leaks had been knocking policy efforts back—by a step or more—at regular intervals. But there were also regular reminders of the severity of the cybersecurity threat, which served to propel the policy efforts forward.

On the same day as the latest Snowden-based *New York Times* report, the Office of Personnel Management (OPM) announced that it had discovered the breach of its networks, exposing private data of at least four million current and former federal employees. To some industry sources, the breach highlighted a disconnect between the Obama administration's demands on the private sector on issues such as data-breach notification and cybersecurity in general. "People who live in glass houses should not throw stones," a tech industry source jibed.

The White House bristled at the suggestion, responding quickly to a reporter's inquiry with a huffy assertion that the administration was following the mandates of its own proposals on breach notification.

"I'd caution you that discovering an intrusion and verifying that [personally identifiable information] may have been compromised are two different things," an Obama administration official told InsideCybersecurity.com. "OPM discovered the incident in April, but only became aware of potentially compromised data in May. Notification will be completed within the thirty-day period consistent with our legislative proposal."

The White House also used the occasion to prod Congress to get moving on information-sharing and data-breach notification legislation, shrugging off any suggestion of "glass houses."

Industry sources suggested, hopefully, the OPM breach could offset the political damage inflicted by the latest Snowden leak. But lawmakers like Sens. Patrick Leahy (D-Vermont) and Wyden were having none of that.

"I want to look more at what happened at OPM, but I worry that it's always, 'Pass this law immediately, because otherwise we're'—fill in the blank," Leahy said during an interview for C-SPAN's *Newsmakers* program, as reported by *National Journal*.

"You'd almost think ISIS was marching up Pennsylvania Avenue during this last debate, if we didn't pass it immediately," Leahy said of the recent Patriot Act debate. Now, Leahy said, he wanted the Judiciary Committee to get a chance to review CISA before it reached the floor.

"Take a breather," Leahy said. "There are always going to be attacks. There is always going to be hacking."

Wyden said the OPM hack was "a bad excuse to try and pass a bad bill."

Mitch McConnell rolled the dice again. As the Senate labored through an increasingly partisan dispute over a Department of Defense policy bill, McConnell emerged from Republican senators' weekly luncheon on June 9 to announce that the cyber information-sharing bill would be added as an amendment to the defense bill in the coming days.

"[O]ur view is that this is a debate that needs to go on for a while," McConnell told reporters gathered outside the Senate chamber. "The national defense of the country is extremely important given the cyber attacks that occurred earlier in the week. It's the intention of Chairman Burr of the Intelligence Committee to offer cybersecurity to this bill, a bill that came out of Intelligence 14–1. So we'll be doing both NDAA, National Defense Authorization Act, and cybersecurity in the course of this debate."

McConnell said he was inspired to act by the recent OPM hack. "It might not deal with every aspect of what happened a few days ago," McConnell said, "but Congress is going to act on cybersecurity on this bill in the very near future."

Feinstein, Burr's partner on the bill, had no immediate comment on the maneuver. Neither did the White House, except to point a reporter toward a veto threat hanging over the defense bill due to other issues.

But senators who were leery of the cyber bill were now apoplectic.

"I am deeply concerned that the Republican Leader now wants the Senate to pass this information sharing bill without any opportunity for the kind of public debate it needs," Leahy said in a statement. "This is not the transparent and meaningful committee process the Republican Leader promised just months ago."

Leahy added:

> I agree that we must do more to protect our cybersecurity, but this information sharing bill should not be considered as a last-minute amendment to yet another bill that was negotiated and considered behind closed doors. . . . The American people deserve an open debate about legislation that would dramatically expand the amount of information about them that companies can share with agencies throughout the federal government.

The online privacy community erupted as well.

"That's a huge problem, both for privacy and transparency," said Rottman of the American Civil Liberties Union. "CISA would create huge exceptions to basic due process protections and would allow even more personal information to flow to intelligence agencies. There needs to be a debate."

Nojeim of the Center for Democracy and Technology added: "It would be more than unfortunate if Senate consideration of necessary privacy amendments to the cybersecurity bill were thwarted by a truncated debate of the bill because it was tacked on to the Defense Authorization Act."

This was either a bold or a reckless parliamentary move by McConnell, his second in recent weeks. The Kentuckian, after eight frustrating years as minority leader, had vowed as majority leader to make the Senate a busy, productive place with lots of votes. He said he wasn't afraid of occasionally losing a vote, a novel and quasi-courageous position for a Senate leader. The catch here, though, was that the cybersecurity bill wasn't facing any procedural roadblocks and didn't need to be protected by the armor of a procedural maneuver that would restrict senators' ability to offer amendments. What it needed was time on the floor to allow serious policy issues to be debated.

Most industry lobbyists held back comment immediately after McConnell's announcement, quite aware that McConnell's gambit on NSA reform had blown up in the leader's face a week earlier. They wanted to do everything in their power to push the cyber bill along, but they were terrified that their long-sought legislation would get caught up in the intense animosity between McConnell and Minority Leader Harry Reid.

A framed photo of an old miner's shack hung on the wall in Reid's Capitol office. The Democratic leader would jab a finger at the photo of his childhood home in Searchlight, Nevada, and tell visitors: "That's where I'm from." He loved a scrap, and in particular he loved a scrap with his "dear friend" from Kentucky.

Now, Reid charged, McConnell was merely trying to "check off the box" on cybersecurity and didn't care about trying to reach a legislative agreement. But in a timeless legislative tradition, the majority leader appeared to be simply adding elements that would increase votes for the troubled defense bill. McConnell, like Reid, was a student of parliamentary procedure and had an equal taste for political combat. The risk in the current maneuver was that McConnell wouldn't succeed in adding enough votes to advance the Pentagon measure, while at the same time poisoning the waters around the bipartisan cybersecurity bill.

Feinstein came to the floor the next day, June 10, to urge Republicans to reconsider the gambit. This was a serious, perhaps fatal defection. "The Senate Select Intelligence Committee produced a bill in the last Congress but it didn't receive a vote," Feinstein said. "Chairman Burr and I have been determined not only to get a vote, but to get a bill signed into law. And it should be evident to everybody that the only way we'll get this done is if it's bipartisan."

Feinstein said she had a pledge from Harry Reid not to block a vote on the Cybersecurity Information Sharing Act as a stand-alone measure. "So the bill is ready for floor consideration," she said. "Now a number of my colleagues would like to propose amendments, as is their right. And I expect I would support some of them and would oppose some of them. But the Senate should have an opportunity to fully consider the bill, to receive the input of other committees with jurisdiction in this area."

If the Senate leader pushed ahead with the cyber bill as an amendment to the defense package, "We're in real trouble," Feinstein warned.

Armed Services Chairman John McCain took to the Senate floor to assert that the cybersecurity bill belonged in the defense measure—and required immediate action amid growing cyber threats to the nation. Pointing to the fourteen to one Intelligence Committee vote for CISA in March, McCain called the bill a "crucial piece" of an overall cyber deterrence strategy. McCain noted defense-related provisions in CISA to argue that the measure was germane to the defense bill.

But Feinstein warned that adding CISA to the defense bill would prevent senators from debating and amending the cybersecurity measure—and undermine painstaking efforts to build bipartisan support. Feinstein added, "Now, unless we do this, we won't have a bipartisan vote, I believe, because like it or not, no matter how simple—and I've been through two bills now—this is not an easy bill to draft because there are conflicts on both sides."

Wyden, the one vote against CISA in committee, offered a detailed policy critique of the cyber legislation—while sharply criticizing the Republicans' procedural move in bringing it up as part of the defense debate.

A controversial bill like CISA "should be subject to open-ended debate . . . not stapled onto other legislation," Wyden said. "Think about whether this is an appropriate process," Wyden urged.

He called the substance of the bill "a placebo" and "a Band-Aid on a gaping wound." Wyden cited significant shortcomings on privacy and civil liberties protection. He said that could be addressed with a language change specifying that any personally identifiable information shared with the government must directly describe a cyber threat.

The current language said companies must scrub data "known at the time of sharing" to be personally identifiable information. Industry groups supported this formulation. However, Wyden asserted that would discourage companies from scrutinizing data before sharing.

Supporters of the legislation were in real trouble. McConnell used a parliamentary maneuver to tee up the cyber bill as an amendment, promising to allow votes on further changes. But the move only served to solidify Democrats against the action. And all of the animosity between Reid and McConnell was on display.

On the morning of June 11, McConnell opened the Senate by saying the Senate would "soon" consider the "fully vetted" cybersecurity measure. He noted the fourteen to one vote in committee, said the measure had advanced in a "transparent" way and was posted online for all to read. "We shouldn't wait for the administration to fumble away another four million Social Security numbers" before action, McConnell jabbed, referencing the OPM hack.

This cyber bill was "smart, transparent, bipartisan, fully vetted," McConnell said. It would be open to amendment. But it was urgent the Senate move it along and get it into conference with the House.

Harry Reid's response just seconds later on the Senate floor?

"Talk about cynicism and hypocrisy," Reid shot back. "He comes to the floor today and blames Barack Obama for the hacking the Chinese did. We tried for five years to get a cybersecurity bill, the Republicans blocked us."

This was not going well for supporters of the cyber bill as Reid blasted McConnell's stewardship of the Senate and even raised the GOP's fundraising connections to the conservative Koch brothers. The leaders were throwing haymakers at one another.

There were two entwined problems from Democrats' perspective. First, the defense bill was part of a deeper budget policy dispute with Democrats and the White House on one side and Republicans on the other. Adding the cyber bill here wouldn't change that underlying dispute, or persuade Democrats to let the defense bill pass without changes.

Second, CISA supporters like Feinstein were well aware of the political sensitivities around their bill and thought they needed plenty of sunshine on the Senate floor to address concerns that they were moving yet another surveillance bill, as Wyden charged. A quick debate over CISA as an add-on to the defense bill, with only one amendment allowed to the long and complex cyber measure, just wouldn't accomplish the goal of demystifying and building support for desperately needed cyber information sharing.

McCain inherited this CISA problem from his leadership; he was usually perfectly happy to extend his jurisdictional reach into cybersecurity, but this was holding up his top priority: moving the defense bill. The signs were becoming obvious that McConnell's ploy was destined to fail. McCain, McConnell, and Reid spent the morning of June 11 in negotiation, often huddled in a mass with a changing cast of other interested senators at the front of the Senate. While McCain continued to assert the propriety of adding the cyber bill to the defense bill, he was looking for a way out.

When Sen. Tom Carper issued a statement denouncing McConnell's maneuver, the GOP leadership could basically turn out the lights. Carper was a leading voice on cyber policy and a supporter of CISA, who still wanted to see some tweaks to the bill.

"While I appreciate Majority Leader McConnell's willingness to move forward with cyber information sharing legislation, tucking it into the National Defense Authorization Act with almost no debate is not the right approach," Carper said. "I believe that proceeding in this way would hurt this critical bill's chances to get signed into law in a timely manner. I strongly encourage Senator McConnell to consider this bill under regular order so that we can have the full and open debate on this issue my colleagues and the American people have been expecting all year."

The U.S. Chamber of Commerce released two letters to senators in two days urging passage of the CISA amendment. Privately a well-connected business source expressed bewilderment at McConnell's tactic. "I don't think they get sixty votes," the official said. "I don't get it."

By mid-afternoon on June 11, McCain was ready to wrap this up and move on. He came to the floor and proposed moving up the cloture vote to that afternoon. There was no reason to wait until after midnight or until the next morning when the outcome was becoming clear.

Reid had a counteroffer: Withdraw the amendment and bring the cyber bill to the floor, under regular order, immediately after the Senate completed work on the defense bill.

"We have acted in a responsible way . . . when out of the blue came this cybersecurity amendment," Reid said. "The cybersecurity bill is a major bill in its own right, a major bill."

"The past is never dead. It's not even past," Faulkner wrote. He might've been writing about the U.S. Senate.

"We tried for five years to get a cybersecurity bill," Reid said, revealing as much anger and exasperation as he ever had on the Senate floor. Of course, Reid never showed any interest in bringing up a bipartisan cyber information-sharing bill in 2014 after McConnell helped thwart movement on a broader, bipartisan cyber bill in 2012.

The issue had history in the Senate and, substance aside, the history wasn't encouraging.

McConnell thanked his "good friend" for the offer and made his own proposal: The Senate would finish the defense authorization bill, proceed to a defense spending bill, and then move to cybersecurity.

"Putting it after defense appropriations is a false promise, a facade," Reid shot back. "We're not going to get to defense appropriations." The Pentagon spending bill had even more political problems than the authorization bill now on the floor. Democrats already had announced they would use their parliamentary tools to block the defense spending bill if McConnell brought it up next.

"We set the schedule," McConnell pointedly reminded his colleagues. The appropriations bill would be on the floor next, and cybersecurity would be left hanging unless Democrats agreed to support moving it as part of the defense debate.

Finally, the leaders agreed to hold the vote immediately on whether to consider the cyber bill as an amendment to the defense measure. The result was preordained: The motion received fifty-six votes, four short of the sixty-vote super majority needed to advance the proposal.

The Senate returned to its defense debate and cybersecurity was back on ice.

An industry source said in an e-mail: "Wacky. Unnecessary. Things could slip to September. That wouldn't be good."

But there were some positive signs from the procedural fiasco.

For one thing, Reid said the cyber bill would only need two or three days of debate as a stand-alone measure. Wyden, the chief Democratic opponent of the bill as reported by the Intelligence Committee, agreed there would be no obstacles to passing the bill if a full debate were allowed. Reid said Feinstein could work out problems over the bill with Democratic members of the Judiciary and Homeland Security and Governmental Affairs committees.

The procedural thickets of the Senate could be navigated. Amassing the necessary vote total to pass an information-sharing bill could be accomplished too.

Analyzing the vote tally, at least five, and perhaps many more, of the thirty-seven Democrats that voted against proceeding to CISA as an amendment to the defense bill seemed certain to vote in favor of the legislation under regular order. That list would include Feinstein, three other senators who voted for the bill in committee but opposed the floor move, and Carper. Seven Democrats crossed lines to vote in favor of the cloture motion, so they almost certainly would support the bill if and when it came up again. Some of the Democrats who voted "no" wanted changes to the exemption from Freedom of Information Act disclosure, an issue that could be addressed in the amendment process.

Among the three Republicans who voted against proceeding, Sens. Mike Lee of Utah and Dean Heller of Nevada raised substantive concerns related to use of data in noncyber criminal investigations. Both staked out anti-surveillance positions during the NSA debate. Now, industry lobbyists were confident their concerns with CISA could be addressed through the amendment process. That would be important, not only in moving the bill but in the broader policy context of separating cybersecurity information sharing from the issue of government online spying.

Sen. Rand Paul of Kentucky was the third GOP "no" vote, but he was a different story.

"Many agree with the underlying purpose of the bill but want it to go through the full amendment process," said one lobbyist.

When that would happen was anyone's guess. A few days after the Senate voted to block CISA as an amendment, Sen. McConnell walked away from a reporter without comment when asked about prospects in July for the cyber bill. Pursued down a Capitol hallway, McConnell barely broke stride to say, finally, the cyber bill "is important, it's a priority, we will continue to look for a way forward." He wouldn't comment on timing and quickly spun away into his office near the Senate floor.

The Senate was going to consider defense bills, an education bill, and a highway bill, and cyber wasn't on the table, for now. Memories in the Senate are long and parliamentary maneuvers are not soon forgotten. Days earlier, cybersecurity had been a matter of paramount urgency, necessitating extraordinary procedural moves to get it passed. Now it was just another item on a to-do list, tucked away somewhere.

"I hope Sen. McConnell would put it on the floor quickly," Sen. Charles Schumer (D-New York) told reporters a few minutes after the fleeting encounter with McConnell. Democrats would accept time limits around the cyber bill and move it quickly across the floor, he reiterated.

From "the other chamber," House Homeland Security Chairman McCaul said he was urging Senate leaders to get on with it. He expected Senate action in July and urged senators not to waste time passing something President Obama would veto.

"The president would sign our bill into law," McCaul said of the House Homeland Security-crafted bill.

Industry advocates quickly moved to regroup, while online privacy and civil liberties organizations sharpened their lines of attack against the CISA proposal. Despite Wyden's cooperative tone on the Senate floor, groups like the Center for Democracy and Technology were still gearing up for a major campaign to obstruct the progress of CISA.

But that was how policy was made in the U.S. Senate.

11

THE PROMISE AND PERIL OF "STRONG ENCRYPTION"

I know many in our privacy and technology communities are highly skeptical that any reform can be accomplished without unacceptably undermining both the privacy interests of our citizens as well as the international competitiveness of our technology companies. These are, no doubt, fundamentally important considerations. But as a start, we need to have an open and honest conversation that examines the costs and benefits both of potential reforms, as well as continuing down the path we are headed. And we need to do so with humility and respect for those who come to the issue from different perspectives.

—Sen. Charles Grassley (R-Iowa), who called a July 8, 2015, Judiciary Committee hearing on the policy issues raised by strong encryption

Some have suggested that technology companies should build special law enforcement access into their systems. But we also have to consider the risks of this approach. Strong encryption has revolutionized the online marketplace and protects American businesses and consumers from cybercrime, espionage, identity theft, stalking, and other threats on the Internet. Undermining strong encryption could make our data more vulnerable.

—Sen. Patrick Leahy (D-Vermont), July 8, 2015

Other cyber policy issues, such as Chinese hacking, were very much on Congress's radar, but as always it was unclear how effectively the legislative branch could engage. One question lawmakers seemed interested in probing—as productively as ever—was whether rapidly evolving technology was an answer or part of the problem. Tech wouldn't be the answer in and of itself. And tech was posing questions for the political system that seemed intractable.

"Strong encryption," the development of a new technology that promised to keep communications private and secure from end to end, was a case in point.

As these technologies quickly evolved, IT companies and privacy advocates expressed alarm that the government was seeking to mandate built-in vulnerabilities allowing investigators to get at communications protected by strong encryption. The first cyber bill introduced in the Senate in 2015, S. 135 by Sen. Ron Wyden, was intended to "prohibit Federal agencies from mandating the deployment of vulnerabilities in data security technologies." That was an effort to prohibit the government from planting bugs in commercial devices. It served notice that Congress was watching, but the legislation wouldn't move.

Online privacy advocates framed the data encryption debate as "law enforcement versus cybersecurity."

Federal law enforcement leaders wanted access to information locked up by increasingly sophisticated encryption technology. FBI Director James Comey posted a blog on July 6, 2015, in which he argued that "universal strong encryption" will be good for society, but must be balanced by consideration of security concerns.

"To protect the public, the government sometimes needs to be able to see an individual's stuff, but only under appropriate circumstances and with appropriate oversight," Comey wrote. He called for an "informed" debate in which the potential costs of encryption—such as a diminished ability to track terrorists—were understood.

Comey's posting provoked a strong reaction from the tech sector and privacy advocates.

"It was interesting to read Comey's op-ed in *Lawfare*, especially that the sides continue to talk past one another," commented a tech sector source. "We continue to say front doors, backdoors, trap doors are technically infeasible and would be exploited by bad actors and cybercriminals, [but] he continues to push for it. I joke they want a DC solution, like there is a compromise to be found on the laws of gravity."

The online privacy community pushed back as well, arguing that such "backdoors" would fundamentally undermine cybersecurity. These groups repeatedly challenged the FBI and Department of Justice (DOJ) to spell out exactly what they wanted in terms of ability to access encrypted data.

"The FBI wants to set up the issue as pitting crime fighting versus privacy," Nojeim of the Center for Democracy and Technology (CDT) said. "Really it's security versus security. Will privacy security be compromised" by the FBI's law enforcement interests, he asked. "What's interesting is what the FBI isn't saying," Nojeim said. "What are they proposing?"

Nojeim said mandatory, built-in backdoors in technology for law enforcement use was a nonstarter. He said any backdoor for the FBI would be accessible to the National Security Agency as well—severely damaging U.S. technology brands in overseas markets. "Any U.S. product operating under this regime will be seen as inherently suspect," he predicted.

The Information Technology Industry Council agreed and in June 2015 sent a letter to President Obama opposing any efforts to undermine encryption.

Further, Nojeim said any kind of access protocol for law enforcement eventually would be cracked by cyber bad actors. Would this be the next Stuxnet, a weapon or tool developed for the United States that escaped into the cyber wild with all kinds of dangerous ramifications?

"Are you going to undermine all of cybersecurity to achieve law enforcement goals?" asked Joseph Hall, CDT's chief technologist. He said it was time for the FBI to "put up or shut up" on what exactly it wanted.

"No solution has been put forward and we don't think there is one that doesn't create bigger problems," Nojeim said.

"If you have a backdoor, someone will find it," warned Internet pioneer Vint Cerf.

At a pair of hearings on July 8, 2015, Department of Justice and FBI officials tried to get off the defensive and recast the debate. They sought to assure lawmakers they were not seeking "backdoors" into U.S. technological products to investigate criminal or terrorist activities, but rather wanted to ensure that service providers themselves could respond to court orders by accessing customers' encrypted communications.

Comey and Deputy Attorney General Sally Quillian Yates testified before the Senate Judiciary Committee on the law enforcement challenges raised by rapidly evolving encryption technologies that allowed users to "go dark" in cyberspace. They also provided an informal closed-door briefing for committee members before the hearing.

Yates said the Obama administration was not seeking a legislative response, saying there was no "one-size-fits-all solution." Instead, she said, DOJ and the FBI were trying to engage on a "company-to-company basis" on individual approaches. Currently, she said, strong encryption technology was creating "safe zones" that put online criminal and terrorist activity beyond the reach of lawful warrants.

"Our goal is not to mandate a legislative solution" but to have each provider look at possible answers that fit their circumstances, she said. The government wasn't "asking for the keys," she added, and didn't want "special access." She said companies often keep this data for their own business purposes and asked that law enforcement and national security also be considerations when it comes to retaining data.

Comey said there was "an urgent need" to have this conversation about how the nation should respond to the emergence of strong end-to-end encryption. He described encryption as "a great thing" for the nation and the economy, but called for an honest dialogue involving Silicon Valley and others to address law enforcement's concerns.

Judiciary Chairman Grassley said it was critical to start "an open and honest conversation" on this issue that respects different points of view. "Today I hope the Senate takes a first step at seeing if any consensus is possible on this important and complicated issue," Grassley said.

Judiciary ranking member Leahy echoed the thought, but expressed deep concern about pressuring tech companies to provide backdoors. He called for more hearings—and for hearing from technology industry witnesses.

Tech groups were not invited to testify but weighed in nonetheless.

"We appreciate law enforcement has legitimate needs for information during criminal investigations and the technology industry works with local, state, and federal law enforcement to comply with lawful requests for information during such investigations," Information Technology Industry Council president and CEO Dean Garfield said in a statement. He said:

> We reiterate our commitment to a dialogue with the administration and law enforcement regarding their concerns, but we also encourage policy makers to consider that weak encryption is essentially no encryption, leaving all consumers vulnerable to breaches of privacy and cybercrime. We therefore caution the administration against pursuing

policies that encourage or require companies to weaken encryption technologies, including requiring so-called "back-doors."

Hinting at both the practical and political complexity of the issue, Sen. Al Franken (D-Minnesota) noted that there was little data on what if any negative impact encryption was having on criminal investigations. On the other side of the issue, Sen. Sheldon Whitehouse (D-Rhode Island) warned there would be "a price to pay" in innocent victims if law enforcement was stymied by strong encryption.

After the Senate Judiciary Committee hearing, the panel's top Democrat cast doubt on the likelihood of a legislative response on the issue. "The Bush administration and the Obama administration have wrestled with the same issues," Leahy told Inside Cybersecurity.com. "They want to keep us safe," but run up against policy obstacles ranging from privacy concerns to impacts on the competitiveness of U.S. technology products.

"I have sympathy for law enforcement because this is a tough problem," Leahy said. "But people can go to other countries to buy products" if U.S. tech devices contain "backdoors" allowing law enforcement to access data that may be screened by advanced encryption.

Leahy said the past two administrations had been unable to craft a legislative response—and, he noted, the Justice Department witness said the Obama administration wasn't seeking legislation at this time.

Leahy noted another obstacle to any effort to mandate any kind of access to encrypted communications: "What about the technology?" he asked. "In six months it's completely new."

A congressional source expressed doubt that the Judiciary Committee would seek a legislative response and pointed to Grassley's comments that he was most interested in starting a dialogue at this stage.

Rep. Adam Schiff of California, the top Democrat on the House Intelligence Committee, agreed that legislation was improbable. But he said an answer needed to be found, even if the solution was to consciously continue the status quo.

"Last week, I went to Silicon Valley, where I held a series of very productive sessions with a number of leading tech companies," Schiff said at a September 10 hearing with Comey on a panel of witnesses from the intelligence community. "I'll continue to have these conversations, and I encourage others to sit down with them as well. We in DC just can't tell tech to figure it out. We have to work with them and others to find the best mix of incentives, standards, and technological solutions."

Schiff put the question of next moves to Comey.

"First of all," Comey said, "I very much appreciate the feedback from the companies. We've been trying to engage in dialogue with companies, because this is not a problem that's going to be solved by the government alone; it's going to require industry, academia, associations of all kinds, and the government."

> I hope we can start from a place we all agree there's a problem and that we share the same values around that problem. When I hear people talk about the crypto wars, it throws me, because wars are fought between people with different values. I think we all share the same values here. We all care about safety and security on the Internet, right? I'm a big fan of strong encryption. We all care about public safety.

Comey agreed that this was a very difficult policy issue to resolve but added:

> I don't think we've really tried. I also don't think there's an "it" to the solution. I would imagine there might be many, many solutions depending upon whether you're an enormous company in this business, or a tiny company in that business. I just think we haven't given it the shot it deserves, which is why I welcome the dialogue. And we're having some very healthy discussions.

A tech industry source, contacted after the hearing, laughed at Comey's description of a robust dialogue. "I'm hoping a member of the panel was lucky enough to press him on what he meant by that," the source said.

After the hearing, Schiff told reporters: "I was impressed by the companies' position—it's hard to refute. But what was unusual, more than one of the companies said government should provide its answer in order to advance the discussion." The tech sector, Schiff said, is unlikely to advance a policy position other than its opposition to any mandated "backdoor."

President Obama seemed to agree on the need for resolution during a September appearance before the Business Roundtable—though he acknowledged how elusive an answer was proving to be.

"One of the big issues . . . that we're focused on, is this encryption issue," Obama said. "And there is a legitimate tension around this issue." Obama explained:

> On the one hand, the stronger the encryption, the better we can potentially protect our data. And so there's an argument that says we want to turbocharge our encryption so that nobody can crack it. On the other hand, if you have encryption that doesn't have any way to get in there, we are now empowering ISIL, child pornographers, others to essentially be able to operate within a black box in ways that we've never experienced before during the telecommunications age. And I'm not talking, by the way, about some of the controversies around [National Security Agency surveillance]; I'm talking about the traditional FBI going to a judge, getting a warrant, showing probable cause, but still can't get in.

According to the president, law enforcement, the tech community, and others were engaged in "a process . . . to see if we can square the circle here and reconcile the need for greater and greater encryption and the legitimate needs of national security and law enforcement."

Obama summed up: "And I won't say that we've cracked the code yet, but we've got some of the smartest folks not just in government but also in the private sector working together to try to resolve it. And what's interesting is even in the private sector, even in the tech community, people are on different sides of this thing."

The president may have been overstating the divisions among the techies, who seemed in agreement on one rather large point: They weren't interested in negotiating a standard or even in putting their own proposal on the table.

An industry source, asked about the policy perambulations, nodded and said this was the type of issue that hovers above policy discussions but doesn't go anywhere in a legislative or federal policy sense. The *Washington Post* reported in the fall of 2015 that federal officials had devised four possible policy approaches—and discarded them all.

Strong encryption seemed destined for the rather large basket of cybersecurity policy issues that soak up lots of debate time but do not lend themselves to actual solutions. Such issues can distract policymakers from urgent business, with no payoff. In any case, there would be no legislative payoff anytime soon.

12

CYBER TENSIONS DEFINE THE U.S.-CHINA RELATIONSHIP

Responsible competitors help to sustain the system where research and development are rewarded, where intellectual property is protected, and the rule of law is upheld, because nations that use cyber technology as an economic weapon or profits from the theft of intellectual property are sacrificing tomorrow's gains for short-term gains today.

—Vice President Joseph Biden, June 24, 2015,
U.S.-China Strategic and Economic Dialogue

The question of what to do about China was another matter of cross-cutting importance, with myriad policy implications and few readily available answers in the summer and fall of 2015.

Gen. Martin Dempsey, the chairman of the Joint Chiefs of Staff, called Russia the number one strategic threat to the United States. In cyberspace, that honor went to the Peoples' Republic of China.

Chinese government fingerprints were all over the breaches at the Office of Personnel Management (OPM) and Department of Homeland Security (DHS) contractor USIS, originally known as U.S. Investigation Services. Major news outlets reported the Chinese were probably building a huge database on American government employees. Whether or not that was, in fact, the Chinese interest in the U.S. government employee files, China's hackers were finding their way into every nook and cranny of the government's computer networks. They hacked the private e-mails of top U.S. officials. The Chinese were also mapping the U.S. natural gas pipelines and electric grid.

And we could only assume the U.S. government was doing the same to China. But there was a distinction.

"It's one thing to poke around on the weapons side, we have an interest in doing that too," Sen. Tom Carper said in an interview. "It's quite another to steal the personally identifiable information of our government employees or our intellectual property, our seed corn. That is very troubling."

If cybersecurity was the defining issue in the U.S.-China relationship, it was an open question, in 2015, when and how the two nations would move to a next phase after the cyber dialogue ground to a halt following the U.S. indictments of five Chinese military officers for cyber espionage.

"China's cyber behavior is the number one element of the Sino relationship," Gen. Michael Hayden, the former CIA and NSA chief, said at the American Enterprise Institute (AEI) in 2014. Hayden, now of Chertoff Group, vigorously pushed back against what he called a false equivalency between U.S. espionage activities and China's actions. Contrary to China's approach, Hayden said, "We spy to keep you safe. We don't spy to make you rich."

Then-House Intelligence Chairman Mike Rogers (R-Michigan) at the same event said human rights issues were important, but "the first three issues with China should be economic espionage, economic espionage, and economic espionage."

Lawmakers clamored for stronger responses to China's cyber activities. Generally though, the approaches by both Congress and the Obama administration were much more nuanced than confrontational. Every year Congress passed—and the president would sign—legislative language attached to an annual spending bill that required federal agencies to apply special scrutiny when purchasing technology products made in China. It was a mild irritant in the U.S.-China relationship, and it made life a tad more difficult for U.S. technology companies operating in China. Attorney General Eric Holder testified that the requirement had a positive benefit for security.

After the OPM hack, some in Congress demanded economic sanctions on the Chinese. The Obama administration in early 2015 actually spelled out a new policy on sanctions that could be applied to bad actors on cybersecurity in the international arena. Under the order, the Treasury Department could hit countries, individuals, or other entities with sanctions for malicious cyber activities. But this was a very blunt, very public weapon and the administration didn't appear to reach for it.

"It's not so easy," said Eggers of the U.S. Chamber of Commerce. "How do you push back and still encourage trade and investment and avoid the economic de-globalization that's going on?"

There was another problem: The OPM hack might be characterized as old-fashioned nation-state espionage. Government officials let it be known in July 2015 that they wouldn't publicly name China as the perpetrator. (Officially, that is; Director of National Intelligence James Clapper had already done so in a public setting.) There were practical reasons: The U.S. government was living in a glass house on this one; it would have to respond accordingly.

The reaction on Capitol Hill bordered on incredulous. "The fact that we're not willing to name names is a terrible mistake," said Sen. Cory Gardner (R-Colorado), who chaired a Foreign Relations subcommittee with jurisdiction over both China policy and cybersecurity issues. "When Sony got hacked, we got an executive order," he said in exasperation. A direct assault on the U.S. government would get no response?

China, in the eyes of Gardner and many other lawmakers, needed to know that such cyber activities affecting everyday Americans were beyond any norms in international behavior.

The Justice Department tried to send a message in 2014 by indicting five members of the Chinese military on economic espionage charges, claiming they were stealing trade secrets.

"This case should serve as a wake-up call to the seriousness of the ongoing cyber threat," then-Attorney General Holder said. "These criminal charges represent a groundbreaking step forward in addressing that threat. This indictment makes clear that state actors who engage in economic espionage, even over the Internet from faraway places like offices in Shanghai, will be exposed for their criminal conduct and sought for apprehension and prosecution in an American court of law."

Those members of the military would never appear in a U.S. courtroom and China responded by suspending a much ballyhooed bilateral dialogue on cybersecurity.

Rep. Rogers, at that 2014 AEI event, said China was "punching back" in cyberspace after the indictments and said the U.S. private sector "is absolutely vulnerable."

Using indictments to make a point—targeting individuals rather than the Chinese government itself—could be seen as way to maintain room for government-to-government talks and efforts on cyber.

President Obama, during a joint press appearance with Australian Prime Minister Tony Abbott in June 2014, stressed that China must abide by global "norms" of behavior, a formulation the administration used repeatedly in discussing China and cyber issues. "Obviously, both the United States and Australia have enormous trade relationships with China, and we both agree that it's important to continue to see China prosper and rise," Obama told reporters. "But what's also important is that as China emerges as this great world power that it also is helping to reinforce and abide by basic international law and norms."

Christopher Painter, the State Department's cybersecurity policy coordinator, said at the AEI event that China, among other nations, had agreed that international law applies to cyberspace. He said the U.S. government's interest was in building up institutions and legal structures on cyber at home and abroad. "Reputational harm is there" for the Chinese, he said, suggesting that cyber crime, as practiced against the United States by a foreign power, no longer would get a free pass.

There were also benefits in collaboration, for both countries. High-ranking officials including Commerce Department general counsel Kelly Welsh promoted cybersecurity tools like the National Institute of Standards and Technology (NIST) Framework during visits to Beijing. It was the kind of helpful suggestion one shared with a friend. U.S. officials suggested, obliquely, that China was helping to "stifle" dangerous activities in cyberspace by North Korea, as InsideCybersecurity.com's Christopher J. Castelli reported.

Some of that assistance may have been inadvertent and unintended by China. The only way into North Korea's closed Internet system was through China's own networks. A widely suspected U.S. hack-back that temporarily brought down North Korean systems after the Sony Pictures attack was probably only possible because the U.S. side had infiltrated those Chinese networks, according to a source. If China had actually allowed the United States to get at North Korean networks through that pathway, neither side would ever admit it.

The Obama administration was trying to balance carrots and sticks. In 2015, presidential candidates ranging from Ted Cruz to Hillary Clinton shouted that China only understood the stick. It got a lot more complicated for those who had to actually implement the policy.

The answer, such as it was, would continue to evolve. It would involve a long-haul effort on the public stage to craft those international norms of behavior. It would also involve a long twilight struggle, to paraphrase President Kennedy's Cold War description, to inflict as much or more pain on adversaries as we were receiving. Cyber deterrence would be a crucial concept going forward, especially in the China relationship, but for now remained an amorphous idea.

By the late summer of 2015, the administration had determined its decision not to call out China in the aftermath of the OPM breach was untenable, the *New York Times* reported. "The decision came after the administration concluded that the hacking attack was so vast in scope and ambition that the usual practices for dealing with traditional espionage cases did not apply," the *New York Times* said.

The administration officials didn't say so, but the intensely negative political reaction at home—and U.S. military and intelligence leaders' near inability to hold their tongues about their frustrations—may have had an impact too.

Regardless, the administration didn't have a ready response in its cybersecurity playbook.

"But in a series of classified meetings, officials have struggled to choose among options that range from largely symbolic responses—for example, diplomatic protests or the ouster of known Chinese agents in the United States—to more significant actions that some officials fear could lead to an escalation of the hacking conflict between the two countries," the *New York Times* reported.

The Obama administration liked to portray itself as the architect of the nation's first holistic strategy on cybersecurity. Critics like McCain frequently said the strategy was more of a Potemkin Village, and was particularly lacking in the area of deterrence. By the summer of 2015, the administration still hadn't provided Congress with a long overdue report on deterrence strategy. China, North Korea, and others were taking advantage in an unceasing campaign of cyber hostility.

The stumbling response to the OPM episode provided McCain with plenty of ammunition to charge that the Obama administration had no strategy at all to counter this threat.

But the cyber strategy toward China, as the U.S. Chamber's Eggers pointed out, would affect numerous national priorities and couldn't be formed in a policy vacuum, even amid outrageous activities by the other side.

There was, for instance, a summit meeting coming in September 2015 between Obama and Chinese president Xi Jinping. It would be the Chinese leader's first state visit to the United States. Obama and Xi had reached a landmark agreement on global warming during the U.S. president's November 2014 trip to China. Could a cybersecurity breakthrough be next?

The two sides had been preparing the ground for this visit for over a year. There was no interest, on either side, in an acrimonious breakdown over OPM hacks, no matter how much invective was flowing from Capitol Hill.

Lu Wei, minister of the Chinese Cyberspace Administration, said during a visit to the United States in December 2014 that the United States and China had far more in common than they had differences over cybersecurity policy. In an appearance at George Washington University, Lu said he had met with top White House and other officials despite the suspension of the U.S.-China cybersecurity working group. "What I can tell you is, I am here and I have already started that dialogue," he said.

Lu said the two countries had become "one community of common interest" in Internet policy. The two countries agreed on 90 percent of issues, he said, and areas of disagreement were often exaggerated. "We have reached important consensus during this visit," Lu said. He said the sides agreed to pursue "common rules" to avoid mutual condemnations, to fight cyber theft, and to "strengthen the rule of law."

"But we cannot repeatedly condemn each other," he said, arguing that no country could say it was free of hackers and cyber crime. "I told [U.S. officials] I am here with a sincere heart, with friendship and candidness," Lu said. "I told our U.S. friends, we can't fight like teenagers anymore." Asked about cyber attacks as a tool of policy, Lu said: "I have never engaged in such activities for such purposes. The Chinese government is very engaged against hackers, against cyber attacks, and cyber theft."

U.S. officials didn't believe it, of course, and Lu was miscasting the policy disagreement. The U.S. side wasn't up in arms because the Chinese government was insufficiently cracking down on illegal hackers; the U.S. side was up in arms because the Chinese government *employed* those hackers. In any case, the U.S. officials felt they had little choice besides taking up the offer to engage with Chinese counterparts whose vision and goals in cyberspace were profoundly different.

Lu was a skilled, glad-handing politician. He said at George Washington University that he enjoyed visiting Beijing's bustling university campuses late at night and mingling with the young technologists. He visited with Facebook's Mark Zuckerberg during his trip to the United States. But Lu, of course, was China's chief censor. His daily activities went far beyond the government spying and Internet interference that American digital-rights activists complained about in debates over U.S. cybersecurity policy. Lu's agency gobbled up Chinese citizens' personally identifiable information for breakfast.

Here's how ForeignPolicy.com described Lu on its Pacific Power Index page:

> As China's Internet czar, Lu Wei has championed both censorship and China's new model of "Internet sovereignty," the idea that a government has the right to determine what online content can enter its virtual borders. That may sound retrograde, but the confident Lu has a keen grasp of how information moves in Chinese cyberspace, and, as a result, he knows exactly how to stop it. It's a model that other authoritarian regimes, and even nominally democratic Turkey, may already be looking to as they step up their own Internet policing. And as gatekeeper to China's 600 million-plus Internet users, Lu may even have the bargaining power to bring Western Internet companies to heel.

As U.S. cybersecurity policymaking staggered along, China had already articulated its vision of commercial and civilian cyberspace while its cyber-warriors and spies aggressively advanced the country's interests in the shadows.

"China is looking for shortcuts to catch up with us economically," one particularly clear-eyed Senate leader on cyber issues said shortly before the 2015 Obama–Xi summit. "When their economy gets more mature, their interest in cybersecurity will coincide with ours. We're not there yet."

The *Washington Post* reported on August 31, 2015—weeks before the summit—that U.S. officials had decided they must, in fact, use their sanctions authority to send a message to China. But they would not link the sanctions directly to the OPM breach, which was still viewed as falling into the area of legitimate espionage activity. It was a carefully nuanced position and as such offered limited satisfaction.

House Intelligence ranking member Adam Schiff told reporters after an early September hearing that, in order to have a credible deterrence policy, the United States must impose sanctions on China for some of its hacks. "We should underscore that there is an increasing cost for such activity," Schiff said. But such sanctions should not be imposed until after the upcoming visit by the Chinese president. Announcing the sanctions beforehand "would be so in-your-face it would disrupt the rest of the summit," Schiff said.

Schiff had just emerged from a hearing at which NSA director Michael Rogers testified that the threat of sanctions and other actions was having a moderating impact on the behavior of Iran and North Korea. Surely such tools could be brought to bear in the most critical relationship in cyberspace.

Paul Stockton, the former high-ranking Defense Department official, said use of the sanctions tool spelled out in Obama's April executive order would in fact be a major turn. "The first shoe to drop," against China and other aggressive actors in cyberspace, was the decision to assert sanctions authority in that executive order, Stockton said.

"Now the second shoe is dropping," Stockton said in September 2015. "The administration is preparing to apply it to Chinese companies. That new tool is going to get used."

Stockton acknowledged a cost to U.S. companies in China, but said those firms were already facing discriminatory policies there. The necessary calculus, he said, would always be how to inflict an appropriate level of pain to positively influence behavior without provoking an unacceptable backlash.

Eyeing the upcoming summit, Stockton said U.S. officials should take the Chinese up on their offer to collaborate in cyberspace. "But we need to tell the Chinese, we know where these attacks are coming from and you must take concrete steps" to reduce the hacks emanating from China.

With an eye on the policies advanced by Lu Wei and the Chinese government as a whole, Stockton agreed this was a very difficult proposition because of the vast philosophical differences between the countries.

"Negotiating a common approach won't be easy," Stockton said. "It's worth a try but we need to make clear that the Internet must allow a free flow of information, it must empower individuals and it must never be a tool of repression."

President Xi sought to set the tone for the visit in a *Wall Street Journal* interview published on September 22, saying both the United States and China were victims of the global hacking plague. And, Xi said, there would always be disagreements between the countries. But it was beneath the dignity of two great powers to let those differences define the relationship.

Xi told the *Wall Street Journal*:

> In approaching China-U.S. relations, one should see the larger picture and not just focus on differences, just as a Chinese saying tells us, "When important things are addressed first, secondary issues will not be difficult to settle." Together, China and the United States account for one-third of the world economy, one-fourth of the global population, and one-fifth of global trade. If two big countries like ours do not cooperate with each other, just imagine what will happen to the world.

That evening, in a speech in Seattle, Xi called for making common cause against cyber crime. The next morning, the Office of Personnel Management revealed that 5.6 million electronic fingerprint records were stolen in the massive hack uncovered the previous spring—more than five times the number previously reported. "Federal experts believe that, as of now, the ability to misuse fingerprint data is limited," OPM said in a statement. "However, this probability could change over time as technology evolves."

Since that hack was never formally attributed to China, the announcement on the eve of Xi's arrival in Washington, DC, was probably mere coincidence. But cyber policy never developed in a news vacuum.

Xi arrived in Washington, DC, on September 24, as Pope Francis was departing after a celebrated visit to the White House and Capitol Hill. Xi and Obama dined that evening at the Blair House, across the street from the White House. David Jackson of *USA Today*, the White House pool reporter that night, said the dinner lasted two-and-a-half hours, "longer than expected." Obama, Biden, Secretary of State Kerry, and a passel of other senior administration officials walked back to the White House deep in conversation.

The next day, the Chinese and U.S. governments elaborated on their earlier climate change agreement, but there was also a major announcement on cybersecurity. A framework for future relations in cyberspace had been reached, though its effectiveness would have to be tested. Immediately, it pushed off the question of economic sanctions and instead created a new collaborative process—and gave the United States an agreed-upon benchmark for measuring behavior.

It might be frustratingly ambiguous in many ways, as most diplomatic agreements are. But it was more than observers were expecting.

According to a September 25, 2015, White House fact sheet, the two countries agreed

> that timely responses should be provided to requests for information and assistance concerning malicious cyber activities. Further, both sides agree to cooperate, in a manner consistent with their respective national laws and relevant international obligations, with requests to investigate cybercrimes, collect electronic evidence, and mitigate malicious cyber activity emanating from their territory. Both sides also agree to provide updates on the status and results of those investigation to the other side, as appropriate.

The oftentimes cyber rivals put this in writing: "The United States and China agree that neither country's government will conduct or knowingly support cyber-enabled theft of intellectual property, including trade secrets or other confidential business information, with the intent of providing competitive advantages to companies or commercial sectors."

That got at the crux of the international dispute and provided the benchmark for assessing behavior.

The nations agreed to "further identify and promote appropriate norms of state behavior in cyberspace within the international community." And they agreed to

> establish a high-level joint dialogue mechanism on fighting cybercrime and related issues. . . . As part of this mechanism, both sides agree to establish a hotline for the escalation of issues that may arise in the course of responding to such requests. Finally, both sides agree that the first meeting of this dialogue will be held by the end of 2015, and will occur twice per year thereafter.

"Today's agreement marks encouraging progress toward better protecting our nation's ideas and ingenuity," Carper said in a statement. "It also represents a significant step toward building a long-term and robust pact on cybersecurity with China. That being said, we can't just believe what China says. We also have to see what they do and continue to monitor their actions in cyberspace very closely."

Carper added:

> I know some of my colleagues will say that this agreement doesn't do enough. But we must start somewhere and this is more than a good start. As a former naval flight officer who served our nation for five years during a hot war in Southeast Asia and for another eighteen years until the end of the Cold War, I am reminded of our negotiations on nuclear arms reduction limitations. With that initiative, we took a modest but meaningful first step by stopping atmospheric testing. At the end of the day, we ended up with a lot more. Likewise, we shouldn't be satisfied by this agreement alone; more must be done.

Sen. Dianne Feinstein expressed more skepticism: "There's a difference between an agreement on paper and having the Chinese government, including the People's Liberation Army, actually stop conducting and supporting cyber attacks on U.S. companies. The Senate Intelligence Committee will be paying very close attention to how faithfully this agreement is implemented."

And Sen. Devin Nunes came close to kicking dirt on the agreement:

> The new agreement between the United States and China regarding economic espionage would be a big step forward if China abides by it. Unfortunately, in light of its many long-running cyber-theft enterprises, there is little reason to believe China will live up to its commitments. These cyberattacks will almost certainly continue until the Obama administration puts forward a credible deterrence policy.

The Chinese said they wanted to make common cause against criminal hackers, terrorists, and rogue states. It was a significant starting point, in terms of the always delicate U.S.-China relationship. But cybersecurity policymaking involved much more than security. As the U.S. political system grappled with the sometimes conflicting demands between security and liberty, the Chinese were still asking the United States to turn a blind eye to government dictates in cyberspace that neither the American public nor the political system would even remotely consider. International cybersecurity partnerships were as difficult as any aspect of cyber policy, requiring stakeholders to confront bedrock principles as they sought to define a twenty-first-century policy-scape.

A U.S.-China partnership on cybersecurity might not be fully possible until the Chinese faced the same kind of economic theft that was being perpetrated against the United States. "They're catching up to us [economically] and at some point they'll have to worry about someone stealing from them," Carper said in an interview. In the meantime, Carper said, the Chinese were determined to find economic shortcuts. "They want to play in the Super Bowl without even playing an exhibition game."

But a shared interest between the two countries was a lot closer than most people realized.

13

HELP WANTED, DESPERATELY, FOR CYBERSECURITY

In many ways, cybersecurity is similar to 19th century medicine—a growing field dealing with real threats with lots of self-taught practitioners, only some of whom know what they're doing.

The evolution of the practice of medicine mandated different skills and specialties coupled with qualifications and assessments. In medicine, we now have accreditation standards and professional certifications by specialty. We can afford nothing less in the world of cybersecurity.

—From "A Human Capital Crisis in Cybersecurity," November 2010, Center for Strategic and International Studies Commission on Cybersecurity for the Forty-fourth Presidency

In the summer and fall of 2015, University of California, Los Angeles; Rutgers University; and the University of Connecticut were among the latest targets of cyber attacks. Universities, insurers, health care providers, and every other industry were in desperate need of cybersecurity professionals. So was the U.S. government.

China faced no manpower limits as it challenged the United States for preeminence in cyberspace. That was far from the case in the United States. While enlightened corporate and government leaders stressed cybersecurity as an existential issue within their enterprises, they also faced a critical shortfall in skilled technologists.

One of the "easy" cybersecurity bills passed in December 2014 at the end of the 113th Congress gave the Department of Homeland Security

(DHS) new authority to recruit and retain cybersecurity experts. Several years earlier, Congress gave the Department of Defense (DOD) special powers to go around the cobwebbed civil service rules to recruit and pay certain skilled civilian professionals. Now DHS would have the same authority as it built a cybersecurity workforce. Another "easy" bill passed at the time required DHS to assess its cyber workforce and develop a manpower strategy.

The competition for cyber professionals within industry—and between industry and government—was intense. One development from the Office of Personnel Management (OPM) breach was newfound interest in putting a dedicated cybersecurity adviser at the elbow of department and agency leaders. That trend could extend to the private sector as well; cybersecurity expertise was already becoming a ticket to a seat on corporate boards of directors.

Advertisements for college degrees in cybersecurity frequently graced the walls of the Metro system in Washington, DC. Trend Micro found cybersecurity positions growing twelve times faster than the rest of the U.S. job market in 2015. Frost & Sullivan estimated a global workforce shortfall of 1.5 million cybersecurity professionals by 2020.

"It's clearly a seller's market," former White House official Robert Knacke blogged from the annual Def Con hackers conference in Las Vegas in the summer of 2015. "Unfortunately, the market for talent doesn't work the way that the market for firewalls works. More forensics experts cannot be rolled out of a cleanroom. Training takes time and money and in this field much of the learning is best done on the job."

The Defense Department's plan to train six thousand cyber warriors was well and good, Knacke blogged, but every one of them would be "snapped up by the private sector as soon as their enlistment contracts are over without making a dent in the workforce demand." Knacke called for a collaborative effort on the industry side to provide free training for cyber professionals. "Perhaps it is time for the many rivals . . . to band together and train the workforce so that there is someone to respond to the millions of alerts of malicious cyber activity their devices generate each day," he blogged.

In the spring of 2015 Booz Allen Hamilton and the Partnership for Public Service issued a report finding nearly 93,000 federal government employees who could be characterized as cyber professionals, "which means one in every twenty-two workers deals in this field." That was the civilian government and wouldn't include those Pentagon cyber warriors.

Calculating how many cybersecurity professionals there were in the private sector was more difficult, if not impossible. The National Institute of Standards and Technology (NIST) jumped on the question of defining what constitutes a job in cybersecurity, laying the basis for better assessing the state of the workforce. It was a complicated challenge.

At an Institute for Information Infrastructure Protection workshop in 2011, Hewlett-Packard's William G. Horne pointed to his own company's 325,000 employees at the time and said, "there's no database I can query to find out how many of those people know government and risk management and how many people know incident response."

Cybersecurity was obviously a growth industry, regardless of the sketchy metrics, but one that still needed to figure out how exactly it would be staffed. The federal government launched the National Initiative for Cybersecurity Education, or NICE, as a promising vehicle for promoting cybersecurity as a field of study. Within that process there was an opportunity to expand outreach to communities not typically represented in this space. Cybersecurity policy conferences and other events attracted participants from all walks of life, naturally, but the audiences were largely white and male. Diversity was coming, but slowly.

The marketplace was moving in this direction and government could lend a hand. In January 2015 Vice President Joe Biden and Energy Secretary Ernest Moniz traveled to Norfolk State University to announce a new program to bolster cybersecurity offerings at historically black colleges and universities. A $25 million grant would be shared among thirteen schools participating in the Cybersecurity Workforce Pipeline Consortium.

More publicity needed to be brought to the opportunities available in the cybersecurity profession. The people who were making a living in cybersecurity, both in government and private industry, had a compelling story to tell. By 2014, Obama administration officials were appearing with increasing frequency on college campuses to encourage young people to choose a career in cybersecurity.

DHS's leadership was particularly active in reaching out to the university community, and Secretary Jeh Johnson flagged it as a personal priority. "The Administration, including the White House but also DHS, DOD, and other relevant agencies, considers outreach on cybersecurity issues an important element of our work," National Security Council spokeswoman Laura Lucas Magnuson said in a statement to InsideCybersecurity.com in 2014. "As part of those efforts, we frequently engage with universities to encourage a conversation about cybersecurity."

National Security Council official Samara Moore appeared before a packed lecture hall at George Washington University in April 2014 to urge students to help fill the cybersecurity workforce gap, as part of an outreach effort that was often overshadowed by other cybersecurity priorities. Moore spoke on a panel with several high-ranking corporate cybersecurity executives at a George Washington University event "celebrating women in cybersecurity."

Appearing on stage with Moore was an all-star lineup: Leslee Belluchie, a former Defense Department official who founded National Security Partners; Deborah Bonanni of Intelligent Decisions Inc., who was National Security Agency chief of staff from 2006 to 2013; and Gina Loften of IBM and Cheri McGuire of Symantec, cyber executives who were both active in initiatives such as creation of the NIST Framework.

Moore said Big Data, the Internet of things, and multiple other developments "present significant opportunities" in the field of cybersecurity, adding that "the workforce is already challenged today to meet the demands." The needs were varied, Moore said; the complex field required people with "the technical skill set"—coders, hackers, and system developers—as well as people "who can translate the technical side to the business side. We need business people who understand how [cyber issues] can affect their enterprise."

Bonanni said women comprised 40 percent of the NSA workforce and 40 percent of then-NSA Director Keith Alexander's senior leadership staff. Once she returned to the private sector, Bonanni said, she would sometimes find herself the only woman in a meeting for the first time in twenty-five years. McGuire said the cybersecurity workforce needed people with risk management, communications, compliance, and social science skills. "It's about policy, not just the technical side," she said.

"We need to think about how to talk to the CEO, the CISO, and the CFO about how they see risks," Loften said. "I see cybersecurity evolving across the entire enterprise; it's not just the CISO."

Moore touted cybersecurity as a field in which practitioners could go from doing system assessments at a chemical plant to making policy at an enterprise level—or at the White House. She had a bachelor's in accounting and information systems from Virginia Tech and a master's in engineering management and systems engineering from George Washington University. She hadn't expected to land in the White House—or necessarily to land in the field of cybersecurity. But that's where the need and the opportunities propelled her. Moore would later leave government service to become senior manager for critical infrastructure security at the energy company Exelon.

Her path was a model that should be offered to more students from all backgrounds.

The nation's cybersecurity policy was full of gaps, but filling this one—the workforce gap—could provide an economic boon and help address long-held worries about the United States losing its educational and thus its technological edge, all while preparing both government and businesses for the long struggle in cyberspace.

14

SENATE DEBATE TAKES SHAPE, THEN—SURPRISE!—STALLS

The Internet makes a lot of good things possible, but it also makes it possible for corporations and governments to exploit us in ways they never could before. The debate over CISA is not about hackers, or China, or cybersecurity—it's about whether we want to further normalize ubiquitous monitoring, warrantless surveillance, and unfettered manipulation of our vulnerabilities, or if we want to protect the Internet as a promising platform for freedom and self expression.
—Evan Greer and Donny Shaw, Fight for the Future,
July 29 blog in the *Hill*

There was no compromise in sight on the preeminent cyber legislative issue—information sharing—as the summer of 2015 began.

Amid the ongoing political impasse on Capitol Hill, GOP candidate Jeb Bush decided the time was right to insert cybersecurity into the 2016 presidential campaign. The Office of Personnel Management (OPM) breach had revealed a "cultural failure" on cybersecurity within the Obama administration, Bush charged. The president was failing to lead on the stalled legislation in Congress, Bush asserted. Using Medium.com to get a high-tech splash on a high-tech issue, Bush on June 22, 2015, posted an extensive critique of the Obama approach to cyber.

Other GOP candidates, including Florida Sen. Marco Rubio, used the OPM breach to lambaste the administration as soft on China. But Bush was the first to launch into an extensive policy discussion on cybersecurity.

"The President can issue an Executive Order or give a speech about cybersecurity, but without sustained leadership and determined implementation—including a concerted effort to work with the Congress—we will not adapt to meet the growing threats," Bush said in the post. "Recent high-profile intrusions into private and government networks suggest we are not meeting this challenge."

Bush noted that vulnerabilities within the OPM system had been identified as much as a year earlier and asked whether any agency officials would be held responsible for not fixing the problems.

"We are not powerless unless we choose to be," Bush wrote. "It would be a start for the President to show leadership on Capitol Hill, and to throw his weight behind the House's effort to improve cybersecurity information sharing between the government and the private sector—a critical impediment to cybersecurity according to experts."

Bush said: "For three Congresses in a row, the House of Representatives has passed information-sharing legislation only to see it stonewalled by Senate Democrats. . . . President Obama should step up, show some leadership, and work with Congress to pass this legislation—a key step towards creating a more robust public–private partnership."

As noted earlier, cybersecurity legislation that included information-sharing provisions was filibustered by Senate Republicans in 2012, while the Senate Democratic leadership refused to bring up a bipartisan Intelligence Committee bill in 2014.

Bush asserted that Obama had underfunded both the Department of Defense (DOD) and intelligence community in his budgets, increasing the nation's cyber vulnerabilities.

And the candidate blamed the president for failing to engage with the private sector. "We need a President with the experience and trust necessary to mobilize public and private resources to ensure that our critical infrastructure, networks, and communications remain secure," Bush wrote. "These efforts will help guarantee America remains on top throughout the ongoing technological and communications revolutions that will transform fundamental aspects of our world, economy, and society."

The post was a mild declaration of cyber policy, but between the lines it didn't venture very far from the general consensus that already existed within the administration and on Capitol Hill. Information-sharing legislation had broad support and the public–private partnership concept was central to the Obama strategy. Bush's broadside whizzed past the Capitol without noticeable effect.

Democratic candidate Hillary Clinton took her first swipe at cybersecurity over the July Fourth holiday weekend, bemoaning Chinese theft of U.S. defense secrets and commercial property. "They're also trying to hack into everything that doesn't move in America. Stealing commercial secrets, blueprints from defense contractors, stealing huge amounts of government information. All looking for an advantage."

The former secretary of state didn't have an answer, necessarily, except that it was time to get tough on China. Where her policy would depart from Obama's—or her own when she served as Obama's top diplomat—was left unsaid.

As Congress returned from its July Fourth recess, insiders worried that the coming five-week stretch would have significant implications for the fate of cybersecurity legislation in 2015, and perhaps into the next year as well. There was a narrow window for legislation and anything that fell over to 2016 would face long odds amid election-year scheduling and politics.

"Legislating by crisis" was a catchphrase often attached to Congress's deadline-driven approach to budget and other issues, but thanks to the Senate's inability to move an information-sharing bill, cybersecurity legislation was slipping into this category. If a cyber information-sharing bill didn't make it through the Senate in July or early August, the legislation would be one of many priorities jostling for floor time on the crowded fall calendar.

Over the July Fourth break, business lobbyists met with staff for Senate Republican and Democratic leaders to beg for just two days of floor time for the Senate Intelligence Committee-passed information-sharing bill. That would be cutting it close in the Senate, they knew, but they had to get the bill to the floor.

At least three major, discrete cybersecurity issues were on Congress's plate, if only lawmakers would act: information sharing, data-breach notification, and enhanced criminal penalties for cyber bad actors. Leaders of the congressional homeland security committees were also looking at a direct legislative response to the OPM breach by accelerating deployment of the EINSTEIN 3 detection and response system across government agencies.

The full House had passed an EINSTEIN provision in April as an amendment to the McCaul information-sharing bill, and Sen. Tom Carper and Homeland Security and Governmental Affairs chairman Ron Johnson (R-Wisconsin) were in discussions on how to move a Senate version. But Sen. Johnson had other priorities as well: He put the Mexican border crisis, avian flu, national debt, and regulatory reform on the committee's July agenda.

The pace on information-sharing frustrated advocates of that legislation, but data-breach notification bills were on an even slower track. In the aftermath of blockbuster consumer data breaches in 2014, it appeared consumer-friendly notification legislation might be primed for quick action. Here was an issue where Congress could provide direct comfort to voters who'd been hit in the pocketbook by malicious hacks. Alas, jurisdictional and substantive issues between the House commerce and financial services committees were hanging up data-breach legislation in that chamber, while the issue couldn't get a toe-hold in the Senate commerce, judiciary, or banking committees.

The Federal Trade Commission (FTC), in the meantime, would continue issuing guidances and dangling the threat of prosecution over the heads of companies that handled sensitive consumer data.

The Senate Judiciary Committee scheduled an early July hearing on modernizing criminal law to fight cyber crime. Sens. Lindsey Graham (R-South Carolina) and Sheldon Whitehouse (D-Rhode Island) championed the issue for years, but so far had been unable to move legislation. Across the Capitol, the House Judiciary Committee hadn't announced any plans on the issue, once again revealing the chronic lack of coordination on cyber policy that would constantly thwart legislative efforts.

"I want to partner with Sen. Whitehouse if I can and come up with legislation," Graham said at the conclusion of the hearing. He noted that the senators had draft legislation but did not mention any timing for introduction. "We can't just play defense," Whitehouse said, noting that "many of our key cyber laws are as much as thirty years old."

With a month to go before the summer break—and with only a short season for legislating in the fall—lawmakers were increasingly hard-pressed to achieve their cybersecurity objectives before time ran out. But sometimes Congress's own self-made messes created opportunities. An ongoing partisan war over the federal budget for fiscal year 2016 had basically halted the annual appropriations process to fund government. It meant another shutdown showdown was probable in the fall of 2015, but in the meantime there was a sudden surplus of available Senate floor time. Cybersecurity might just slip onto the July agenda after all.

Senate leaders from both parties expressed optimism on July 8 that cybersecurity information-sharing legislation would reach the floor that month. It was Majority Leader Mitch McConnell's decision, of course, and lobbyists were thrilled when he listed cybersecurity as one of the promising areas for bipartisan action along with education and a couple of other bills. "We're going to make a major effort to ferret out those things we do agree on and those are some examples," McConnell said. Pushing through bipartisan legislation was the "theme" of this Republican majority, McConnell said.

"There's a good chance we'll take up the cybersecurity bill" in July, Majority Whip John Cornyn (R-Texas) told reporters after the first Senate Republican Conference policy luncheon following the July Fourth recess. Senate Minority Whip Dick Durbin (D-Illinois) also expressed optimism the bill would be addressed on the floor in July, saying it "comes up regularly in our meetings." Intelligence chairman Richard Burr (R-North Carolina) said the bill would come up "as soon as we can get a slot" and added that "I think July looks good."

As much as they wanted to believe, industry sources weren't buying into the optimism so quickly. Their conversations with Senate offices weren't always quite so upbeat, they told reporters on the down-low. There was a rumor afoot that McConnell would give supporters forty-eight hours for debate, in early August, shoved up against the beginning of the summer recess. That way, the leader could test advocates' assertion that the measure was widely supported. It would also impose a hard stop on the debate that could prevent fights from breaking out on extraneous issues like retail breach notification or a re-do of the NSA battle.

If lawmakers needed a nudge from the real world, actual and perceived threats continued unabated. On July 8, as senators were making positive noises about acting on cybersecurity, the New York Stock Exchange went down for over three hours, United Airlines was forced to ground flights due to an unspecified computer problem, and the *Wall Street Journal*'s Web site was taken down. There were no established links between the events and no evidence that a cyber attack was behind them. But that didn't stop the speculation or screaming headlines.

"Day of 'technical' glitches puts lawmakers on edge," the *Hill* newspaper declared. "Lawmakers are having a hard time swallowing the idea that a major stock exchange, a global airline and a prominent media outlet coincidentally suffered major outages on the same day," the paper reported. "The Obama administration said there were no signs the outages were caused by nefarious outside actors, but lawmakers were having a tough time buying it could all be a coincidence and are vowing to look into the matter."

"I think it has the appearances of a cyberattack," said Sen. Bill Nelson of Florida, the top Democrat on the Senate Commerce Committee.

The cyber-panic would recede fairly quickly. United Airlines was suffering from chronic technical problems in its reservation system. Concern over the other events faded as it became apparent that "routine" issues were behind the failures.

Perhaps it would still take "the Big One" to move the political system, but these mini-big ones were coming with increasing frequency and growing implications. So-called routine failures in an airline's reservation system disrupted travel plans of a half-million people; a problem with "loading" the *Wall Street Journal*'s homepage stoked dark speculation.

By this point, the specter of "the Big One" was enough to cause at least mild cyber-panic. Maybe the political system had enough evidence in hand to do something.

It certainly helped push cybersecurity into a category where Majority Leader McConnell saw value in producing some kind of legislative answer from what he characterized as the freshly invigorated, GOP-controlled Senate. After rapping the Obama administration for "total incompetence" in the hacking at the Office of Personnel Management, McConnell on July 12 told a *Fox News Sunday* interviewer: "These cybersecurity issues are enormously significant. What we're going to do is before August, take a step in the direction of dealing with the problem with information sharing bill that I think will be broadly supported."

Word of the comments trickled out slowly after a balmy summer weekend, and generated skepticism.

Still, industry groups needed to do their due diligence. Business lobbyists met with Sen. Mike Lee (R-Utah) on July 13 with a simple request: Please temper your rhetoric against the legislation. Please don't paint it as an NSA bill, thus galvanizing opposition to business's top cyber priority. Lee was a Tea Partier on many issues, but he was also a friend of the business community. "I think we got him to come around," a business source said.

On the substance, Lee was concerned that a provision in the Cybersecurity Information Sharing Act (CISA) allowing law enforcement to make use of cyber data to investigate serious violent felonies "expands the scope of the bill too much" and could be misused, according to an industry source. That wasn't industry's issue, but lobbyists understood it "repels some senators," the source said, and thus "weakens the political traction for the bill."

Lee and other civil liberties advocates also believed the bill gave the government "too much wiggle room" to use the data in various ways not directly related to cybersecurity, the source said.

On July 13, Cornyn came close to putting a date on the planned debate. He told the *Hill* newspaper the bill would be on the floor sometime the week of August 3, just before the Senate decamped for summer recess on August 7.

"I think it will be on the floor this work period," Dianne Feinstein told InsideCybersecurity.com a couple of days later. Chuck Schumer, a key member of the Democratic leadership, said he would support the bill as reported by the Intelligence Committee. "I'd like to see the bill strengthened a little bit, but I'd take it right now because we've done nothing on cyber for a long time," he said in a brief interview outside the Senate chamber.

Schumer was on track to replace the retiring Harry Reid as Democratic leader in the next Congress and his positive comments on the legislation were significant. The *New Yorker* remembered the inconclusive debates of 2012 and often suggested industry obstructionism was a root cause of the nation's cyber vulnerabilities. Now he was offering a strong show of support for a pro-industry cyber bill, representing a long stride away from his advocacy in years past for the Lieberman–Collins approach.

Whenever the debate got underway, senators including Ron Wyden, Rand Paul, Patrick Leahy, and Sen. Dean Heller (R-Nevada) were all expected to push amendments that could degrade the liability protection in the bill and increase industry's responsibilities to ensure personal privacy.

"We will have privacy amendments," Wyden told InsideCybersecurity.com as he loped to his office in the Dirksen Senate Office Building.

Wyden was a lanky former college basketball player and reporters frequently had to jog to keep up with him. But the senator, first elected in 1992, was always polite and helpful even as he zipped away down corridors.

Cybersecurity was a serious problem, Wyden acknowledged, noting that a company in his state, Solar World, was hacked by the Chinese. "Information sharing can play an important role," he said, "but without adequate privacy protections, it's a surveillance bill."

CISA advocates always bristled at those words. Knocking down that perception was one of their top priorities, which is why the NSA debate carried such importance for the cybersecurity bill.

Wyden said there would be "a number of strong amendments" on privacy and civil liberties when CISA reached the floor. "I don't believe I'll be alone," he added, suggesting he would have plenty of allies.

Feinstein, encountered the same day on her way to the Senate floor, said bill sponsors had "bent over backwards" to address privacy concerns. "We put thirteen privacy amendments in the bill already, based on input from the privacy community," Feinstein said.

Perhaps privacy issues would need to be revisited in the future, she said. "That's a discussion for another day."

Sen. Richard Blumenthal (D-Connecticut), an ally of Wyden's on civil liberties issues, said the information-sharing debate offered a unique opportunity to improve individual privacy rights in the cyber age. "We should have a full debate," Blumenthal said. "Few significant measures are done in forty-eight hours."

Once again, the procedure could be as important to the debate as the substance.

And, as optimism spread about the legislation's chances, the cyber information-sharing bill began to look like something more than a complicated, contentious measure: It began to look like a Christmas tree that could hold those other cyber-related priorities.

Perhaps the EINSTEIN legislation could be added to strengthen government networks. Whitehouse announced that he would try to add the data-breach notification and cyber crimes bills as amendments to CISA. Some in industry cringed: Would this add votes or hopelessly tie up the information-sharing measure?

"We have a very good chance" to move cyber legislation this year, Whitehouse said at an event on July 15. He said the "core" information-sharing measure should be bolstered by "thoughtful amendments" on cyber crimes and breach notification.

The data-breach proposal by Whitehouse, Carper, and Roy Blunt (R-Missouri) was backed by the financial sector. The retail industry favored a rival measure that passed the House Energy and Commerce Committee. Retail groups might drop their support for CISA if the Carper-Blunt-Whitehouse plan was added.

This was getting messy.

Sen. Tom Cotton (R-Arkansas) was working on a proposal to expand the number of government agencies that could receive cyber threat indicators directly from industry with related liability protection. His amendment would allow direct sharing between industry and law enforcement entities.

As meticulously crafted by the Senate Intelligence Committee, CISA restricted direct electronic sharing to the National Cybersecurity and Communications Integration Center (NCCIC) portal run by the Department of Homeland Security. The House-passed version potentially allowed sharing with multiple government entities, but not with the Defense Department or National Security Agency.

"Limiting it to DHS is too narrow," said an industry source who suggested the Cotton amendment would be the only one with broad industry support. However, online privacy groups that already opposed CISA could be expected to erupt over any expansion in the number of acceptable government portals.

In turn, the financial and technology industries were two sectors that were perfectly happy with the restrictions in the Senate bill and didn't support an expansion that would trigger even more opposition on the Senate floor.

As Sen. McConnell assessed how much time the bill would need, and the potential for controversial amendments, industry lobbyists now urged Senate leaders to allow several days of floor debate in order to build political support for a measure that was frequently, if unfairly, linked to separate debates over government surveillance.

"I think we've shifted peoples' thinking on this," said one industry source. "We're telling them, this is not FISA [the Foreign Intelligence Surveillance Act], this is not that surveillance issue you were dealing with a few weeks ago."

Perceptions around cyber information sharing were vitally important and the bill's advocates didn't want to be seen as ramming the measure through the process without careful consideration and ample debate time.

Industry lobbyists from the Protecting America's Cyber Networks Coalition met with McConnell's staff on July 16. Unsurprisingly, McConnell's employees were as inscrutable as the majority leader himself. The lobbyists reported on their efforts to canvass Senate offices and to educate members and staff about the substance of the bill. "We said we'll do whatever we can to help and that we're hitting as many [Senate] offices as we can," said one industry participant in the meeting.

One of McConnell's aides casually noted that December had been a good month for cybersecurity legislation the previous year. That could be interpreted as an ominous remark. Was the leader backing away from summer action on the bill?

"I didn't like that suggestion," the industry lobbyist said. "Those were mom-and-apple-pie bills last year. CISA isn't mom-and-apple-pie."

The source said business lobbyists were "getting good vibes" from Democratic and Republican Senate offices alike. But they couldn't quite pin down McConnell's intentions. After the meeting with staff, the source said, "I came away not discouraged, but not encouraged either."

The source mulled the legislative calendar. Three weeks wasn't really three weeks in the Senate. "What do they have, nine working days left?" the source asked. The summer could slip away still.

As August drew near, possible amendments went from a trickle to a flood. That signaled a growing confidence among senators that the cyber bill was actually headed to the floor. But it was also creating the probability of an unruly debate, which McConnell would be anxious to keep within certain parameters.

A bipartisan group of senators led by Sen. Susan Collins (R-Maine) announced a new bill to address the breaches at the Office of Personnel Management by giving the Department of Homeland Security clear, direct authority to drive cybersecurity upgrades at other agencies. They intended to offer it as an amendment to CISA.

Some senators believed they had already accomplished that in legislation signed into law the previous year.

"I'm glad to see my colleagues engaged on such an important issue," Carper said.

It's my understanding that this legislation attempts to build on the FISMA modernization bill that the Homeland Security and Governmental Affairs Committee worked so hard to pass last year. I look forward to reviewing the bill and working with all the sponsors on improving security of our federal networks, including overseeing the implementation of my FISMA legislation that became law in December.

Collins was also considering an amendment to require industries designated by DHS as "critical infrastructure" to report to the government on cyber attacks. Such a proposal would provoke strong opposition from industry.

Online privacy advocates were finalizing their amendment wish lists: In addition to excluding the NSA from the sharing process and limiting law enforcement uses of shared data, they wanted to strike language on "defensive measures" that they believed would allow private companies to "hack back" and fight their own wars in cyberspace. They also wanted to get rid of an exemption from disclosure of sharing activities under the Freedom of Information Act. Otherwise, they said, there would be no way to police what the government and industry were doing with this new power.

"It would be an extraordinarily heavy lift to get CISA, specifically, to be privacy neutral," the American Civil Liberties Union's (ACLU) Gabe Rottman said in late July. "The bill is currently far beyond the pale—it would literally enable and facilitate the kind of surveillance revealed over the past couple of years. Worse, this would pump even more sensitive information to government agencies, increasing the chances of another OPM hack."

And still more issues were being pushed into the equation.

Sen. Cory Gardner (R-Colorado) said he might try to address the congressional oversight structure around cybersecurity during the information-sharing debate.

"We're trying to direct the State Department to create a [cybersecurity] strategy," Gardner said, pointing to an amendment he successfully added to a State Department bill. "Maybe we need to do the same thing in Congress."

Gardner said a select committee on cybersecurity comprised of the leaders of standing committees with extensive cyber portfolios could help better organize lawmakers' approach to the issue.

As the Senate worked through a late July debate on a major transportation bill, the cyber policy world was watching McConnell for signs of how he would structure the CISA debate and what kind of fence he would place around amendments. The majority leader let industry lobbyists know that he wanted a "clean" bill, or as clean as possible. Now, before McConnell had even announced a floor date, there were amendments growing in three distinct piles.

Amendments like the one contemplated by Cotton would have a significant impact on how an information-sharing law actually worked, but the amendment didn't undermine the purpose of the bill. This amendment fell into pile number one: generally supportive proposals that tweaked the bill around the edges.

Pile number two held amendments from bill foes like Wyden and Rand Paul. They didn't expect to win—if their amendments on privacy and other issues actually got votes—but they wanted a thorough debate. If they could kill the underlying bill in the process, all the better.

The third pile held amendments on issues that were cybersecurity in nature but not directly related to information sharing. For senators and lobbyists who had been struggling for years to make incremental progress on discrete cyber issues like information-sharing, these unrelated amendments were the most dangerous. If the Senate became preoccupied with a debate over consumer data-breach notification—an issue that had bogged down without resolution in multiple Senate and House committees—the CISA bill might stall and get yanked from the floor.

Legislation on DHS's role, and the EINSTEIN program in particular, was less controversial. With a rump caucus of senators unveiling their own plan, Sens. Johnson and Carper moved to ensure the Homeland Security and Governmental Affairs Committee remained in charge of any proposals related to DHS. Despite the chairman and ranking member's polite words, they were clearly rankled that the Collins group, which included Sen. Mark Warner (D-Virginia) and a number of other Homeland Security Committee members, had jumped outside of regular channels in releasing their proposal.

But Carper was a master at stepping back from confrontation and getting his colleagues to focus instead on making progress. After he and Johnson agreed to fold the Collins legislation into their own measure, the Homeland Security Committee on July 29 unanimously passed its EINSTEIN bill.

Still, the twists wouldn't let up and suddenly the big cybersecurity vehicle for all of these measures, CISA, appeared to be veering off the road on the way to the Senate floor.

Making clear that the privacy community was at war over CISA, a coalition put together a Web site called stopcyberspying.com and planned to bombard Senate offices with anti-CISA faxes. "Congress is stuck in 1984," the group's said on the Web site. "It doesn't seem to understand modern technology. So we're going to communicate with it in a way it'll understand: With faxes. Thousands and thousands of faxes."

With the subtlety of a brick through a window, the group was using a 1984 technology to oppose what it claimed was an Orwellian *1984* piece of legislation. The campaign claimed to generate over 6 million faxes to Senate offices within days, raising at least one question: Why were senators keeping so much fax paper on hand in 2015?

At the same time, the ACLU, Center for Democracy and Technology (CDT), New America Foundation, and other civil liberties groups—which the Obama White House would like to consider as friends—wrote to the president urging him to issue a veto threat against CISA, just as he did against the CISPA bills in the House in previous years. They were looking for a sign of where the administration stood this time around, as was everyone involved in the debate.

And then, outside factors once again intruded on an orderly march into a Senate debate on cybersecurity. As a few news outlets reported breathlessly on whether the CISA bill would come up in two or three or five days, Majority Whip Cornyn dropped a bombshell, saying it wouldn't come up at all before the summer break. A transportation bill had to be finished, and then there would be an abortion debate, and an important veterans' bill needed to be completed. They were all weighty, important issues. Cybersecurity, on the other hand, was once again a third-tier issue for lawmakers regardless of their protestations.

After the Senate Republicans' July 28 weekly policy luncheon, Cornyn told reporters there wasn't enough time to take up the complex and controversial bill before August 7, the Senate's planned departure date, the *Hill* reported. Cornyn pledged a renewed effort to bring up the bill when Congress returned in September.

"If CISA does get pushed to September, it would be disappointing because every delay throws getting the bill passed into question," an industry source said, before reaching for a positive spin. "But, many in the private sector are confident that Senate leadership—both Senators McConnell and Reid—is committed to acting on CISA as soon as possible. They recognize the importance of the bill to business and U.S. economic security. It has to happen."

That belied industry sources' gnawing fear that the Senate debate would drag out into the fall, that the eventual House–Senate negotiations over a final version of the legislation wouldn't begin until late September or October, and that the whole thing would be knocked off the agenda by year-end budget and political issues. After that, a bill this controversial simply wouldn't get to the floor in 2016 while a full-blown presidential election campaign was underway. If it didn't happen in the fall of 2015, the next best chance would probably be the inevitable lame-duck session at the end of 2016.

The online privacy groups itching for a fight also saw an advantage in the delay.

"There is a decent chance that CISA will not come up" before the recess, Wyden said on a conference call organized by the digital privacy group Access. "The Republican leadership keeps going back and forth because they can't decide among themselves. But whether it comes up now or at the very beginning of September, it is coming up."

Wyden added: "It's definitely a temporary win to have this bill not come up next week." The delay "gives us a month" to ramp up the opposition, Wyden said. "Members are going to hear about the concerns about this bill," he warned his colleagues. "A lot of members are getting interested in offering amendments."

Amid the uncertainty about floor prospects, lawmakers across Capitol Hill were spreading their bets on what would happen with the cybersecurity legislation. Early in the week of July 27, the CISA bill was widely seen as the big train that would carry multiple cyber initiatives. Senators were ready to haul everything from consumer data-breach notification to cyber criminal law reform to the Senate floor. Later in the week, some lawmakers were quietly preparing to unpack their individual initiatives from that train.

The leaders of the House and Senate homeland security panels began setting up their bills to secure the dot-gov domain so they could move either as amendments to CISA or as stand-alone bills in the fall. "We're monitoring the Senate but we could move separately in the fall if we have to," a House Homeland Security Committee source said.

The source emphasized that the homeland panel's legislation built off the Department of Homeland Security-oriented cybersecurity bills signed into law the previous year. Those bills sailed to passage and were signed into law without controversy. It was a poignant if unspoken counterpoint to the political fireworks surrounding CISA. "That was step one and this is step two," the source said of the effort to secure the dot-gov domain. The new bills would "allow DHS to proactively protect the government's networks."

These proposals clarified the Department of Homeland Security's power to fix cybersecurity holes like the ones that allowed the massive breaches at the Office of Personnel Management. The Senate version cleared the Homeland Security and Governmental Affairs Committee on a unanimous vote on July 29. The House version would be ready to go as well, as soon as the CISA outlook became clear.

The last week of July, just a week away from summer recess, was always a confusing time of shifting priorities and schedules in the Senate. Virtually every senator had a priority he or she hoped to slip across the finish line before the Senate shut down for a month. Cyber was competing with a hundred parochial issues; could it transcend that dynamic and finally advance as an issue that should have a hundred advocates in the Senate?

Perhaps it could. Two days after Cornyn's pronouncement—and moments after Wyden's conference call—McConnell came to the microphones outside the Senate chamber to take a victory lap after passage of a major transportation bill. The Senate would move next, on Monday, August 3, to a bill defunding Planned Parenthood, he said. But, he added casually, if that was blocked by Democrats, as expected, they would take up cybersecurity.

"If we are unable to get on the defund Planned Parenthood vote on Monday, hopefully we will get on it, but if we don't we'll turn to cybersecurity next week and see if we can achieve something additionally for the American people before the August recess," McConnell said.

McConnell wasn't going to be intimidated by 6 million faxes. But he could be dissuaded by prospect of an uncontrollable floor debate.

Feinstein and other supporters of the bill raised concerns about trying to shoehorn the debate into a couple of days before recess. "I have mixed feelings about it," Feinstein told the *Hill*. "I'd obviously like to get it done. We're working with people. Whether it can get done in a short floor time or not, I don't know."

Schumer, on the other hand, said Democrats would accept a reasonable time limit and that he was eager to get this debate started, even if it wasn't finished before recess. But Wyden, Leahy, Paul, and others were preparing for a fight—over process as well as substance.

By Friday, July 31, Senate staffers who worked on cyber issues were preparing for a floor debate, even though the situation was "about as clear as mud," in the words of one aide. An industry source offered updates throughout the day: Debate was on; it was off. Best to hold off on reporting anything.

The White House was hanging back on issuing the customary Statement of Administration Policy on legislation about to hit the floor. "We are encouraged by the progress and reiterate that it should be brought to the floor for consideration as soon as possible," a senior administration official said.

The official declined to comment on whether the administration wanted to see additional privacy and civil liberties protections. The White House had long suggested it would be satisfied to see CISA clear the full Senate and open the way to three-sided negotiations involving the administration and the House and Senate to develop final language. But the ferocious opposition from the digital privacy crew might have altered that calculation just a bit. This was a legacy issue, after all, and Obama didn't want to wrap up his term as an enemy of online privacy.

That evening, Carper attended "Senator Carper Bobblehead Night" at the minor league ballpark in Wilmington, Delaware. As he tried to follow the Senate Republican leader's on-again, off-again plans for cyber, Carper could empathize with the bobbleheads.

Carper was a patient, level-headed legislator. He sprinkled simple axioms throughout his conversations but loved tackling complex policy questions. He'd gone through Ohio State as an ROTC cadet at the height of the Vietnam War in the late 1960s and served a total of twenty-three years in the Navy, including three war-time tours in Southeast Asia as a flight officer aboard a P-3 Orion reconnaissance plane. Afterward, he'd earned an MBA at the University of Delaware and gone on to represent the state in the U.S. House for five terms before serving two terms as governor. Carper joined the Senate in 2001 and had no illusions about how difficult it was to move a complicated bill through the chamber.

But this was getting ridiculous.

The Senate returned on Monday, August 3, but as the day progressed Mitch McConnell didn't give any indication of his next steps. "High drama," a Senate source joked. "It's like a Lifetime Channel movie."

Burr and Feinstein did their part to make it as hard as possible to delay action, circulating a "manager's amendment" that sought to neutralize many of the hot-button issues around CISA. It might also take away some of the reasons why industry supported the information-sharing bill in the first place. But the important thing now was to get it through the Senate and to the next stage of negotiations.

Under the manager's amendment, shared information couldn't be used to investigate "serious violent felonies," which the sponsors called "a very significant privacy change." The new language sought to limit uses to tightly specified "cybersecurity purposes." Burr and Feinstein agreed to partially eliminate the exemption from disclosure under the Freedom of Information Act, and to put new restrictions around the uses of "defensive measures" by private entities.

The secretary of homeland security would join the attorney general in writing the rules around sharing; this responsibility was handed to the attorney general in the version that passed the Intelligence Committee in March.

The revised bill also sought to limit the types of industry-generated information that could be shared outside of a "portal" maintained by the Department of Homeland Security. DHS Deputy Secretary Alejandro Mayorkas, in a letter late the previous week to Sen. Al Franken, expressed concern that the Burr–Feinstein bill still allowed too much sharing to take place directly between industry and other agencies. The DHS portal at NCCIC needed to be the main portal, Mayorkas said, in order to ensure efficiency as well as uniform treatment of sensitive personal data.

The changes may have weakened the bill, at least slightly, from industry's perspective, but the business world wasn't backing off at this late stage. Instead, groups like the U.S. Chamber of Commerce (Chamber), Securities Industry and Financial Management Association, and Financial Services Roundtable put out letters saying how much stronger the bill was with those controversies resolved.

"Among other things, the managers' amendment further limits the sharing of cyber threat data to 'cybersecurity purposes,'" the U.S. Chamber wrote.

Closely related, the revised measure eliminates the government's use of cyber threat indicators to investigate and prosecute "serious violent felonies," thus putting to rest false claims that CISA is a "surveillance" bill. The managers' amendment also ensures that the use of defensive measures does not allow an entity to gain unauthorized access to a computer network. The bill writers have worked diligently to address the concerns of privacy and civil liberties organizations.

The online privacy community grudgingly acknowledged some improvements, but the changes didn't go far enough to earn their support or even temper their opposition. Personal information could still be shared, CDT's Greg Nojeim asserted. The NSA would still get the data. There were plenty of unresolved issues.

The tighter definition of "cybersecurity purpose" was a "significant improvement," Nojeim wrote in a blog posted late on August 3, as were stricter limits on government uses of cyber threat indicators.

The language on "defensive measures" was improved, Nojeim wrote, but it was still not adequate and should be removed entirely. He said the bill continued to "marginalize" the Department of Homeland Security's role in cybersecurity, echoing Mayorkas's complaints to Al Franken.

Critically, CDT believed the legislation needed stronger requirements to remove personally identifiable information from threat indicators and tighter restrictions on National Security Agency access to the data.

Franken's office said the bill was still a mess, regardless of the manager's amendment. The privacy community wasn't moving either.

The White House, on the other hand, offered encouragement for senators to pass the bill before adjourning for the summer.

"While there are still areas of concern that we hope to address, the bill's sponsors have made a good faith effort to address some of our biggest concerns," a senior administration official told InsideCybersecurity.com. "We are very encouraged by this progress and want to work with Congress to ensure that cybersecurity legislation preserves the long-standing, respective roles and missions of civilian and intelligence agencies and contains appropriate privacy protections."

The official added, "Cybersecurity is an important national security issue and the Senate should take up this bill as soon as possible and pass it."

That indicated a possible disconnect in the administration's position. Mayorkas, reflecting DHS's perennial concern over its place, may have written before Burr and Feinstein had finished work on the manager's amendment. In any case, the White House was satisfied at this stage.

At the appointed hour on Monday evening, senators began voting on a motion to proceed to a bill defunding Planned Parenthood. Lobbyists and online privacy activists alike were gathered around screens across the capital, watching for what McConnell would say after the inevitable defeat of the Planned Parenthood bill. That bill, as expected, was blocked.

The majority leader asked for recognition. Without elaboration or any signs of emotion, the tight-lipped Kentuckian entered a motion to invoke cloture on S. 754, the cybersecurity bill. With that, he spun off and left the Senate floor.

The debate was on, though. The cloture motion would require a vote in two days on limiting debate. In the meantime, the question was whether McConnell and Reid would come to some kind of agreement on how to structure this debate.

Interest groups quickly filled senators' in-boxes with messages of support or opposition.

The Retail Industry Leaders Association urged lawmakers to add the amendment by Sen. Cotton that would expand the acceptable "portals" for industry-to-government sharing to include the FBI and Secret Service. But most industry groups simply asked senators at long last to pass the bill. The U.S. Chamber of Commerce wrote to senators urging support for the bill. As an added inducement, the Chamber said it would consider this a "key vote" in its vote ratings.

On August 4, McConnell opened the Senate on an optimistic note. If senators pulled together, he said, they could pass the bill before adjourning for the summer. He underscored the urgency by reading from an Associated Press article about the vulnerabilities in federal computer networks. The Senate could help "rescue" the Obama administration "from the cybersecurity dark ages," McConnell said, a line that brought smiles from his GOP colleagues and made Democrats on the Senate floor grimace.

McConnell asked colleagues who wanted to amend the measure to begin discussions and said "with cooperation" the Senate could pass the measure before adjourning at the end of the week.

Reid, in his opening remarks, said he would discuss "a way of proceeding in a dignified manner" to CISA, but warned that was "easier said than done." Democrats were "willing to proceed" to the bill once they receive "assurances" on amendments. He pointed to a Monday letter from Wyden urging Reid to stand up for "an adequate process" for considering "a reasonable number of amendments."

This was not an optimistic note, and it went downhill from there.

Reid sharply criticized McConnell for limiting the minority's ability to offer amendments on unrelated legislation. The Republican leader, Reid charged, had used a legislative device known as "filling the amendment tree" to limit debate far more times than Democrats ever did when they were in the majority. Next, he blasted the Republican for blocking the 2012 version of cybersecurity legislation in 2012. The long memories of the Senate were not working in favor of the bill.

As senators went into their weekly Tuesday policy luncheons, there was still no agreement on how many amendments would be voted on, and the clock was ticking toward that cloture vote the following day. The two leaders, through staff and emissaries, were trading offers and discussing the process with their respective caucuses.

When they emerged from their separate closed-door luncheons, there was still no deal, but McConnell continued striking the optimistic notes. He would ask for unanimous consent to call off the cloture vote and proceed to debate on "a limited number" of amendments. Remember, McConnell told reporters, the Democratic leader had said in June that this was "a two-day bill."

Reid came next to the mics. "Accomplishment as well as maturity are in short supply" in the GOP-controlled Senate, he said. He questioned whether Republicans really wanted this cybersecurity bill and said they seemed "afraid" of the issue. In 2012, Reid said in an ominous flashback, McConnell had teed up Obamacare repeal as the first amendment to that cybersecurity bill. This time, the Senate had wasted time on the Planned Parenthood vote and now was trying to cram the debate over cyber into a few hours prior to the summer break. McConnell "wants to drag it out until vacation" and then "push it over" into the crowded September agenda.

Moments later, the two leaders were at their desks on the Senate floor, separated by a few feet, but unwilling to look at one another.

"Now is the time to allow the Senate to debate and pass" the cyber legislation, McConnell said. He and Reid were largely alone on the floor, watched by a few dozen tourists in the galleries and attended to by a handful of aides and pages. No other senators were about; this was a leadership game.

McConnell proposed allowing each side to offer ten amendments, but Reid objected, saying the offer included no guarantee that the Democratic or Republican amendments would actually receive a vote.

"The Republican leader is my friend," Reid said gravely, "and I don't mean in any way to disparage him. But I don't know how he can make that offer with a straight face."

Reid called for an agreement to actually begin debating and voting on amendments, saying this would be the only way to pass the bill that week. Reid and other Democratic leaders said their caucus was united on the terms for debate, casting doubt on whether the underlying bill could win sixty votes the following morning to advance absent a deal between the leaders.

McConnell responded by offering to continue the negotiations. "There may be a way forward," he said, choosing to find a tiny patch of common ground in the supposed mutual desire to address cybersecurity before the August break.

Reid agreed, but the talks would produce no breakthrough Tuesday evening.

Possible amendments were continuing to proliferate, as Sens. Lee and Leahy announced they would try to add their proposal to reform the Electronic Communications Privacy Amendments Act, the federal government's main law on e-mail privacy. Homeland Security and Governmental Affairs Chairman Johnson confirmed he would move to add his committee-passed bill on DHS authorities and tools. Over seventy amendments were filed by Tuesday night.

Wyden took to the floor to reiterate that he planned a major fight over civil liberties and privacy protections. The bill was portrayed as a voluntary information-sharing measure, Wyden said, but that was "only partially true." Companies might have the option of participating or not, he said, but their customers would have no say in the matter. And it was their information that would be bouncing between companies and government.

McCain came to the floor a few minutes later, seething.

"I tell my colleagues on the other side of the aisle . . . by blocking this legislation, you're putting this nation in danger by not allowing the United States to act against a very real threat to our very existence," McCain said, nearly shouting. "So I say, Mr. President, this is a shameful day in the United States Senate. I urge the Democrat leader to come to the floor and allow us to consider amendments [and] move forward with this legislation because the security of the United States of America is in danger."

Wyden had located a seam in the bill—the distinctly involuntary role played by ordinary citizens in the information-sharing process—that he would try to relentlessly exploit in his rhetoric against the measure. McCain added his sense of personal outrage to the sense of urgency being emphasized by the bill's supporters. These were the two poles at either end of the debate.

Schumer, approached as he awaited the subway train that shuttled between the Capitol and Senate office buildings, expressed his enduring hope that a deal would be reached. "I hope so," he said, but "it's not fair for [McConnell] to fill the amendment tree." Under the Republican's plan, "pending" amendments would "go away" as soon as the GOP leader filed another cloture motion, Schumer said.

He turned away from the reporter to speak into his mobile phone.

"'Pending' means nothing," Schumer said before returning to his phone call.

Schumer very much wanted a cyber deal; the financial industry in New York City was sending out releases on a daily basis to help push the bill along. But one of the reasons Schumer wanted to get it cleared had nothing to do with cybersecurity: The likely successor to Harry Reid as the Senate's top Democrat—and one of the party's most visible, influential leaders—had to make a momentous decision on whether he would support or oppose Obama's nuclear accord with Iran when the issue was debated in September. Later that week, Schumer would announce his opposition to the Iran deal, bringing on furious denunciations from the White House and its allies and from throughout the liberal community. The New Yorker smiled tightly at the reporter as he signed off his phone call and jumped on the Senate subway car. Cybersecurity legislation wasn't his biggest worry at the moment.

On Wednesday morning, McConnell opened the Senate at 9:30 a.m. with a discussion of how the chamber would handle the Iran debate in September, before turning to cybersecurity. The vote on the cloture motion was scheduled to take place in one hour. In the meantime, McConnell thought it worthwhile to remind his colleagues of what was at stake.

The threat in cyberspace, he said, was "personally violating . . . financially crippling . . . and just plain creepy."

Luckily, there was an answer at hand, he said, pointing to the CISA bill. He noted the White House's "strong support" for the measure. He reminded listeners that Feinstein—"the top Democrat on the issue"—had added "important privacy protections."

And, McConnell, said, he had made "a fair offer" for debating amendments. Frankly, McConnell added with a little, humorless chuckle, "everyone was taken aback" when Reid rejected the offer. McConnell urged fellow senators to ignore this procedural spat and vote with him on proceeding to the CISA debate.

Reid, in his opening remarks, focused on Iran and the possibility of a government shutdown. He didn't say a word about cybersecurity.

Feinstein came to the floor next, saying she was "very disappointed" by the failure to reach agreement thus far. This critical legislation was hung up by procedural issues that "people don't care about." The CISA bill wouldn't end cyber attacks, Feinstein said, but it would greatly enhance the ability of government and industry to identify and respond to the threats. Just as she began to riff on the privacy protections added to the bill, McConnell returned to the floor and asked to interrupt.

If senators would agree, the cloture vote would be postponed until 2 p.m. It seemed talks were afoot. But 2 p.m. would come and go. Sen. Thune led a press conference with committee chairmen to tout the Republicans' successes after seven months in the majority. He hailed 165 roll call votes so far in 2015, contrasting that with the gridlocked, Democratic-run Senate of the previous year. A vote on passing the cybersecurity information-sharing bill was not among those 165, of course.

Senate Democrats and Republicans met separately behind closed doors to discuss the final moving pieces of the work period before the recess. As those meetings broke, Paul Kane of the *Washington Post* tweeted that senators were going home; the work period was over and there would be no more votes.

Finally, at 3:27 p.m., McConnell and Reid were back on the floor, looking exhausted. McConnell asked for unanimous consent to withdraw the cloture motion. Without fanfare he announced the deal: "At a time to be determined by the majority leader in consultation with the Democratic leader," the Senate would return to CISA.

"At a time to be determined" meant September, perhaps, but certainly after the debate on Iran. The two leaders had reached agreement on considering an Iran resolution, and included a side deal on how they would start the CISA debate, though not when.

McConnell continued: Each side would be permitted to offer ten amendments; he proceeded to list the Republican proposals that would be debated when CISA returned.

Reid didn't object; his only ask was for one additional amendment on the Democratic side. McConnell nodded.

Under the deal, the first amendment would be the manager's amendment by Burr and Feinstein. Other amendments to be debated would include the one by Cotton allowing companies to share directly with the FBI and Secret Service as well as with the Department of Homeland Security. The list seemed tight, excluding extraneous issues but allowing a serious debate on privacy and other controversial aspects of the legislation.

Activist groups quickly issued triumphant news releases.

"This is a victory for our basic right to privacy," said Nathan White of the digital privacy group Access. "Credit goes to the activists who have generated more than six million faxes demanding that the Senate slow down and consider the privacy implications of this overly broad, dangerous cyber surveillance bill." White called the delay "a clear failure for CISA and its proponents" and said: "Activists' voices will only get louder during the August work period. Senators will hear opposition to this bill in every state."

The U.S. Chamber acknowledged the setback in a release from senior vice president for emergency preparedness Ann Beauchesne.

"The Senate may have left town without passing cybersecurity legislation, but the need for it remains," she said. "Cyberattacks are being launched on a daily basis from various sources, and CISA would help companies achieve timely and actionable situational awareness, which will improve the business community, and the nation's detection, mitigation and response capabilities. We remain committed to seeing this legislation over the finish line, and urge the Senate to swiftly take up and pass CISA after recess."

Carper, who had been laboring for years to pass cybersecurity legislation, saw a bright side.

"I am encouraged by the significant progress the Senate made this week on this critical issue, and I would like to commend Senators Burr and Feinstein and their staffs for their leadership and tireless efforts on their cybersecurity information sharing bill," Carper said in a statement. "While we do not agree on everything in this legislation, I greatly appreciate the compromises that have been made to make the bill stronger."

And that was it. The drama of the previous days drained away as senators wrapped up a few loose ends and turned their thoughts to the summer recess. Cybersecurity was an issue for another day.

"I would love to have finished cybersecurity this week," McConnell said the next day, "but we have now an agreement that will allow us to finish it in September."

Wyden, though, would have the last word on the rapidly emptying Senate floor as lawmakers scrambled for the exits on August 5. There was a fundamental misunderstanding about this cyber bill, Wyden repeated, returning to a line of argument that he was sharpening and would brandish in the coming months: This was not a "voluntary" cybersecurity bill, as portrayed. There was nothing voluntary about it for companies' customers, whose data could be shared with the government at the business's discretion. He would propose a notification amendment, requiring that individuals be informed whenever their personal data was shared as part of a "cyber threat indicator."

Wyden was satisfied with the process, for the moment. "Now," he said as the Senate chamber grew quiet and lonely,

> so that all concerned understand where things are, there are going to be more than twenty amendments to this badly flawed bill. Those of us who want to make sure that there is a full airing of the issues, have come to understand that there is no time limit that has yet been agreed to on those amendments. So there's going to be a real debate. And of course that is what the United States Senate is all about. And I particularly want to commend the millions and millions of advocates around the country who spoke out—I understand that there were something like six million faxes that were sent to members of this body.

He was just warming up:

> I start with the basic proposition, Mr. President, that we have a very serious set of cyber security threats, as I touched on seeing it at home. Second, information sharing can be valuable. There is certainly a lot of it now. It can be constructive. Information sharing, however, without vigorous, robust privacy safeguards will not be considered by millions

of Americans to be a cybersecurity bill. Millions of Americans will say
that that legislation is a surveillance bill.

It wasn't voluntary for citizens, Wyden exclaimed, and the abuses it
would enable were beyond legal remedy. "As written, the cybersecurity
legislation prevents law abiding Americans from suing private companies
that inappropriately share their personal information with the government."

With that shield, Wyden said, companies would be far less motivated
to remove personal data from the threat indicators they wanted to share.
Then it would go into a big vat of data within government agencies,
accompanied by questionable safeguards. The sanctity of this personal
information would be subject to the whims of potentially "over-zealous"
bureaucrats as well as industry security officers.

What was this debate about?

> When I say personal information, I'm talking about the contents of e-
> mails, financial information, basically any data at all that is stored
> electronically. CISA, as the bill is called, would allow private compa-
> nies to share large volumes of their customers' personal information
> with the government after only a cursory review. And colleagues who
> want to look at that provision ought to take a look at page 16 of the
> bill. And we were told repeatedly that this legislation was voluntary.

Not so, Wyden said. "While the fact is it is voluntary for the companies. But for the citizens of Pennsylvania, the citizens of Oregon, those
across this country, it's not voluntary. The people of Pennsylvania won't
be asked first whether they want their information sent to the government.
Oregonians won't have the chance to say whether or not they want that
information sent. For them, this legislation is mandatory."

Wyden offered an example: "Imagine that a health insurance company
finds out that millions of its customer's records have been stolen. If that
company has any evidence about who the hackers were, or how they stole
this information, of course it makes sense to share that information with
the government."

On the other hand, he said,

> that company shouldn't simply say here you go, and hand millions of
> its customers' financial and medical information over to a wide array
> of government agencies. The records of the victims of a hack should

not be treated the same way that information about the hacker is treated. If companies are sharing information for cybersecurity purposes they ought to be required to make a reasonable effort to remove personal information that isn't needed for cybersecurity before that information is handed over to the government.

CISA would require companies to remove data "known at the time of sharing" to include personal information. Industry lobbyists preferred that definition to "reasonable," which could be interpreted—by bureaucrats or juries—in various, shifting ways.

"Now I want to talk about just one other issue specifically that I think senators are not familiar with, and that is the issue of cyber signatures," Wyden said. "Cyber signatures are essentially recognizable patterns in online code. A number of informed observers have raised the concern that once individual cyber signatures are shoveled over to the government by private companies they could be used as the basis for broad surveillance affecting law abiding Americans."

This was a sensitive area, Wyden acknowledged. "Now I'm not going to confirm or deny any of the press reports that have raised concerns about cyber signatures being used in this way," he said. He was an Intelligence Committee member and restricted in what he could share. He could, however, turn that restriction into a rhetorical advantage with heavy hints.

"But I believe senators should understand that this is certainly, and it's been widely discussed in the public arena, a theoretical possibility," he said. "And that helps underscore the importance of including a strong requirement for private companies to remove unrelated personal information about their customers before dumping data over to the government."

And then there was a "secret" Department of Justice legal opinion that Wyden believed would show the government's expansive view of what it could do with citizens' private information. Wyden had been agitating for disclosure, without success, for much of the last year.

"This opinion interprets common commercial service agreements and in my judgment it is inconsistent with the public's understanding of the law," Wyden said.

So once again, Mr. President, we have this question of what happens when the people of Pennsylvania, Virginia, or Oregon think that there's a law because they've read it in the public arena or on their iPad at home, and then there is a secret interpretation. I've urged the Justice Department to withdraw this secret Department of Justice opinion that relates directly to the cybersecurity debate. They've declined to do it. I suspect many senators haven't had the chance to review it, and I would urge, as I have done before, on this type of topic, I would urge senators or their staff to take the time to read it. Because I believe understanding the executive branch's interpretation of these agreements is an important part of understanding the relevant legal landscape on cybersecurity.

Wyden wrapped up with a final kick at the bill, namely, that it wouldn't work.

"And I'm going to close by talking about the question of effectiveness," he said.

Because I think we all understand that we are facing very real cyber threats. I'm of the view this bill in its present form would do little if anything to stop large sophisticated cyberattacks like the Office of Personnel Management hack. And I don't think senators ought to take just my word for it here. In April, sixty-five technologists and cybersecurity professionals expressed their opposition to the bill in a letter to Chairman Burr and Vice-Chairman Feinstein. Referring to the bill and similar bills they wrote and I quote "We appreciate your interest in making our networks more secure. But the legislation proposed does not materially further that goal and at the same time it puts our users' privacy at risk."

Wyden concluded:

We'll have a chance in the fall to look at ways to address cybersecurity in a fashion that I think does respond to what our people want, and that is to show that security, and in this case cybersecurity, and liberty are not mutually exclusive. That sensible policies worked out in a bipartisan way will respond to the needs of this country in what is unquestionably a dangerous time. With that Mr. President I yield the floor.

It was a pointed reminder of what to expect in the fall.

"It's too bad he's not crazy," an industry source said of Wyden, just a little bit worried. "He's a pretty smart guy."

There was a good fight coming.

15

AT LONG LAST, THE POLITICAL SYSTEM ARRIVES AT AN ANSWER

I spent countless hours crafting and debating cyber legislation back in 2012—the last time we attempted to pass major cyber legislation. This body has come a long way since that time. We understand that we cannot improve our cyber posture by shackling the private sector, which operates the majority of our country's critical infrastructure, with government mandates. As I argued at that time, heavy-handed regulations and government bureaucracy will do more harm than good in cyberspace. The voluntary framework in this legislation represents the progress we have made in defining the role of the private sector and the role of the government in sharing threat information, defending networks, and deterring cyber-attacks.

—Sen. John McCain (R-Arizona), Senate floor speech, August 4, 2015

The Department of Homeland Security (DHS) may have been desperate for success stories, but so was Congress. In mid-August 2015, a Gallup Poll showed Congress with a 14 percent approval rating—not its lowest on record, but pretty dismal and suggestive of the need to reel off some accomplishments. Senate leader Mitch McConnell's national unfavorable rating was 41 percent, compared to a 22 percent favorable rating. Lawmakers would be looking for areas of possible success when they returned in the fall.

The Senate failed to advance cybersecurity legislation in early August, but the agreement on a process for considering the bill in the fall provided a silver lining. The procedural deal between the Senate's leaders could, potentially, contribute enormously to the ultimate success of the bill.

First, the agreement obviated the need for a cloture vote on proceeding to the Cybersecurity Information Sharing Act (CISA), removing one obstacle. The bill could be brought directly to the floor by the leaders. Second, McConnell and Democratic leader Harry Reid agreed on a list of amendments that would be in order for consideration once the bill was taken up. The amendments focused on the content of the CISA bill and closely related issues, and extraneous proposals were excluded. Third, the agreement seemed to provide ample time for debate, after debate on the Iran nuclear agreement and perhaps amid skirmishing over the federal budget.

"I could see CISA slip until October," an industry source said, given the realities of the Senate's September agenda and a looming showdown over government funding. But the prospect wasn't as alarming as it would've been a few days earlier. "The fact that they hammered out an agreement on amendments is notable," the source said. "Maybe we'll have to live with something on privacy, but I think most of these amendments get defeated."

The timing was still subject to any number of outside influences, as well as to the vagaries of the always potentially combustible McConnell–Reid relationship. Some kind of time agreement between McConnell and Reid for actually voting on and getting through those amendments would still be needed. But supporters of the CISA bill looked at the amendment list and saw a pathway to victory—as they wondered what took the Senate leaders so long to reach this point.

Amendments on limiting legal immunity for companies that shared threat indicators, privacy protections, securing federal computer networks, and fighting cyber crime would be in order. But separate issues raised by senators such as consumer data-breach notification and Electronic Communications Privacy Act reform were off the table. Likewise, Sen. Rand Paul's bid to stoke unrelated debates over defunding "sanctuary cities" and allowing firearms on military bases was disallowed. The proposal by Sen. Susan Collins to add mandatory cybersecurity reporting requirements for some critical infrastructure operators did not make the cut.

"We set up expeditious consideration of the cyber bill" for when the Senate returned in September, McConnell said.

The Republican list included at least three problematic amendments from industry's perspective: a Paul proposal to limit businesses' liability protection, one by Sen. Dean Heller (R-Nevada) that would set a stricter requirement on removing personally identifiable information, and a proposal by Sen. Jeff Flake (R-Arizona) to sunset the bill's provisions after six years. The House-passed legislation included a seven-year sunset.

There was also the Cotton amendment on direct sharing with the FBI and Secret Service, which many industry groups supported.

The most contentious Democratic amendments included two by Ron Wyden strengthening the requirement to remove personally identifiable information and requiring notification when a customer's personal data had been shared. Sen. Al Franken would offer an amendment to tighten the definition of the "threat indicators" that could be shared. Sen. Patrick Leahy would offer an amendment to eliminate exclusions from the Freedom of Information Act, closing a loophole left open in the manager's amendment by Richard Burr and Dianne Feinstein.

Sen. Tom Carper would offer the Federal Cybersecurity Enhancement Act, the bill approved by his committee that would accelerate deployment of the EINSTEIN system across government agencies and make clear DHS authority to compel other agencies to make cybersecurity improvements. Carper would also offer an amendment clarifying the Department of Homeland Security's authority to scrub incoming data of so-called personally identifiable information (PII).

Supporters of CISA pointed to a two-stage "scrubbing" process already contained in the bill, which would require companies to remove data "known at the time of sharing" to include personal information, followed by a second scrub at federal agencies receiving the threat indicators. The data first would go from the private sector to DHS's National Cybersecurity and Communications Integration Center (NCCIC), which would then share it with the other federal agencies "without delay."

Burr and Feinstein said this process addressed concerns about "direct sharing" between the private sector and entities such as the National Security Agency (NSA). But critics said it opened the door to vast amounts of personal data falling into the hands of intelligence and law enforcement agencies with no intervening "scrub" at DHS.

Carper's amendment would create space for DHS to take a look at the threat indicators before sending them along to other agencies, specifically to determine whether PII was included. Carper's amendment specified that DHS must share the information among other agencies without "un-necessary" delay, leaving it up to the department to determine what con-stituted a "necessary" delay.

DHS's advocates on the congressional homeland security committees said the department was far ahead of other agencies in developing the capacity to review data and strip out PII. Some industry lobbyists be-lieved this was more about protecting DHS's turf, rather than ensuring an effective information-sharing process.

"DHS is supposed to be the agency with the expertise so they should perform a privacy scrub," a Senate source asserted. "The concern is under the current language it is not entirely clear DHS would be afforded the flexibility to conduct an automated privacy scrub that may require DHS to modify or remove irrelevant PII as it sends the info around to other agencies."

Industry lobbyists questioned the impact of including an additional stop at DHS before threat indicators could be put to use, but quietly agreed they might accept the limited Carper amendment as one price for getting the bill through the Senate.

Sen. Christopher Coons (D-Delaware) would offer an amendment that took a harder line, mandating a scrub of personal information at DHS. Industry groups saw this as much more time-consuming and onerous than the Carper amendment.

It was classic Carper: a one-word solution that seemed to cut through the noise.

The great significance of this amendment list was that it allowed de-bate on the weighty philosophical issues raised by the bill, along with chances to adjust the functionality of the legislation by degrees. Reluc-tantly, almost by accident—and only because of the need to deal quickly with the separate Iran matter—the Senate had arrived at a place where it could constructively engage on an issue of national import.

If it could actually just get on with it.

Industry supporters of CISA got ready to work over the summer re-cess, with plans for constant, traditional outreach to Senate offices bol-stered by a social media campaign to counter bill opponents on their own cyber turf. "They have a month, but we have a month too," said an industry source. There needed to be a message of the week countering the "surveillance bill" narrative with a "myth versus fact" campaign.

On August 11, the Protecting America's Cyber Networks Coalition sent out its first broadside attempting to wrestle the narrative away from the online privacy activists. The coalition included forty-eight industry groups representing much of the U.S. economy and most critical-infrastructure sectors.

"The idea behind the myth-versus-fact piece is to describe CISA in accurate and positive ways—in ways that are true to the bill," an industry insider explained. "Opponents describe the bill in ways that are false. We've selected five myth-versus-fact combinations to counter such false claims, and we plan to push them out over the coming weeks in the run-up to a vote in September." CISA was so important, the industry source said, because individual companies in the private sector were forced to play an outsized role in defending networks against sophisticated international attacks. "Companies are confronting nation-states and their proxies, criminal gangs, and rogue hackers on the Internet," the source said. "They are also managing these and other cyber threats to their data and devices." The source added: "Frankly, businesses are supplying security in environments that used to be supplied by national governments. Companies must have timely situational awareness and legal clarity to defend against the bad guys. CISA would be a key tool in businesses' cybersecurity toolbox."

The first coalition posting challenged bill opponents' assertions that the legislation would allow sharing of broad types of information; that it authorized surveillance; that it would allow companies to "hack back" against cyber attackers; that it didn't require companies to remove personal data from shared information; and that businesses would be "encouraged" to share with the Defense Department and National Security Agency.

The industry side was trying a frontal assault on every point used against CISA.

The release included a string of data that the coalition said was typical of the kind of cyber threat indicators shared between industry and government.

"The caption below isn't a series of typos. It shows a typical example of cyber threat information—technical and sterile data—that businesses share and receive from industry and government partners to counter cyberattacks. It contains no personal information—and that's the point," according to the coalition.

It looked like this:

```
alert tcp $EXTERNAL_NET any -> $HOME_NET $HTTP_PORTS
(msg:"ZBC DDoS - HTTP Header Structure with
Hex Byte URI seen"; flow:established,to_server; content:"Keep-
Alive|3a 20|"; http_header; fast_pattern; content:!"gzip";
http_header; content:"Connection|3a 20|Keep-Alive"; http_header; no-
case; pcre:"/[\?&][a-f0-9]{5,6}$/U"; classtype:webapplication-
attack; sid:40000006; rev:4;)
alert tcp $EXTERNAL_NET any -> $HOME_NET $HTTP_PORTS
(msg:"ZBC DDoS - KamiKaze";
flow:established,to_server; content:"CLIENT-IP|3a 20|"; http_header;
fast_pattern; content:"Via|3a 20|"; http_header;
content:"X-FORWARDED-FOR|3a 20|"; http_header; classtype:web-
application-attack; sid:40000007; rev:1;)
```

This is what the fight is about, the industry side was arguing. Privacy protections are very important, the CISA supporters said repeatedly. But now they were not going to sit back while the opposition turned cyber info sharing into something that it most emphatically was not.

The online privacy crew shrugged it off. "I didn't find it very convincing," said Nathan White of Access. Things were going their way, the digital rights groups were convinced, more than ever.

Industry representatives thought it a smug response, and that CISA foes were already chalking up a victory. "I wouldn't say anything's a given in the Senate," one business source said. "I'd say 'smugness' captures the attitude in their camp."

Behind the scenes, industry advocates were monitoring social media and finding few signs of the promised anti-CISA campaign. The chatter was minimal, and it was all inside the Beltway. The online privacy camp seemed to be on vacation.

This source expressed the industry side's frustration: "They aren't quite capturing the nuances of our argument. They don't even want to talk about our needs—and we're always willing to talk about how to improve the privacy protections."

The source added: "We need to remember who the bad guys are, this is aimed at overseas bad actors."

In the existing threat environment, the source said, it was simply a fact that the National Security Agency would get the kind of data it needed to battle "a dangerous adversary." But under CISA, it wouldn't be a straightforward handover of the data; there would be steps to ensure the government wasn't tossing around personal information.

"What the bill does is require Uncle Sam to review it first," the source said. "It doesn't just go directly to Admiral Rogers" at the NSA.

That may have been true, but late on August 15, the Snowden effect slammed into the CISA debate once again.

The *New York Times*'s latest bombshell from the Snowden leaks detailed the cozy relationship between AT&T and the national security establishment. The story was posted online Saturday evening and appeared on the front page of the Sunday paper on August 16. The upshot was that plenty of data was going to Adm. Rogers and others at the NSA and other intelligence centers without a great deal of concern for privacy considerations.

"While it has been long known that American telecommunications companies worked closely with the spy agency, newly disclosed N.S.A. documents show that the relationship with AT&T has been considered unique and especially productive. One document described it as 'highly collaborative,' while another lauded the company's 'extreme willingness to help,'" the *New York Times* reported in collaboration with ProPublica.

The article continued: "AT&T's cooperation has involved a broad range of classified activities, according to the documents, which date from 2003 to 2013. AT&T has given the N.S.A. access, through several methods covered under different legal rules, to billions of emails as they have flowed across its domestic networks."

AT&T declined to comment to the *New York Times*. But in terms of this story's impact on cybersecurity, that didn't really matter. Perceptions were key at the intersection of cybersecurity and surveillance, and here was another episode that fit snugly into the online privacy community's narrative: A surveillance-oriented government and its willing partners in industry were constantly charging up to or over the line when it came to protecting citizens' online privacy rights.

It didn't matter that the executive branch *said* it had changed its policies and that the USA Freedom Act had been signed into law. Look at what the government and the telecom industry have been doing already— and they're asking for *more* authority to dig into peoples' data?

"If the Cyber Information Sharing Act were to pass, companies like AT&T would be encouraged to share more of their customers' data with law enforcement and surveillance agencies in the United States without concern about any privacy laws," said Peter Micek, senior policy counsel at the digital rights group Access. "In fact, the bill creates legal incentives to encourage companies to give more and share more private data. This news should put an immediate halt to consideration of CISA."

An industry source fired back, saying: "In my mind, there's no reason to slow pushing CISA for one second. The *Times* story is limited to a company. The policy and legal underpinnings are different."

The source stressed: "CISA is not about surveilling law-abiding citizens but about guarding U.S. cyber networks, respecting privacy, and sharing threat data at Internet speeds. There ought to be no impact on CISA. The bill should get taken up the first week the Senate gets back."

By early Monday morning, August 17, industry groups that supported CISA were stressing to reporters the distinction between "surveillance" activities as opposed to government and private-sector sharing of cyber threat indicators. "This is common-sense legislation, it's not at all about personally identifiable information or surveillance," said a financial-sector source. Those issues had already been addressed in the USA Freedom Act debate, the source said with some exasperation.

Another source, also from the financial community, said firms had no interest in handing over personal data as part of an information-sharing regime under CISA. "This is about technical threat indicators," the source said. Industry representatives put on a brave face, saying the short legislative calendar in the fall, not the steady drip of ruinous leaks from Edward Snowden, were still the biggest obstacle to passing CISA.

There was the McConnell–Reid consent agreement to proceed and the White House had said nice things about the bill. There were plenty of signs that senators wanted to get it done. The crowded fall agenda was still the main problem, not this new story about AT&T, a company that was a highly active and well-respected member of industry's cybersecurity inner circle.

But behind the scenes the mood was very worried, if not approaching panic. E-mails whipped between the offices of trade association officials who were leading the industry campaign for CISA. Some felt the latest story killed CISA; others noted it was posted on a sleepy weekend in mid-August.

Industry representatives heatedly debated whether to take on the charges directly or hope that it would settle down on its own. In a bit of cyber-irony, AT&T announced its "Digital You" campaign on August 17, a new program aimed at giving consumers—and especially parents—new tools to secure their digital lives. Such positive gestures didn't have much sway in the bare-knuckled policy arena though.

Amie Stepanovich of Access published a piece in *Wired* hammering at the "involuntary" nature of the bill, when it came to consumers' unwitting participation in the program or even for companies that signed a cooperative agreement with the government. The legislation "sacrifices peoples' privacy and security at the altar of corporate liability protection," Stepanovich wrote.

"AT&T just galvanized the civil liberties groups," an industry lobbyist said glumly. It would be another bullet to fire at the legislation, but the privacy-rights community was feeling confident that it had plenty of ammunition.

The industry coalition charged back into the fight with an August 19 posting that once again tried to explain "cyber threat indicators" and how they were far different from personal, private information. "CTIs, according to the bill, describe or identify malicious reconnaissance, a method of defeating a security control or exploitation of a security vulnerability, malicious cyber command and control, the actual or potential harm caused by an incident, among other types of cyber threat data," the coalition wrote.

That might include domain names or Internet protocol addresses. It could be log data, which the coalition described as the "exhaust gas of an information system." It could include signatures, "recognizable, distinguishing patterns associated with a cyberattack (e.g., a binary string in a virus or a particular set of keystrokes used to gain unauthorized access to a network)," or time stamps or a Web address.

But it wasn't the content of someone's e-mail.

"In those rare instances where an individual's personal information might happen to be embedded within CTIs or defensive measures, CISA mandates that public and private entities remove such personal information unrelated to a cyber threat when sharing CTIs and defensive measures," the coalition wrote.

"The bottom line is that CISA is about protecting America's cyber systems. It is not a surveillance bill, which some privacy advocates wrongly argue by stretching the intent of CISA to unrecognizable lengths.

The fact is that CISA does not authorize the government to surveil individuals or target crimes unrelated to cybersecurity."

As the dog days of August stretched out, hackers began publicly revealing the contents of their haul from an attack on the Ashley Madison Web site, which promoted itself as an adultery-enabling service under the slogan "Life is short. Have an affair." E-mail content and the embarrassing personal details of more than 30 million alleged customers were released into cyberspace.

Now here was a scandal that might motivate Congress to act! Or so snickered the cynics.

In the immediate, sometimes grim reality of cyberspace, within days a couple of suicides were linked to the releases, the data inspired blackmail schemes aimed at hapless customers who had, apparently, entered extensive personal data in hopes of scoring a fling, and a mayor in Alabama felt compelled to resign.

The CEO of the Ashley Madison parent company stepped down about ten days after the hacked content began seeping out through the Web. Despite the tawdry nature of the business, the resignation demonstrated the risk that cyber insecurity posed to the upper leadership of virtually any organization. From Sony Pictures to OPM to Ashley Madison, it was becoming the norm for CEOs to take the fall after massive hacks.

The Ashley Madison hack didn't have much visible impact on Capitol Hill in late August. The prospects for the cyber information-sharing legislation were as murky as ever, with senators back in their states, many staff on vacation, and an industry coalition gamely trying to win a message war that the other side didn't seem to feel much need to counter. *Politico*'s Tim Starks posted an item on August 28 noting "dour vibes" around the bill on Capitol Hill. An industry lobbyist dashed off an e-mail to the reporter playfully demanding to know his source on congressional "vibes." Things were going very well, the lobbyist asserted. But the lobbyist was paid to keep hope alive; Starks was calling them as he saw them.

A well-connected senator, off the record, said September was extremely unlikely for floor action. He heavily qualified the prospects for action in the later months of the year, offering one thin reed of hope: Congress would likely be in session right up until Christmas Eve.

After running through a check list of "show votes" on other issues, the Senate finally turned to cybersecurity in the fall of 2015. With little fanfare and minimal histrionics, the legislation by Burr and Feinstein sailed through in late October, setting the stage for negotiations with the House and ultimate passage of a major cybersecurity bill that President Obama would sign into law.

Lawmakers added privacy protections and folded in the "EINSTEIN" legislation that would speed up the implementation of advanced cybersecurity technology throughout the government. In the end, Congress came up with a workmanlike product that could accomplish a modest goal, a result that belied the almost apocalyptic debate of the preceding years.

Congress could be maddeningly inward-looking and childishly distracted, but it wasn't alone on the cybersecurity-policy playing field. The policy was going to march ahead regardless of what lawmakers managed to accomplish. Besides the latest titillating news produced by illegal hacks, the last full week of August 2015 also produced a string of hugely significant cybersecurity policy developments that would, naturally, be overlooked amid the summer doldrums, the Donald Trump watch on the presidential campaign trail, and the latest episodes of homicidal rage that would dominate the Web and the airwaves.

As Congress fiddled, cybersecurity policy was actually still being made in new collaborative efforts between government and industry, but also in regulatory moves by the federal bureaucracy and in courtrooms. It was, as always, a menagerie of partnership, legal brickbats, and regulatory muscle-flexing.

As noted earlier, on August 24, a U.S. appeals court stamped its approval on the Federal Trade Commission's authority to enforce cybersecurity standards. Two days later, the Pentagon released a new rule requiring its contractors to report breaches on their networks. Just a couple of weeks earlier the White House Office of Management and Budget proposed new rules for all government contractors on improving the cybersecurity of their supply chains. The federal government awarded over $305 billion in contracts in the 2015 fiscal year, so its ability to influence cybersecurity habits—in this case, the habits of its vast network of vendors—was unparalleled within the U.S. economy.

That was the disciplinary and regulatory side of government's approach; there were also developments on the partnership side. The same week in late August, the Federal Communications Commission's (FCC) industry-led advisory council got to work on its next collaborative endeavor on cybersecurity, addressing information sharing, "security by design," and the telecom sector's cyber workforce. As information-sharing legislation lagged, the FCC's leaders wanted to independently work with industry to see if barriers to sharing could be reduced.

The Commerce Department announced the details of a new "multistakeholder process" aimed at getting cybersecurity researchers and vendors of security products on the same page when it came to revealing vulnerabilities in software. And the Department of Homeland Security reached a decision on a private-sector entity to establish rules of the road for the new information sharing and analysis organizations created under Obama's executive order of the previous February.

The policy needs wouldn't disappear in the absence of congressional action, and multiple interests—within and outside government—would push the policies in a variety of directions. Many of those efforts would be discretely effective. But what was lacking was the overarching policy guidance that only Congress, as the representative of the nation's myriad interests, could produce.

"Why has this been so hard? I'm stumped," a financial-sector source said in the late summer of 2015, as the CISA bill's fate still hung in the balance. "Everyone says the next breach will be the one that changes the political calculation. But what's the magic number? The government has already literally lost the crown jewels."

And still, Congress stumbled and could only offer partial answers. At long last, completion of the information-sharing legislation wasn't a final victory, but would mark another step toward completion of a policy arc that began with Obama's 2013 executive order. The legal fears that inhibited sharing of threat indicators would be addressed; at the same time, the National Institute of Standards and Technology (NIST) voluntary framework of cybersecurity standards would guide industry efforts, rather than a top-down regulatory command structure as was envisioned just a few years before.

There were missing pieces, most notably tangible incentives to encourage expensive investments in cyber defenses by individual companies, which would in turn benefit entire industry sectors and the United States as a whole. But once Congress finally acted on information sharing, even more responsibility for cybersecurity clearly would be in industry hands. At that point, industry and its government partners would just have to make it work.

16

THE UNFINISHED JOURNEY

We are all for improving the safety and security of the Internet. Your own choices, your practices [and] the practices of Internet service providers are all part of the fabric that we have to maintain. The things that you do to protect your own safety and security and privacy affect me, too, because if you don't do a good job of it, you become an avenue through which phishing attacks can be made.
—Vint Cerf, chief Internet evangelist at Google, National Press Club, May 4, 2015

By 2016 government and industry alike could claim a series of policy accomplishments. Any improvements in the cybersecurity policy landscape only set the stage for the next round of challenges, of course, and the essential question remained whether policy accomplishments translated into better security in cyberspace. The White House put out lengthy fact sheets and the Department of Homeland Security boasted of hundreds of meetings with stakeholders, but were we any more secure? The business community stressed the benefits and need for a nonregulatory, industry-led approach, but was it actually effective? Congress toted up hearings and bills passed, but the effect, if any, was far from certain.

Cybersecurity posed a surging river of questions that twisted in surprising directions and never, ever, slowed down.

On the government side, cyber policy was first articulated under the Bill Clinton administration, became an upper-tier priority under the George W. Bush administration, and at times dominated policy discussions during the Obama administration. But the current governmental approach, priorities, and structure for dealing with cybersecurity still might not get it done.

The verdict wasn't in yet on the voluntary approach to driving cybersecurity improvements in the private sector. By 2016, the verdict wasn't even in on whether the federal government truly believed in a voluntary approach, or whether it could or would maintain such an approach.

Some of the flagship efforts launched under the banner of the National Institute of Standards and Technology (NIST) framework of cybersecurity standards quickly revealed inherent strains, regardless of the sturdiness of the NIST product itself. By late 2015, for instance, it was unclear whether the Federal Communications Commission (FCC) could actually provide the confidentiality guarantees that industry needed before handing government highly detailed reports about companies' cyber efforts. In the FCC's eyes, such reporting was a key to assuring that the communications industry was actually using the NIST framework-based "working group 4" report released earlier in the year.

Without an adequate system for assuring effectiveness, industry lawyers believed the FCC almost certainly would decide to fall back on a more traditional mandatory approach to requiring beefed up cybersecurity controls in the communications sector. Government and industry lawyers would dominate the process, it would be battled out over years and probably trigger multiple lawsuits. The year-long FCC–industry collaborative process would be for naught.

Such an outcome was averted as the FCC, the Department of Homeland Security (DHS), and industry representatives figured out a way to hold the assurance meetings under a legally sound cloak of privacy. But the difficulty in settling this point demonstrated, once again, the inherently precarious nature of government–industry collaboration in the risky, costly world of cybersecurity.

Viewed in a different light, the constant tension between a private sector-led approach and the threat of government intervention provided motivational sparks that kept industry moving forward to improve the nation's cybersecurity. In any case, industry wouldn't have much choice when an activist government such as the Obama administration was in power. Yet another experiment in cybersecurity policy would be in store if and when the next Republican administration came into office. Would a more hands-off government approach, devoid of a regulatory threat, lead industry to slack off?

Some on the security side didn't think that was the right question. As seen under George W. Bush, a Republican administration might not be shy at all about requiring cybersecurity improvements.

The Obama administration as part of the executive order in 2013 made sure federal agencies had the regulatory authority they needed to drive cyber improvements, if they decided that was necessary. But the threat of regulation was kept in the holster into 2016.

"The voluntary part of the [2013] executive order was all about politics," a former Obama administration official, who was oriented toward the security side, said in late 2015. "This is a Google White House, a Microsoft White House. They think the national security types stifle innovation."

Melissa Hathaway, who worked in both the Bush and Obama White Houses, cited a conundrum in the business community. Industry leaders desperately feared and opposed regulatory mandates, but also cried out for specific guidance on what they should do to improve cybersecurity. Businesses were reluctant to make investments that their competitors weren't making—and spending on cybersecurity was still, in many ways, a choice. Critical sectors still needed guidance and it wasn't clear that "voluntary" would achieve the goal.

A source from the tech sector, speaking on background, was harsher in the assessment of the Obama White House and its commitment to a voluntary, industry-led cyber strategy. "I don't believe a word they say," said the source, who worked for a critical infrastructure entity. "They talk about partnership but everything they do is counter to partnership."

Government–industry collaboration quickly soured when the Obama administration took office in 2009, this source charged. "'Partnership' is just a way for them to get what they want from business." The process of collaborating on securing critical infrastructure—in both cyber and physical space—was far more robust under both the Bill Clinton and George W. Bush administrations, according to this source. "With this administration, there's a belief that government can provide the solutions and should be at the center of everything," the source said.

In previous administrations "it was about finding common ground," the source said. "Slowly but surely the government side became the dominant partner."

From the 2013 National Infrastructure Protection Plan to the 2014 NIST framework to the 2015 proposal on information sharing and analysis organizations, or ISAOs, this source reflected a view that was widely—if quietly—held in industry: "Partnership" was a one-way street for the Obama administration.

"Nobody in industry was clamoring for a NIST framework; it pulled away a lot of resources. And, they say the framework is voluntary but if we don't do it they'll make it mandatory," the source charged. "They're asking us to write our own regulations," the source said of the Obama administration's allegedly voluntary approach to cybersecurity.

"Likewise, with the ISAOs, we provided a lot of input on what the [existing] ISACs could be doing better and they ignored it," according to the source.

"After fifteen years," the source said in late 2015, "this is the worst I've ever seen it on government–industry partnership" on security issues.

Questions about the Obama administration's commitment to a "voluntary" approach emanated from a few corners of the largely unregulated technology sector. Stakeholders from heavily regulated communities such as telecom, finance, or energy were often quicker to praise the NIST framework and other initiatives.

For them, any commitment to an industry-driven, risk-management approach was a breath of fresh air.

"Was the framework a distraction? No way," said a telecom industry source who was closely involved in the NIST process. "You have to remember, we were just coming off Lieberman–Collins, which was a very prescriptive approach to the policy. This, by contrast, was collaborative, it was industry-driven."

Participants enjoyed the NIST framework process, the source asserted. The blowup aimed at DHS during the San Diego workshop was the only negative moment at those meetings over the course of a full year, this source said. "I've never seen that before in government—a truly productive dialogue over a year."

The two points of view, from two industry representatives on the front lines of cyber policy, reflected an unsettled conflict over philosophy when it came to government and industry roles. There were plenty of practical, tangible problems as well.

On the question of how the federal government organized itself, the verdict was already in by 2016—and it was not a positive one. The government was structured extremely poorly to take on the challenge of cybersecurity and virtually all of the stakeholders knew it.

The Department of Homeland Security had the biggest piece of jurisdictional pie, but cybersecurity was just a small part of the department's responsibilities. DHS was an amalgamation of functions whose leaders, going back to the last years of the George W. Bush administration, saw cyber as a potential "win" area. The department desperately needed a success story as it was frequently hammered over issues like the porous border with Mexico and incompetent TSA officers at the nation's airports. But the department's culture was jumbled, its morale low, and mission confused.

DHS's priorities could shift with the political winds. The secretary of homeland security generally had to answer to the president about immigration and transportation security before the conversation ever got around to cybersecurity. Questions surrounding an expensive new campus that would bring together the department's disparate elements often got more attention from Congress than cybersecurity.

DHS needed a win, but it was reasonable to conclude by 2016 that its focus should be terrestrial, and on security at the shoreline and in the skies.

As an alternative, the security of the nation's computer networks and digital life could be in the hands of a new Department of Cybersecurity. Much of the government restructuring discussion during the early years of the Obama administration centered on the supposed need for a legally empowered cybersecurity "czar" within the White House apparatus. The existing White House coordinator position was often portrayed as toothless, though Michael Daniel gave it real power through his collaborative and evangelical efforts.

Creation of a cybersecurity department would obviate the need for a new structure within the White House.

It would, however, raise its own set of issues. "First and foremost," Hathaway observed, "you slow things down. Nothing else goes away and you create a new layer of bureaucracy. You have to merge multiple cultures and we saw how well that worked at DHS."

Hathaway spent substantial time pondering whether a new department was worthwhile and how it would work. Existing entities at other agencies that were "drivers of Internet policy" would have to be folded into a cyber department, she said. That would include the National Telecommunications and Information Administration at the Commerce Department, the Information Assurance Directorate at the National Security Agency, and the State Department's cybersecurity office.

There were ways to bring logic to the government's organization on cyber, Hathaway determined, but the practical downsides argued against building up an entirely new department.

"A Department of Cybersecurity would be threatening to some," commented an industry lobbyist. "People would say, 'What are they going to do to us?'"

A stand-alone department would face tremendous pressure to justify its existence. Many on the industry side believed that would translate into pursuit of a far-reaching regulatory regime insinuating itself into every corner of the U.S. economy.

And on Capitol Hill, DHS had supporters who believed the department was on the right trajectory. Sen. Tom Carper, for one, said strong leadership under Secretary Jeh Johnson and deputies like Phyllis Schneck was creating an environment that brought in more talent. The DHS workforce law passed in late 2014 was beginning to show results, in terms of effective recruitment, by the fall of 2015, Carper said.

New laws made clear that DHS could force improvements at other agencies and the department's cyber information-sharing center now had real operational capacity. "The federal government is as challenged by hacks as other sectors of the economy," Carper said. "We have had a huge struggle to define responsibilities. We want all of the agencies to straighten up and fly right, and we want for DHS to drive the improvements."

But greater focus and attention to the cyber mission were badly needed. As an alternative to a new department, the U.S. Chamber of Commerce's (Chamber) Matthew Eggers suggested DHS's authority should be allowed to "sunset," with Congress stepping back to analyze the various pieces and decide what should be appropriately housed within a centralized homeland security structure.

Departmental reauthorizations are fairly routine in Congress: periodic reviews of mission, authority, and budgeting, performed by the committees that oversee each federal department. Congress has passed a reauthorization bill for the Defense Department every year since the landmark national security overhaul of 1947, which put the structural pieces in place for the government to fight a Cold War.

But by 2016, the Department of Homeland Security had never been through the exercise since its inception in 2002. At the beginning of each new year, the leaders of the House and Senate homeland security panels would declare that DHS reauthorization was a high priority; inevitably it would slide off the calendar. Reauthorization of DHS would be an extremely complicated, time-consuming endeavor, and there were other priorities.

"We don't need a whole new bureaucracy while we do need more focused attention on cybersecurity" within the existing department, Eggers said. Congress could, perhaps, tackle this in a reauthorization process. The challenges of securing cyberspace in the twenty-first century were different from the Cold War challenges of the mid-twentieth century, but the implications could be similar. In any case, the U.S. government was short-changing itself and its citizens by failing to confront the question of how it should line up to effectively pursue cybersecurity.

The government's organizational shortcomings went beyond the problems at DHS.

For one thing, the Obama administration often inadequately expressed its cybersecurity priorities in the annual budget submission to Congress. Any president's budget document was often viewed as a worthless anachronism, dissected and quickly discarded on Capitol Hill. But it was an administration's chief policy tool for organizing its mission and priorities. The Obama budget submissions reflected an emphasis on cybersecurity in the raw numbers, but frequently represented a missed chance to demonstrate the "whole of enterprise" approach to cyber that the administration was demanding of the private sector.

The federal budget could show how a large organization instills security and risk management into both its operations and philosophy. Instead, cybersecurity elements were typically siloed throughout the budget, popping up discretely in documents for each federal agency. There was no directive for managers at different levels of the executive branch to include cybersecurity in their decision-making processes. The Obama administration, meanwhile, was urging that very cultural change on the private sector.

The omissions suggested how easily cybersecurity considerations were trumped by other factors. Corporate managers were well aware of that tension; government officials were often reluctant to acknowledge it might be a legitimate problem for businesses. To its credit, the Obama administration's final budget, proposed in February 2016, included a much more coherent approach to cybersecurity.

By 2016, Congress desperately needed to step up its game on cybersecurity as well.

"Knowledge is a mile wide and an inch deep in Congress," Carper observed. "It's not an issue well understood by generalists, and we are generalists in Congress." Further, Carper said, often times the technologists who do grasp all the nuances of the issue don't do a very good job of explaining it to non-expert audiences, such as a hearing-room full of lawmakers.

A first step, which lawmakers continued to resist, would be streamlining the congressional cybersecurity oversight process through a consolidation of committee jurisdiction, or perhaps by chartering a multi-committee task force. Creation of a new Department of Cybersecurity would produce a logical imperative to engage in congressional reform and help accomplish this. But in the absence of a new department, it still seemed reasonable that lawmakers could self-motivate to clean up their own lines of authority.

"We have overlapping jurisdiction among the Homeland Security, Intelligence, and Judiciary committees, you saw that on FISA [reform of the Foreign Intelligence Surveillance Act] and you see that on info-sharing," a House source said. "Cybersecurity is now a big-ticket item, and as a result, a lot of committees are interested in creating their own turf."

Depending on who was doing the counting, anywhere from eighty-eight to over one hundred congressional committees and subcommittees claimed jurisdiction over cybersecurity issues. DHS officials, careful not to insult the lawmakers who fed their department, would cautiously acknowledge the tremendous amount of time and energy that went into preparing for congressional hearings on cybersecurity and responding to members' requests for information. Consolidation would be nice, senior DHS officials would respond when asked at congressional hearings.

That would involve someone ceding authority over a hot legislative issue. Disputes between the House Homeland Security and the Oversight and Government Reform committees almost sank legislation to strengthen the security of government computer networks in 2014. Consolidation wouldn't be easy.

Whether or not there would be a Department of Cybersecurity, Congress could create dedicated committees on cybersecurity in the House and Senate.

Other congressional panels would continue to delve into cyber issues. The banking committees wouldn't stop looking at financial-sector cybersecurity under such an approach, nor would the transportation committees drop their oversight of the Coast Guard's quite advanced cyber activities. But one committee in each chamber could be empowered to consider cybersecurity issues every week. It could demand accountability from all corners of the federal bureaucracy, not merely those within the narrow jurisdiction of a typical congressional committee.

A look at the homeland security committees' agenda for any given week offered a hint at why this would be desirable.

Border controls, foreign fighters, DHS contracting, regulatory reform, first responders, bioterrorism, government fuel purchase programs, drug trafficking—any and all of these subjects could occupy the homeland security panels' agenda.

The congressional homeland security committees had the same problem as the Department of Homeland Security: responsibility for a vast range of policy issues, covering topics as disparate as allowing passengers to carry shampoo bottles onto commercial airplanes to the care of children brought illegally into the country. Cyber was but a drop in this Olympic-sized pool of duties and troubles.

There was nothing new about the idea of reforming the twentieth-century lines of congressional oversight to recognize the twenty-first-century challenge of cybersecurity. The Aspen Institute amplified the call for reform in the fall of 2013, in a report by a task force led by former Rep. Lee Hamilton (D-Indiana) and former New Jersey Gov. Thomas Kean (R). The retired politicians previously chaired the national commission on 9/11 and had extensive ties and strong credibility on Capitol Hill.

Other prominent voices on security policy weighed in at regular intervals with a clear message: Congress must face up to the need to reorganize around cybersecurity.

"Republican and Democratic leaders need to sit down around a table before the next Congress and say enough is enough," former DHS Secretary Tom Ridge testified in 2013. "We need to consolidate responsibilities so a small group of House members and senators have jurisdiction over DHS."

Former Rep. Jane Harman (D-California), a veteran of the Intelligence and Homeland Security committees, said reorganizing congressional oversight is "absolutely essential and painful to do."

Harman noted, "People in this institution earned their power through their committee positions." Leaders would have to mandate changes that would shrink the authority of some of their members, an unpleasant task. "I don't think we should reorganize the deck chairs [at DHS] but if we can reorganize Congress, this country will be safer," Harman said.

Sen. John McCain repeatedly called for creation of a select committee on cybersecurity; he stopped issuing that call when he assumed the chairmanship of the Armed Services Committee in January 2015, inheriting his own piece of cyber turf.

Reorganizing Congress would be tough, but it wasn't any tougher than asking business leaders to reorient their entire management approach to account for cybersecurity.

"We can't afford any more delay on these issues," Carper said of the broad array of cybersecurity challenges in the summer of 2015. "In the coming days, Congress needs to step up and get to work."

Carper was speaking directly to cyber legislation pending at the time, but even that was easier said than done, in part due to Congress's entrenched existing organizational structure, and in part due to the short attention spans endemic to lawmakers.

Carper saw another way of dealing with this problem: a task force comprised of leaders from the many committees of jurisdiction, empowered by the Senate leadership to forge legislative answers to cybersecurity challenges. "We're often plagued by jurisdictional battles," Carper said. "What we need is a majority leader and minority leader working together to create a task force, so all of these committees don't act as free agents."

Carper summed up his preferred approach: "We need leaders to lead and work together. If they do, we will follow."

New lines of authority certainly wouldn't resolve one of the biggest problems facing Congress: its tendency to "fight the last war" when it came to policymaking. To wit, the vast majority of energy expended on Capitol Hill in recent years on cybersecurity policy was devoted to the information-sharing debate. But observers like Larry Clinton, Robert Dix, and Scott Algeier of the Information Technology Information Sharing and Analysis Center (IT-ISAC) long cautioned that this was just an aspect, a tool, even as they welcomed the related liability protection.

"These efforts are focused on mature companies that can digest information and afford to engage in machine-to-machine automated sharing," Algeier explained. "That doesn't work for smaller entities."

Instead, he said, "we should spend a lot more time on creating a national capability. We need a strategy for enhanced situational awareness nationally."

Information sharing was a tool but it was often portrayed as a goal in and of itself. What was missing, Algeier said, was a unified national strategy that recognized the different needs and abilities of different types of enterprises. "We need concise reports on what to look for, of use to even the small guys—good old-fashioned PDFs," Algeier said.

That was not in the works yet, by the beginning of 2016. "We've proposed ways to do this through the IT-ISAC," Algeier said, "and all we hear is silence."

Others were even more skeptical of lawmakers' focus on information sharing and openly lamented Congress's misplaced priorities. The Center for Democracy and Technology's (CDT) Greg Nojeim said: "We've objected from the outset to the premise of the [information-sharing] bill—preempting all law in the service of cybersecurity. They're not going to change that."

Nojeim agreed there was a "flaw" in the current law that prohibited companies from sharing information for the purposes of helping others' protect their networks and assets, but he said that could be addressed through a much narrower fix. An information-sharing bill, structured along the lines of legislation offered every year from 2012 to 2015, would never be acceptable to the privacy community.

"The surgery on this bill that would be required would be so significant that you wouldn't recognize the bill afterward," Nojeim said.

This was going to provoke a running battle, and stakeholders might want to consider the cost-benefit ratio.

It wasn't just digital privacy activists who were dismissive of the massive time and effort put into the information-sharing debate.

"I don't think it will be useful," Hathaway said of a new information-sharing law. "How does a company get data? Is it data that's useful to them? Is the use to raise their defenses or just to help them qualify for cyber insurance?"

If company officials needed security clearances to access the data, the program wouldn't be scalable across the economy, she said. If it offered blanket immunity for sharing, the incentive to improve one's own cyber defenses would be undermined.

Would the information-sharing law do anything to adjust the economic calculus companies had to make before investing in cybersecurity? Larry Clinton didn't think so. It could improve industry's view of the cyber threatscape, but how many companies would participate in the scheme—and could a small- or mid-sized company (SMB) even make use of the information? The answer was probably no, Clinton believed, unless those companies had a better economic rationale for investing in cybersecurity. And that rationale needed to be developed as part of an overall national strategy on cybersecurity.

Passage of an information-sharing law would be, at best, just an element of such a strategy. Congress, in its wending way, had settled on a solution, but the question had already changed.

And other critics went further, usually requesting anonymity to do so.

"I personally believe that government information sharing regarding cybersecurity is a joke," our observer Lazlo, from the technology security community, said in the spring of 2015, off-the-record. "Many of us in the security community are already sharing intelligence. We don't need a bill to do this."

The leading legislation in Congress created problems, not solutions.

> I personally believe any cyber information-sharing bill expands unnecessary and unfruitful government surveillance, violates our fourth amendment rights, and severely impacts our First Amendment rights. Government information sharing isn't worth the price of our freedom and the dystopian world of having Big Brother. Let's leave that to Russia and China on their own citizens, not America. There you have it.

And, Lazlo added with a wry smile, "so does the NSA."

That's just government. Amid the political foibles and stalemates, business initiatives were moving ahead fitfully.

There were positive signs—developments, in fact, that might've been seen as astounding even a few short years before. Business representatives said this wasn't fully appreciated in the policymaking realm as 2016 dawned.

Larry Clinton saw a major evolution in business's outlook on cyber issues by the spring of 2015. While Clinton continued to bemoan the inability of government, at various levels and branches, to grasp the need for an economic dialogue on cybersecurity, corporate leaders were pushing ahead, he said.

And Clinton had evidence. En route to a June meeting of the North Carolina branch of the National Association of Corporate Directors, Clinton paused to discuss the "great thirst" for information about cybersecurity coming from the upper reaches of corporations.

"This is my sixth event with corporate boards in the last six months," according to Clinton, whose day job also required him to pay close attention to everything cyber that might be brewing in Congress and the federal bureaucracy. But what was happening out in corporate America, from the big firms to the smaller ones, clearly was energizing Clinton. He'd spent over thirteen years at the Internet Security Alliance (ISA) by this point, and had done his turn of duty on Capitol Hill. Clinton, in short, was a man who could distinguish between policy public relations, meant to please this or that audience for the short term, and a real evolution that was going to change the way people did business in the United States.

On cybersecurity, "the corporate people are starting to think about this in a much more sophisticated fashion than some inside the Beltway," according to Clinton.

Part of this stemmed from "an epiphany" that occurred within the business community, perhaps since 2014, that cyber attacks were inevitable and the real question was about risk management. "We're maturing in this space and industry is often ahead of the government policymakers," Clinton said.

Initiatives were sprouting across cyber policy areas and industry sectors. The U.S. Chamber of Commerce frequently updated the list of initiatives underway to use and build upon the NIST framework of standards. Automakers, chemical makers, the communications sector, electricity, gas, IT, water works, mutual funds, oil, retail, hotel keepers—they were all implementing cyber programs based on the NIST framework.

Of interest to executives in all industries, the leaders of the insurance sector were moving ahead with new products, but also with plans for deepening relationships with clients that could lead to dramatic new approaches to corporate cybersecurity strategy. This was a development the Obama White House and Department of Homeland Security had fervently hoped for as an essential companion to the NIST framework and other initiatives flowing out of the 2013 executive order.

In short, insurers could use their access and leverage to push companies to improve cybersecurity, probably in a more efficient and less-intrusive way than could be accomplished through government regulation.

Peter Hancock, president and CEO of American International Group (AIG), in April 2015 gave a seminal speech on what insurers could offer beyond merely "shouldering" a portion of companies' cyber risks. Major insurers were in a unique place to pull together "collective intelligence" on the cyber threat environment, Hancock said, in what was something of a manifesto on cyber from the insurance perspective.

The insurance industry could nudge discussions on broader economic-societal issues such as a possible over-reliance on digital interconnectivity. For instance, whether all of the data within an enterprise should be interconnected required "strategic thinking" and not just a decision by the IT office, Hancock said. An enlightened insurer could raise such an issue with a corporate executive, who otherwise might have allowed a critical internal cybersecurity policy decision to be made by default.

Insurers had a role to play in discussions around other strategic issues like encryption and deterrence, Hancock said. On the latter, Hancock said "going after the bad guys" is an expensive proposition for an insurance company, but legal and other actions undertaken by insurers could have a strong deterrent effect that would pay dividends over time. He predicted more efforts in this area. Further, insurers' willingness to provide more and more comprehensive types of cyber coverage would rise along with the maturity of their customers' efforts to fend off cyber threats, Hancock said.

Insurers were self-motivated, to be sure, but their sophisticated curiosity about how industry was approaching its cyber needs was a positive development that suggested the market would in fact be able to produce answers. DHS frequently tried aligning itself to progress in the insurance industry as it attempted to demonstrate the effectiveness of its own initiatives to support the private sector. But insurers had sorted out the needs and opportunities on their own, a good thing in a policy environment so dependent on the initiatives and follow-through of private industry.

But were the high-profile industry commitments to enhanced cybersecurity really enough?

There were lots of discussions about the appropriate metrics to answer that question, but what it boiled down to would be extremely difficult to measure. We could add up the initiatives and meetings, but did it really reflect an internalization, on a broad enough scale, of the type of risk management mind-set that would be needed going forward?

ISA's Clinton declared himself an optimist, though perhaps a qualified optimist.

"The progress in industry isn't that companies are hiring more IT people," Clinton said. "It's that boards are engaged and taking a sophisticated approach to risk management. These are big issues, and if we allow ourselves to focus on the small issues, we won't make the kind of progress we need to make."

Here was the qualification: "The system itself is getting technologically weaker," Clinton warned in the spring of 2015. "The attackers are getting better. The economics are increasing the motivation to attack."

The campaign to raise awareness of the cybersecurity challenge, in corporate boardrooms, congressional offices, and across the federal government, had the makings of a success story. But Clinton and others knew more was needed and that the campaign to secure the nation's critical infrastructure and Americans' digital lives had only just begun. As Clinton said frequently to government and business audiences, cybersecurity was an economic challenge and the government still hadn't gotten around to figuring out an incentive structure that would help industry invest wisely.

"Small-ball is not going to get it done," Clinton warned.

But tackling the large-scale economic factors consistently proved beyond the reach of elected officials and bureaucrats alike. DHS's work on providing incentives barely got off the ground. On Capitol Hill, the debate continued on whether any additional incentives were needed at all.

Republicans and Democrats in late 2015 tangled over the relatively narrow question of whether to provide companies with some legal protection on cyber through an anti-terrorism law known as the SAFETY Act. Would such coverage incentivize companies to improve cybersecurity or to sit on their hands?

Rep. John Ratcliffe, who chaired a cybersecurity subcommittee, said the SAFETY Act could help ensure "the costly threat of litigation" doesn't inhibit improvements in cybersecurity. But Rep. James Langevin suggested private-sector system administrators still weren't widely adopting even the simple "best practices," like two-step authentication, and questioned the purpose of using the SAFETY Act. Liability protection under the act could dissuade companies from pursuing new technologies and best practices, Langevin said.

If this question—access to a limited government insurance program—triggered such a debate, it seemed extremely unlikely that the government would be able to provide more impactful economic incentives. And why should the government? asked many Democratic lawmakers including Langevin. Companies had economic and reputational self-interest as a powerful motivator to improve cybersecurity. Langevin felt that should be backed by regulation, not tax breaks or other carrots to do what was necessary in any case.

Regardless, the political system wasn't in a place to begin mandating cyber regulations as 2016 dawned. "The government shouldn't even begin to think of imposing standards on the private sector until it can maintain the security of its own systems," House Intelligence Chairman Nunes said pointedly.

So, much of the policy responsibility would remain in private hands. And it remained to be seen if this would work out.

Addressing the congressional and executive branch organizational questions, and filling out the teams of skilled professionals needed to protect cyberspace, might be the easy parts. We've only begun to get into the most vexing and intractable cybersecurity policy challenges. These span the policy horizon from the impact of new technologies on policy choices to how cybersecurity shapes the United States' most critical global relationship: the partnership, competition, and outright conflict with China in cyberspace.

From China to encryption, the U.S. political system and stakeholders from multiple industries, academia, civil liberties groups, and elsewhere must formulate policies that get beyond reactive scrambles to avert disaster in the moment. In all of these policy areas, the collaborative approach taken in the NIST framework process could be instructive, but it was not a panacea. It was risk management, a mind-set, and the government and private sector were placing a huge bet that this strategy would propel innovation while also protecting the crown jewels of the U.S. economy.

It had to be embraced and used, internalized into organizations' very DNA. By the end of 2015, some of the NIST framework's biggest advocates in the private sector were growing concerned about the potential for complacency to seep in. Industry efforts launched in late 2015 to revitalize and further spread the word about the framework reflected more than a desire to make the program work; they represented an intrinsic understanding that policy would be made in this area, and this was industry's one chance to be the author of that policy.

Addressing cybersecurity required nothing less than a cultural change, a dramatic evolution in the public's conception of cyberspace. It required an understanding that there was probably no technical answer that would solve the problem, as smart as America's technologists were and as innovative as the technology industry proved itself to be. It required an enduring commitment to address the issue every day across enterprises. It also might require the government telling industry it must take action, while somehow leaving the details to people who knew more about making this work than did the folks within the federal bureaucracy.

From the emerging "Internet of Things"—and the accompanying, science fiction-like security challenges linked to smart refrigerators and everything else—to the question of how to deter hostile foes in cyberspace, unsettled policy questions were multiplying. And there was no answer, yet, as to whether our leaders, political structures, and business structures could successfully respond to the preeminent security challenge of the twenty-first century. Cybersecurity was in a place, perhaps, not unlike environmental policy in the early 1970s. Then, as now, there was a growing bipartisan consensus on the gravity of the situation and the need to do something on a grand policy scale. Then, as now, the early structures for carrying out policy were being created. Then, as now, there was an evolving democratization of the policy discourse.

Democratization, in the case of cyber, suggested an influential role for small technology and strategic consulting firms—well beyond that of bottom feeders, picking up contract crumbs at the end of a massive corporation's supply chain. In this case, smaller tech and consulting firms could play the essential role of providing services that allow small businesses to secure their own systems. John Abeles's System1, Ola Sage's eManagement, and many others intrinsically understood the needs of so-called SMBs, because they themselves were from that community. They could inform small businesses on their cybersecurity status, elevate their practices, and help secure a vulnerable flank on the cyber battlefield. But Abeles, Sage, and others in this space pointed out that many of their clients had extremely limited resources to focus on cybersecurity. Most companies do not have a dedicated IT person. This would take resources and a commitment from government as well as the private sector.

The policy discourse spread outward in the 1970s to the general public. Remember the 1971 advertising campaign featuring Native American actor Iron Eyes Cody with a tear running down his check? That advertisement, arguably, helped make "environmentalism" a mainstream position in the 1970s. The "Smokey Bear" campaign envisioned by Danielle Kriz and Robert Dix could have a similar impact for cybersecurity. Basic cyber hygiene could become the default setting for the average citizen, just as the vast majority of citizens today wouldn't dream of tossing trash out their car window.

And this time, on this issue, there remained a chance that the policy discourse wouldn't eventually dissolve into the kind of zero-sum politics that took over environmental policy—and most other policy areas—in the nation's capital by the start of the 1990s. This time, perhaps the policy would advance with less overt, some would say onerous and intrusive, regulation and less willingness to cluster into camps of conflict rather into collaborative workshops.

"Voluntary" might come to be accepted as an impermanent state of being that could endure only with constant nurturing and attention from government and industry alike. The threat of regulation and the constant policy accordion of more or less pressure from government might always be there.

And that's because there would always be more than one way of doing this. Policymakers could, for example, look to a tool like the "critical controls" managed and updated by the independent Center for Internet Security. The center, led by former DHS deputy secretary Jane Holl Lute, said its goal was to "create a world in which best practice becomes common practice." Sometimes that could be accomplished through mandatory regulation. Lawmakers like Jim Langevin and some officials within the White House posited that the center's top-ten controls, or a subset, could provide the basis for a regulatory framework. Those controls are incorporated into the voluntary NIST framework; some believe they could be plucked out and applied as mandatory rules for industry.

That would have a profound impact on the policy ecosystem, of course, for good or ill.

Regulation was one road that could be taken. "There's another possible outcome," said the telecom industry source. "The market takes off" around tools and processes such as the NIST framework. The supply-and-demand equation increasingly could lead the private sector to drive the needed cybersecurity improvements, with government figuring out its place in a supporting role.

By late 2015, major technology and defense companies were quietly planning to use the NIST framework as the chief tool for enterprise-level cyber risk management and cloud security. They would use the "profiles" section of the framework, which allowed users to match their state of security to different tiers and plot a plan for improvement, as the basis for its cloud security program. NIST had deliberately left vague the details of the profiles section, in hopes that companies would pick it up and give it an effective real-world definition.

"The key for the framework is getting top level buy-in to drive the culture throughout the entity," the telecom source said. The big companies' work on the framework "profiles" could create a cybersecurity accountability method that went well beyond anything government could mandate in terms of swaying behavior. "It's a fascinating idea," the telecom source said, "to hold executives accountable for cybersecurity through the profiles. A few large companies doing that will have a huge impact."

The policy needs would change at astonishing speeds. The responses would be varied. And they needed to be developed in places like the classrooms on college campuses coopted by NIST during the framework development process. A broad, ongoing, democratic, and nondiscriminatory discussion was needed, because cybersecurity posed a broad, ongoing, democratic, and nondiscriminatory threat.

The precise answers weren't clear by 2016 and they will never be entirely clear. Some were relatively straightforward: finding ways to keep government–industry collaborations fresh and invigorated—and at the forefront of the nation's cyber strategy, for example. Cleaning up the structural lines of authority and responsibility in both Congress and the executive branch seemed achievable.

Others were more amorphous or complex, like promoting a national dialogue highlighting the enormous stakes of the cybersecurity policy debate and somehow compelling stakeholders to determine where the responsibilities of government, companies, and citizens begin and end. Determining responsibilities entailed determining who would shoulder what portions of the massive cost of cybersecurity.

The important thing was posing the right questions, to the right audiences, in a spirit of collaboration. It was absolutely crucial to find a way to keep cybersecurity as a front-of-mind issue—on Capitol Hill and in the White House, in corporate boardrooms and even around kitchen tables.

Because the hacks would keep coming.

"I spent a lot of time tracking Soviet submarines in a P-3 Orion," Carper would recall of his military service in the Cold War. "There was always a huge change in the technology of the subs and our adversaries were always changing up what they were doing."

Carper reflected: "It's very similar today in cybersecurity, the adversary is always changing up. We still have a problem with that."

Successful businesses are known for their adaptability to changing environments. The most effective lawmakers adjust and adapt in order to tease policy solutions through a legislative system prone to stalemate and inertia. Presidents, cabinet secretaries, and policymakers throughout government hammer away at a message until it takes hold. Then try to do it all over again as the policy environment changes.

Cybersecurity is a policy problem that will not drift away. An informed citizenry could engage and demand answers; enlightened leaders in both government and the private sector could respond with energy and innovation. But cybersecurity, and cyber threats, are now a permanent feature of the governing, political, and economic landscape.

Our elected leaders, our government, and our companies and industries should be judged by how effectively they manage this risk and limit the disruptions. But the threat will not go away and the attacks won't stop. Answers must be crafted around that reality.

AUTHOR'S NOTE

In the summer of 2012, as one cybersecurity debate was coming to a heated, inconclusive and temporary end in the Senate, I was working on a variety of energy, health, trade, and defense policy issues at Inside Washington Publishers (IWP), and keeping an eye on my old stomping grounds on Capitol Hill. After fourteen years of immersion in congressional politics, as a reporter and senior editor at *National Journal*'s *CongressDaily* and editor-in-chief of *Roll Call*, I was back at IWP, where I'd gotten my first break in journalism in the pre-digital days.

Cybersecurity wasn't part of my beat in 2012, but the issue kept popping up in each of IWP's core coverage areas. Together with Rick Weber and Dan Dupont, who helped lead the environment/energy and defense groups, respectively, we began exploring how our company could provide IWP's professional readership with useful information on emerging cyber policy.

The result was InsideCybersecurity.com, the first news service devoted entirely to how cyber policy was evolving in Congress and the federal bureaucracy. Much of the day-to-day coverage detailed in this book draws from my reporting for InsideCybersecurity.com.

I am deeply indebted to IWP owner and founder Alan Sosenko—first, for hiring me as a cub reporter in 1989, for his support in launching the cyber news service in 2013, and in his backing for this book. Alan has been a champion of investigative reporting and deep-dive explorations of federal policy for over thirty years. Alan and CEO Robert Harrelson have been enormously supportive of InsideCybersecurity.com, while providing strong, consistent backing for all of the immensely talented teams of journalists at IWP. I hope this book can serve as a modest testament to the "IWP way" that Alan pioneered.

Rick Weber and Dan Dupont contributed mightily to the concept behind InsideCybersecurity.com and to its execution. Christopher J. Castelli has been an outstanding reporter for the news service who has provided unparalleled coverage of policy development at the Homeland Security and Defense departments, and on explosive topics such as cyber deterrence. Joshua Higgins provided much of our coverage of cyber policy development in agencies such as the Department of Transportation. Their reporting and insights have been invaluable in informing this work.

I would also like to thank Hugo Gurdon, editor of the *Washington Examiner*, who invited me to write a column about cybersecurity policy. Hugo realized early on the transformational impact cybersecurity issues were having across the federal policy realm. Some material in these pages is based on columns I wrote for the *Examiner*.

The material in this book draws from exclusive interviews by the author and my running coverage and analysis of policy development. Content originally reported by my InsideCybersecurity.com colleagues is noted. Other material comes from multiple news sources and is attributed in the text of the book. Likewise, research material, government documents, and law firm blog posts are cited and the sources are attributed.

Sources have many motivations for speaking with journalists, but I would like to especially thank everyone who took time to speak with me and help explain the nuances and significance of cybersecurity developments. Particular thanks to Sen. Tom Carper and Rep. Mike McCaul; Robert Mayer, Matthew Eggers, Larry Clinton, Brian Finch, Danielle Kriz, Robert Dix, Scott Algeier, Karl Schimmeck, Jim Linn, Ola Sage, and John Abeles, among many others in the business community; the team at the National Institute of Standards and Technology (NIST), including Adam Sedgewick, Matt Scholl, Kevin Stine, and Donna Dodson; many high-ranking veterans of government including Bruce McConnell and Melissa Hathaway; from the digital privacy world Gabe Rottman and Greg Nojeim; Rochelle Cohen at the Federal Communications Commission (FCC); numerous helpful and conscientious staffers on Capitol Hill, including Jennie Westbrook, Tom Mentzer, Jack Langer, April Ward, and many others who politely declined to be publicly identified; and all the other sources who offered such valuable insights.

Beyond any short-term calculations, it's clear they were all motivated by a strong desire to bring clarity to an extremely complicated, extremely important issue. Without exception, these sources repeatedly stressed the need for the public to understand what was at stake and what policy options were actually available. Amid numerous policy differences, hopefully I've faithfully presented their views.

Charlie Mitchell
December 2015

BIBLIOGRAPHICAL ESSAY

FOREWORD

The *New York Post* first reported the hack of CIA Director John Brennan's personal e-mail account:http://nypost.com/2015/10/18/stoner-high-school-student-says-he-hacked-the-cia/.

The U.S. government defines cybersecurity on the Department of Homeland Security's Web site at:https://niccs.us-cert.gov/awareness/cybersecurity-101.

The nation's sixteen critical infrastructure sectors are described at:http://www.dhs.gov/critical-infrastructure-sectors.

Rep. Mac Thornberry of Texas discussed the cybersecurity challenge in a statement on the 2011 "Recommendations of the House Republican Cybersecurity Task Force":http://thornberry.house.gov/issues/issue/default.aspx?IssueID=44735.

The 2014 annual report of the FBI Internet Crime Complaint Center can be found here:https://www.ic3.gov/media/annualreport/2014_IC3Report.pdf.

The annual IBM-Ponemon Institute Cost of Data Breach Study can be found here:http://www-03.ibm.com/security/data-breach/.

PriceWaterhouseCooper's 2015 assessment of the cost of cyber crime can be found at:http://www.pwc.com/en_US/us/increasing-it-effectiveness/publications/assets/2015-us-cybercrime-survey.pdf.

Larry Zelvin, then director of the Department of Homeland Security's National Cybersecurity and Communications Integration Center discussed the 2013–2014 cyber attack environment in a May 21, 2014, appearance before the House Homeland Security Committee.

NBC News on July 30, 2015, carried an exclusive report on a "secret" National Security Agency map showing the location of Chinese cyber penetrations in the United States, available here:http://www.nbcnews.com/news/us-news/exclusive-secret-nsa-map-shows-china-cyber-attacks-us-targets-n401211.

On August 10, NBC News followed up with an exclusive report that "China's cyber spies" had infiltrated the White House email system:http://www.nbcnews.com/news/us-news/china-read-emails-top-us-officials-n406046.

Lloyd's 2015 report "Business Blackout," on the potential costs of an attack on the U.S. electric grid, can be found here:http://www.lloyds.com/~/media/files/news%20and%20insight/risk%20insight/2015/business%20blackout/business%20blackout20150708.pdf.

Sen. Charles Grassley (R-Iowa) discussed cybersecurity in a September 2014 speech at Iowa State University, which the author highlighted in a column for the *Carroll Daily Times Herald*:http://carrollspaper.com/Content/Opinion-Archive/Opinion/Article/Cybersecurity-Awareness-Stop-Think-Connect/4/4/18823.

Comments by Dave Oxner of the Securities Industry and Financial Management Association are from an August 17, 2015, interview with the author.

Director of National Intelligence James Clapper discussed the cyber threat environment at a September 10, 2015, hearing of the House Intelligence Committee:http://intelligence.house.gov/sites/intelligence.house.gov/files/documents/ClapperOpening09102015.pdf.

CHAPTER I

Quote from North Korean hackers threatening Sony Pictures, as reported by Breitbart News:http://www.breitbart.com/big-hollywood/2014/12/08/hackers-blackmail-sony-pull-the-interview-or-else/.

Blog on House homepage of Rep. James Langevin:http://langevin.house.gov/2nd-district/langevin-hits-rhode/winter-2014-15.

Sen. Bill Nelson (D-Florida) and National Institute of Standards and Technology discussed the effectiveness of the NIST cybersecurity framework at a February 4 Senate Commerce Committee hearing covered by the author for InsideCybersecurity.com.

The FBI on December 19, 2014, issued a statement on the Sony Pictures breach available here:https://www.fbi.gov/news/pressrel/press-releases/update-on-sony-investigation.

Interviews by the author with Sens. Ron Johnson (R-Wisconsin) and Saxby Chambliss (R-Georgia), and with Gabriel Rottman of the American Civil Liberties Union, originally published in part in InsideCybersecurity.com.

Gen. Martin Dempsey discussed cyber vulnerabilities in a February 19, 2015 speech reported on by InsideCybersecurity.com's Christopher J. Castelli.

The author covered then-McAfee executive Phyllis Schneck's July 2013 congressional testimony for InsideCybersecurity.com.

White House cybersecurity coordinator Michael Daniel explained at a January 14, 2014, "cybersecurity summit" sponsored by the Global Law Forum how he was approaching cyber information sharing, covered by the author for InsideCybersecurity.com.

Attorney Brian Finch of the Pillsbury Winthrop Shaw Pittman law firm discussed the fallout from the Snowden leaks in an April 7, 2015, interview with the author.

Sen. Chambliss discussed cybersecurity issues at a September 11, 2014, Ripon Society breakfast and in a brief interview afterward with InsideCybersecurity.com.

Gabriel Rottman of the ACLU discussed his view of problems with cybersecurity legislation in an interview with InsideCybersecurity.com.

CHAPTER 2

President Obama's May 29, 2009, speech on cybersecurity can be found here:https://www.whitehouse.gov/the-press-office/remarks-president-securing-our-nations-cyber-infrastructure.

The *Wall Street Journal* reported on April 8, 2009 on the penetration of the electric power grid:http://www.wsj.com/articles/SB123914805204099085.

Melissa Hathaway, a former official in the Bush and Obama White Houses, discussed cybersecurity policy evolution in an interview with the author.

This Congressional Research Service report from March 2009 discusses elements of the George W. Bush cyber initiative declassified by the Obama administration:https://www.whitehouse.gov/files/documents/ cyber/Congressional%20Research%20Service%20-%20CNCI%20- %20Legal%20Authorities%20and%20Policy%20Considerations%20%2 8March%202009%29.pdf.

Information on the Obama administration's initial cyberspace policy initiatives can be found here:https://www.whitehouse.gov/assets/ documents/Cyberspace_Policy_Review_final.pdf.

And   here:https://www.whitehouse.gov/issues/foreign-policy/ cybersecurity/national-initiative.

The Center for Strategic and International Studies's influential report on cybersecurity for the forty-fourth presidency can be found here:http:// csis.org/files/media/csis/pubs/081208_securingcyberspace_44.pdf.

Bruce McConnell's comments throughout the chapter are from an interview with the author.

The 2009 resignation of Department of Homeland Security official Rod Beckstrom was reported in the *Washington Times* on March 12, 2009:http://www.washingtontimes.com/news/2009/mar/12/cyber- security-chief-resigns-in-protest/?page=all.

The *New York Times* coverage of the 2009 Obama cybersecurity speech noting the new administration's more-public approach to the issue can be found here:http://www.nytimes.com/2009/05/30/us/politics/ 30cyber.html?_r=0.

CHAPTER 3

Fox News in 2009 aired this report on the possibility of an Internet "kill switch" being authorized by cybersecurity legislation:http://www. foxnews.com/politics/2009/08/28/senate-president-emergency-control- internet/.

The Senate Commerce Committee would detail major breaches between 2007 and 2009 in this report:https://www.congress.gov/

congressional-report/111th-congress/senate-report/368/1?q=
%7B%22search%22%3A%5B%22s.+3480%22%5D%7D.

This *Washington Post* story examined Senate legislative efforts in 2009:http://www.washingtonpost.com/wp-dyn/content/article/2009/03/31/AR2009033103684.html.

The first Obama administration cyber proposal, released in 2011, is described here:https://www.whitehouse.gov/the-press-office/2011/05/12/fact-sheet-cybersecurity-legislative-proposal.

This report discusses the content of Sen. Rockefeller's cybersecurity proposal in 2009:https://www.congress.gov/bill/111th-congress/senate-bill/773?q=%7B%22search%22%3A%5B%22s.+773%22%5D%7D.

This report describes the content of a cyber info-sharing bill offered by Sen. John McCain (R-Arizona) as an alternative to Democratic-led efforts:https://www.congress.gov/bill/112th-congress/senate-bill/3342?q=%7B%22search%22%3A%5B%22s.+3342%22%5D%7D.

This article by the news service CSO describes the initial hearing on Sen. Joseph Lieberman's (D-Connecticut) comprehensive cyber bill:http://www.csoonline.com/article/2130936/emergency-preparedness/lieberman--cybersecurity-act-of-2012-will-help-us-protect-critical-infrastruc.html.

This *Daily Caller* article discusses the emerging Republican position against a regulatory approach to cybersecurity:http://dailycaller.com/2012/02/20/mccain-promises-gop-alternative-to-super-regulator-cybersecurity-bill/.

In the summer of 2012, partisanship seemed to take over the cybersecurity discourse on Capitol Hill, according to this *Politico* article:http://www.politico.com/story/2012/06/dems-blame-gop-on-cybersecurity-077394.

The Heritage Foundation released a highly critical assessment of the regulatory aspects of pending cyber legislation:http://www.heritage.org/research/reports/2012/07/cybersecurity-act-of-2012-revised-cyber-bill-still-has-problems.

More reports on the demise of the Senate cyber effort came from *Politico*:http://www.politico.com/news/stories/0812/79305.html.

And from the *New York Times*:http://www.nytimes.com/2012/08/03/us/politics/cybersecurity-bill-blocked-by-gop-filibuster.html?_r=0.

The U.S. Chamber of Commerce's Matthew Eggers discussed the business community's efforts in 2012 on Senate cyber legislation in an interview with the author.

CHAPTER 4

President Obama's landmark cybersecurity executive order can be read in full here:https://www.whitehouse.gov/the-press-office/2013/02/12/executive-order-improving-critical-infrastructure-cybersecurity.

The State Department hack is discussed here:http://readwrite.com/2013/02/20/anonymous-hacks-us-state-department.

The NCC Group report on global hacks is discussed here:http://thenextweb.com/insider/2012/11/12/hacking-attempts-to-pass-one-billion-in-final-quarter-of-2012-claims-information-assurance-firm/.

Bruce McConnell discussed the framework process in an interview with the author.

Matthew Eggers discussed the framework process in an interview with the author.

Melissa Hathaway discussed the framework process in an interview with the author.

Michael Daniel's comments at the RSA conference were reported on by the *Hill* newspaper:http://thehill.com/policy/technology/285095-overnight-tech-cyber-chief-asks-for-industrys-help.

Background on NIST can be found at:http://nist.gov/public_affairs/nandyou.cfm.

NIST's initial request for comment on a cybersecurity framework of standards can be found here:https://www.federalregister.gov/articles/2013/02/26/2013-04413/developing-a-framework-to-improve-critical-infrastructure-cybersecurity.

Details on the April 3, 2013, NIST workshop at the Commerce Department are from the author's notes. These are previously unpublished.

Adam Sedgewick's comments are from the author's previously unpublished notes on a May 12, 2015, panel discussion hosted by the Federal Communications Bar Association.

CNN's report on distributed denial of service attacks against banks can be found here:http://money.cnn.com/2012/09/27/technology/bank-cyberattacks/.

The White House hack was covered by the *Huffington Post*:http://
www.huffingtonpost.com/2012/10/01/white-house-hacked-cyber-_n_
1928646.html.

The *Christian Science Monitor* reported on hostile probes of the natural gas sector:http://www.csmonitor.com/USA/2012/0505/Alert-Major-
cyber-attack-aimed-at-natural-gas-pipeline-companies.

Initial industry stakeholder comments on the NIST framework can be
found here:http://csrc.nist.gov/cyberframework/rfi_comments_2013.
html.

Previously unpublished details of the NIST meeting at Carnegie Mellon were provided by Rick Weber. Adam Sedgewick later discussed the
meeting in an interview with the author for InsideCybersecurity.com.

Coverage of the NIST conference at the University of California-San
Diego was provided by the author. Some of this material was originally
reported in InsideCybersecurity.com.

The initial version of the NIST cybersecurity framework can be found
here:http://www.nist.gov/itl/upload/draft_outline_preliminary_
framework_standards.pdf.

Michael Daniel's White House blog on cyber incentives can be found
here:https://www.whitehouse.gov/blog/2013/08/06/incentives-support-
adoption-cybersecurity-framework.

The author's interviews with Brian Raymond, Adam Sedgewick, Nathan Mitchell, Larry Clinton, and Ola Sage were conducted for InsideCy-
bersecurity.com.

Coverage of the NIST workshop in Dallas was provided by InsideCy-
bersecurity.com's Dan Dupont and Rick Weber.

An article on North Carolina State University's high-tech library can
be found here:http://techincubator.ncsu.edu/2013/03/21/hunt-library-
ranked-in-the-top-25-globally/.

Coverage of industry reaction to the NIST framework was provided
by the author and reported in InsideCybersecurity.com.

The *New York Times*'s coverage of the framework release can be
found here:http://bits.blogs.nytimes.com/2014/02/12/white-house-puts-
out-critical-infrastructure-security-guide/?_r=1.

Politico's coverage of the framework's release can be found
here:http://www.politico.com/story/2014/02/cybersecurity-in-slow-lane-
one-year-after-obama-order-103307.html.

Adam Sedgewick and Matthew Barrett discussed the NIST framework eighteen months after its release in an interview with the author, originally reported in InsideCybersecurity.com.

InsideCybersecurity.com produced a special report on the NIST workshop at Tampa that can be viewed here:http://insidecybersecurity.com/specials/nist-tampa-workshop.

CHAPTER 5

The Reuters report on DHS Secretary Napolitano's August 2009 speech can be found here:http://www.reuters.com/article/2009/08/04/us-usa-cybersecurity-idUSTRE5736ZI20090804.

This article by eWeek discussed the discovery of cyber vulnerabilities in medical devices:http://www.eweek.com/security/fda-dhs-warn-medical-device-makers-hospitals-on-cyber-threats.

This article in *Wired* discusses Napolitano's efforts to bring cyber pros, including white-hat hackers, into the DHS process:http://www.wired.com/2009/06/hacker-dark-tangent-joins-dhs-security-council/.

Napolitano's resignation speech was covered by the *Washington Post*:http://www.washingtonpost.com/blogs/federal-eye/wp/2013/08/28/janet-napolitano-bids-farewell-to-department-of-homeland-security/.

Comments by Bruce McConnell and Sen. Tom Carper (D-Delaware) about DHS's cybersecurity leadership ranks were originally covered by the author in InsideCybersecurity.com.

The *Daily Beast* article on Jeh Johnson's nomination to head DHS can be found here:http://www.thedailybeast.com/articles/2013/10/17/exclusive-jeh-johnson-tapped-to-lead-department-of-homeland-security.html.

Sen. Carper discussed his early conversations with Jeh Johnson in an interview with the author.

The author's coverage of Phyllis Schneck's call for clearer DHS authority and other aspects of DHS's efforts was originally for InsideCybersecurity.com.

DHS official Andy Ozment's June 16, 2015, testimony on the OPM data breach and how the department's security tools work:http://oversight.house.gov/wp-content/uploads/2015/06/Ozment-DHS-Statement-6-16-Data-Breach.pdf.

Christopher J. Castelli of InsideCybersecurity.com covered DHS testimony on the limits of its authority to compel changes at other federal agencies.

CHAPTER 6

The text of FCC Chairman Thomas Wheeler's AEI speech can be found here:http://insidecybersecurity.com/iwpfile.html?file= jun2014%2Fcs06122014_AEI_speech.pdf.

A Motherboard article discusses the history of television hacks:http://motherboard.vice.com/read/headroom-hacker.

This article in the *Hollywood Reporter* discussed industry views of Wheeler:http://www.hollywoodreporter.com/news/new-fcc-chairman-tom-wheeler-652820.

Time's article cited praise for Wheeler in the technology community:http://business.time.com/2013/05/02/tom-wheeler-former-lobbyist-and-obama-fundraiser-tapped-to-lead-fcc/.

This InsideCybersecurity.com story discussed Melissa Hathaway's call for cyber regulation in the telecom sector:http://insidecybersecurity. com/Cyber-Daily-News/Daily-News/former-white-house-cybersecurity-adviser-urges-tougher-fcc-rules/menu-id-1075.html.

Robert Mayer of the U.S. Telecom Association discussed the FCC strategic approach in an interview with the author.

The FCC Web page offered biographical information on retired Rear Adm. David Simpson:https://www.fcc.gov/document/chairman-wheeler-names-admiral-david-simpson-chief-pshsb.

The FCC Web page offered biographical information on Clete Johnson: https://www.fcc.gov/document/fcc-chairman-wheeler-announces-senior-staff-appointments-0.

The author covered Thomas Wheeler's AEI speech and subsequent fallout for InsideCybersecurity.com.

Letter from Rep. Mike Rogers to FCC Chairman Wheeler questioning the commission's claim of regulatory authority over cybersecurity:http://insidecybersecurity.com/iwpfile.html?file=jun2014%2Fcs2014_0130. pdf.

Posting by Wiley Rein attorneys suggesting a new regulatory approach to cyber by the FCC:http://www.wileyrein.com/newsroom-articles-3241.html.

The author's coverage in InsideCybersecurity.com of industry reaction to a *Politico* story on the FCC process:http://insidecybersecurity. com/Cyber-Daily-News/Daily-News/telecom-industry-rallies-behind-working-group-4-cybersecurity-proposal/menu-id-1075.html.

CHAPTER 7

The text of President Obama's January 12, 2015, speech at the Federal Trade Commission can be found here:https://www.whitehouse.gov/the-press-office/2015/01/12/remarks-president-federal-trade-commission.

Federal Trade Commission Chairwoman Edith Ramirez discussed her role in this *Washington Post* interview:https://www.washingtonpost.com/ news/the-switch/wp/2015/06/06/how-the-countrys-top-privacy-cop-is-trying-to-protect-consumers-in-the-digital-age/.

Details on the White House 2015 cyber crime and other proposals can be found here:https://www.whitehouse.gov/the-press-office/2015/01/13/ securing-cyberspace-president-obama-announces-new-cybersecurity-legislat.

BloombergBusiness's profile of Edith Ramirez can be found here:http://www.bloomberg.com/research/stocks/private/person.asp? personId=23838793&privcapId=5410670.

InsideCybersecurity.com provided extensive coverage of the implications of the FTC's enforcement action against Wyndham Worldwide. The commission posted this statement on the U.S. Third Circuit Court of Appeals ruling in the case, along with a link to the court's opinion:https:// www.ftc.gov/news-events/blogs/business-blog/2015/08/third-circuit-rules-ftc-v-wyndham-case.

FTC Chairwoman Ramirez's April 2, 2014, testimony before the Senate Homeland Security and Governmental Affairs Committee can be accessed here:http://www.hsgac.senate.gov/hearings/data-breach-on-the-rise-protecting-personal-information-from-harm.

The 2014 Senate Commerce Committee report on the Target breach can be accessed here:http://www.commerce.senate.gov/public/?a=Files. Serve&File_id=24d3c229-4f2f-405d-b8db-a3a67f183883.

Information on the joint FTC-Department of Justice statement on cyber information-sharing and antitrust can be found here:https://www.ftc.gov/news-events/press-releases/2014/04/ftc-doj-issue-antitrust-policy-statement-sharing-cybersecurity.

White House official Ari Schwartz and private-sector attorney Brian Finch discussed the implications of the DOJ-FTC statement with the author for InsideCybersecurity.com.

CHAPTER 8

Author's notes on September 25, 2013, speech by Gen. Keith Alexander at Billington security conference, Washington, DC.

Author's notes, March 7, 2013, joint hearing of Senate Commerce and Homeland Security and Governmental Affairs committees.

The *Washington Post* coverage of the Edward Snowden leaks regarding government surveillance had a dramatic effect on the cybersecurity debate in Congress:http://www.washingtonpost.com/world/national-security/nsa-broke-privacy-rules-thousands-of-times-per-year-audit-finds/2013/08/15/3310e554-05ca-11e3-a07f-49ddc7417125_story.html.

Author's interview with Rep. Michael McCaul, first reported in InsideCybersecurity.com.

The author reported for InsideCybersecurity.com on Senate Commerce Committee action providing a jolt of optimism for supporters of a broad array of cyber bills.

The author first reported for InsideCybersecurity.com exclusive news on an amendment to the Senate Commerce Committee's NIST bill that could have far-reaching implications.

CHAPTER 9

A White House fact sheet explained the president's February 2015 executive order on information sharing:https://www.whitehouse.gov/the-press-office/2015/02/12/fact-sheet-executive-order-promoting-private-sector-cybersecurity-inform.

Dr. Paul Stockton discussed the need for sanctions and penalties in an interview with author.

Director of National Intelligence James Clapper discussed the role of the Cyber Threat Intelligence and Integration Center in September 10, 2015 congressional testimony:http://intelligence.house.gov/sites/ intelligence.house.gov/files/documents/ClapperOpening09102015.pdf.

The author reported for InsideCybersecurity.com on administration efforts to ease congressional concerns over the new CTIIC.

The DHS announcement that the University of Texas–San Antonio would be the standards-setting body for new information sharing and analysis organizations can be found here:http://www.dhs.gov/blog/2015/ 09/03/dhs-awards-grant-creation-information-sharing-and-analysis-organization-isao.

The University of Texas–San Antonio posted this article on the high ranking for the school's cybersecurity program:http://www.utsa.edu/ today/2014/02/cyberranking.html.

CHAPTER 10

The author's June 8 article in the *Washington Examiner* discussed the impact of the NSA debate on cybersecurity legislation:http://www. washingtonexaminer.com/surveillance-reform-could-tee-up-cyber-bill/ article/2565630.

Content from the author's interview with Ari Schwartz appeared in InsideCybersecurity.com.

Content from the author's interview with Gregory Nojein appeared in InsideCybersecurity.com.

This *New York Times* report on the scope of NSA surveillance bolstered critics of cyber info-sharing legislation:http://www.nytimes.com/ 2015/06/05/us/hunting-for-hackers-nsa-secretly-expands-internet-spying-at-us-border.html?_r=0.

The Center for Democracy and Technology put out this assessment of the link between NSA activities and cybersecurity proposals:https://cdt. org/press/latest-snowden-revelations-highlight-troubling-role-of-nsa-in-cybersecurity/.

Sen. Dianne Feinstein (D-California) put out this statement seeking to refute criticism of cyber info-sharing legislation based on the latest Snowden revelations:http://www.feinstein.senate.gov/public/index.cfm/ press-releases?ID=ff7c9378-e2c7-48ea-9059-233fa1cc9946.

The *Washington Post* provided an in-depth report on the hack at the Office of Personnel Management, which supporters of cyber legislation cited as a clarion call for action on an information-sharing bill:http://www.washingtonpost.com/world/national-security/chinese-hack-of-government-network-compromises-security-clearance-files/2015/06/12/9f91f146-1135-11e5-9726-49d6fa26a8c6_story.html?hpid=z2.

Sen. Patrick Leahy (D-Vermont) strongly and colorfully decried efforts to link the OPM hack with the pending cyber legislation:http://www.govexec.com/oversight/2015/06/leahy-denounces-alarmists-over-latest-opm-cyberattack/114634/.

CHAPTER 11

Senate Judiciary Chairman Charles Grassley (R-Iowa) and ranking member Patrick Leahy (D-Vermont) discussed encryption at a July 8, 2015 hearing:http://www.judiciary.senate.gov/meetings/going-dark-encryption-technology-and-the-balance-between-public-safety-and-privacy.

FBI Director James Comey's July 6, 2015, blog on "LawFare" on the perils of strong encryption, which provoked a strong response from tech groups:https://www.lawfareblog.com/encryption-public-safety-and-going-dark.

The Information Technology Industry Council sent this letter to President Obama urging him to oppose policies that would undermine strong encryption:http://www.itic.org/dotAsset/58fbf8de-cd86-47a0-a114-43a55776d2e6.pdf.

Representatives of the Center for Democracy and Technology discussed the encryption issue with reporters on a conference call covered by the author for InsideCybersecurity.com.

The author covered the July 8, 2015, hearings on encryption for InsideCybersecurity.com.

Rep. Adam Schiff (D-Washington) discussed the policy challenges posed by strong encryption and the tech sector's responses in comments to the author first reported in InsideCybersecurity.com.

The *Washington Post*'s exclusive report on Obama administration policy deliberations on strong encryption can be found here:https://www.washingtonpost.com/world/national-security/obama-administration-

ponders-how-to-seek-access-to-encrypted-data/2015/09/23/107a811c-
5b22-11e5-b38e-06883aacba64_story.html?wpmm=1&wpisrc=nl_tech.

CHAPTER 12

Sen. Tom Carper discussed the difficulties of the U.S.-China relationship
in an interview with the author.

The U.S. Chamber of Commerce's Matthew Eggers discussed the myriad issues tied up in the U.S.-China relationship in an interview with the
author.

The *New York Times* reported on the Obama administration's shifting
position on sanctioning China:http://www.nytimes.com/2015/08/01/
world/asia/us-decides-to-retaliate-against-chinas-hacking.html?_r=0.

The author reported on Lu Wei's appearance at George Washington
University for InsideCybersecurity.com.

Ellen Nakashima of the *Washington Post* reported on August 30 on
the Obama administration's emerging sanctions plan:https://www.
washingtonpost.com/world/national-security/administration-developing-
sanctions-against-china-over-cyberespionage/2015/08/30/9b2910aa-
480b-11e5-8ab4-c73967a143d3_story.html.

Dr. Paul Stockton discussed sanctions policy in an interview with the
author.

The *Wall Street Journal*'s interview with President Xi can be accessed
here:http://www.wsj.com/articles/full-transcript-interview-with-chinese-
president-xi-jinping-1442894700.

Sen. Tom Carper discussed the U.S.-China relationship in a September 10 interview with the author.

CHAPTER 13

The author reported on workforce challenges for InsideCybersecur-
ity.com:http://insidecybersecurity.com/Cyber-Daily-News/Daily-News/
obama-administration-officials-try-to-encourage-the-next-generation-of-
cybersecurity-workers/menu-id-1075.html.

CHAPTER 14

Op-ed in the *Hill* by Evan Greer and Donny Shaw opposing the Senate cybersecurity bill can be found here:http://thehill.com/blogs/congress-blog/technology/249521-cisa-the-dirty-deal-between-google-and-the-nsa-that-no-one-is.

GOP presidential candidate Jeb Bush's initial blog on cybersecurity can be found here:https://blog.statustoday.com/the-president-must-prioritize-cybersecurity-cd4c90cd1fdd.

Democratic presidential candidate Hillary Clinton's criticism of Chinese hacking can be found here:http://www.cnn.com/2015/07/04/politics/clinton-china-hacking/.

The *Hill* newspaper in the summer of 2015 reported on how a series of Internet-related events alarmed lawmakers:http://thehill.com/policy/finance/247312-day-of-technical-glitches-puts-lawmakers-on-edge.

The *Hill* reported on Sen. John Cornyn's (R-Texas) optimism over prospects for action on the cyber bill:http://thehill.com/policy/cybersecurity/247921-senate-gop-whip-eyes-early-august-for-cyber-bill. Shortly thereafter the *Hill* and other news outlets would report that Cornyn reversed himself and said cyber would not come up over the summer. A third twist would come quickly when Senate Majority Leader Mitch McConnell (R-Kentucky) surprised many of his colleagues by trying unsuccessfully to insert the cyber bill into a separate debate over defense spending.

CHAPTER 15

The August 15, 2015, *New York Times* article on the relationship between the NSA and AT&T can be found here:http://www.nytimes.com/2015/08/16/us/politics/att-helped-nsa-spy-on-an-array-of-internet-traffic.html?_r=0.

Amie Stepanovich's article in *Wired* on the Senate cyber bill can be found here:http://www.wired.com/2015/08/access-cisa-myth-of-voluntary-info-sharing/.

Report by *Politico*'s Tim Starks on "dour vibes" around the Senate cyber bill can be found here:http://www.politico.com/tipsheets/morning-cybersecurity/2015/08/whats-on-deck-in-september-210036.

Federal government spending on contracting is detailed here, high-lighting the government's ability to influence corporate behavior by setting stringent requirements on its own vast network of vendors:https://www.usaspending.gov/Pages/Default.aspx.

CHAPTER 16

Internet pioneer Vint Cerf's May 4, 2015, speech at the National Press Club can be seen here:https://www.press.org/news-multimedia/videos/npc-luncheon-vint-cerf.

Gregory Nojeim discussed the flaws in Congress's prevailing approach to cybersecurity issues at a September 2, 2015, Center for Democracy and Technology press event and subsequent interview with the author.

Larry Clinton discussed the issues in a June 1, 2015, interview with the author, some of which was reported in InsideCybersecurity.com.

American International Group CEO Peter Hancock's April 2015 speech on cybersecurity at the NYU Polytechnic School of Engineering. More can be found here:http://engineering.nyu.edu/news/2015/04/09/attacks-multiply-aig-ceo-hancock-calls-stronger-cyber-insurance.

The author covered the SAFETY Act debate for InsideCybersecurity.com.

House Intelligence Chairman Devin Nunes (R-California) discussed possible cyber regulation at a September 10, 2015, hearing.

Information on the Center for Internet Security can be found here:https://www.cisecurity.org/.

Sen. Tom Carper (D-Delaware) discussed parallels between the Cold War and current cyber threats in an interview with the author.

INDEX

Abbott, Prime Minister Tony, 200
Abeles, John, 162, 271, 276
Access Now, 228, 238, 248, 250, 251
Agcaoili, Phil, 68
Alexander, Gen. Keith, 144, 212
Algeier, Scott, 109, 264–265, 276
Allen, Brian, 115
Alperovitch, Dmitri, 49
American Bankers Association, 8
American Civil Liberties Union (ACLU),
    11, 12, 31, 69, 150, 172, 173, 181, 225,
    227, 276
American Enterprise Institute (AEI), 117,
    198, 200
American Water Works Association, 71,
    96, 130
Anthem, 2, 155
AOL, ix
Archuleta, Katherine, 103, 104, 105–106,
    106, 107
Ashley Madison, 252
AT&T, 70, 71, 249–250, 250, 251

Banja, Ajay, 65
Bank of America, 52, 65
Barnett, Adm. Jamie, 121
Barrett, Matthew, 76, 77, 78
Beauchesne, Ann, 238
Beckstrom, Rod, 19
Belluchie, Leslee, 212
Bennett, Steve, 65

Berk, Vincent, 73
Blask, Christopher, 163
Blumenthal, Sen. Richard, 222
Blunt, Sen. Roy, 223
Bonanni, Deborah, 212
Booz-Allen-Hamilton, 63, 210
Boyens, Jon, 53
Brennan, John, ix, 20
Brown, Megan, 118
Brown, Sandra, 53
Burr, Sen. Richard, 171, 177, 181, 182,
    219, 231, 233, 238, 242, 245, 253
Bush Administration. See Bush, George
    W.
Bush, George W., 16–17, 17, 18, 19, 20,
    22, 29, 88, 113, 193, 255, 257, 259
Bush, Jeb, 215, 216–217
Bush, Wes, 65
BuySecure Initiative, 4

Carnahan, Lisa, 75, 76
Carnegie Mellon University, 51, 160
Casey, Tim, 75
Castelli, Christopher J., 164, 200, 276
Cattanach, Robert, 139
Center for Democracy and Technology
    (CDT), 11, 42, 43, 133, 172, 176, 177,
    178–179, 181, 188, 191, 227, 232, 265,
    276
Center for Strategic and International
    Studies (CSIS), 18, 84, 107, 167, 168,

209
Central Intelligence Agency (CIA), ix, xii,
    84, 103, 198
Cerf, Vint, 255
Chaffetz, Rep. Jason, 83, 103
Chambliss, Sen. Saxby, 8, 9, 10, 11, 12, 26,
    34, 38, 148, 150, 152, 153
Charney, Scott, 18
China, xii, 4, 5, 15, 16, 26, 102, 106, 169,
    197–201, 202–208, 209, 215, 217, 266,
    270
Clapper, James, xv, 106, 161, 199
Clinton Administration. *See* Clinton, Bill
Clinton, Bill, 20, 103, 255, 257
Clinton, Hillary, 200, 217
Clinton, Larry, 58–59, 59, 60, 61, 65–66,
    67, 72, 74, 76, 78, 80, 88, 121–122,
    160, 163, 177, 264, 266, 266–267, 269,
    276
Cloud, 2, 273
CNN, 49
Coburn, Sen. Tom, 86, 87, 144, 147
Cohen, Rochelle, 276
Collins, Sen. Susan, 26, 27, 32, 34, 35, 38,
    45, 74, 221, 224, 225, 226, 244, 258
Comey, FBI Director James, 190, 191,
    192, 193–194
Coons, Sen. Christopher, 246
Cornyn, Sen. John, 219, 221, 227, 229
Cotton, Sen. Tom, 223, 226, 233, 238, 245
Cruz, Sen. Ted, 112, 200
Cummings, Rep. Elijah, 103

Daily Caller, 34
Daniel, Michael, 7, 8, 42, 43, 44, 45, 58,
    59–60, 62, 70, 74, 105, 107, 162, 259
Dempsey, Gen. Martin, 5, 21, 197
Denbow, Kimberly, 96
DiMaria, John, 163
Dix, Robert, 97, 98, 100, 160–161, 161,
    264, 272, 276
Dodson, Donna, 53–54, 67, 115, 276
Dow Chemical, 52
Dupont, Dan, 65, 275, 276

Eggers, Matthew, 32, 37, 39, 42, 56, 67,
    70, 199, 202, 260, 261, 276
Energy, Department of, 44, 71, 96, 99, 130
England, Jeff, 75

Enzi, Sen. Mike, 34
Erny, Bill, 57
Executive Order 13636, 41, 44, 56, 85, 87

Federal Bureau of Investigation (FBI), xi,
    3, 12, 17, 18, 31, 84, 99, 190, 190–191,
    191, 192, 195, 233, 238, 245
Federal Communications Commission
    (FCC), xv, 111, 111–112, 113, 115,
    116, 117, 117–127, 129, 132, 135, 253,
    254, 256, 276
Federal Trade Commission (FTC), xv, 129,
    131–136, 137–142, 156, 158, 218, 253
Feinstein, Sen. Dianne, 8, 9, 10–11, 12, 26,
    32, 33, 148, 150, 152, 153, 170, 171,
    179, 181, 182–183, 183, 184, 186, 187,
    207, 221, 222, 229, 231, 233, 237, 238,
    242, 245, 253
Felker, John, 109
Financial Services Roundtable, 8, 150,
    159, 231
Finch, Brian, 8, 138, 139, 276
Flake, Sen. Jeff, 245
Flynn, Patrick, 63
Foreign Policy, 203
Fox News, 220
framework of cybersecurity standards. *See*
    NIST
Franken, Sen. Al, 193, 231, 232, 245
Frost and Sullivan, 210

Gallagher, Patrick, 47, 48, 49, 61, 62, 64,
    144, 146, 148
Gardner, Sen. Cory, 199, 225
Garfield, Dean. *See* Information
    Technology Industry Council
George Washington University, 202, 203,
    212, 213
General Dynamics, 63
Google, 26, 255, 257
Graham, Sen. Lindsey, 86, 218
Grassley, Sen. Charles, xii, 34, 189
Greenberg, Sally, 138
Greene, Robyn, 156
Greer, Evan, 215
Gurdon, Hugo, 276

Hall, Joseph. *See* CDT
Hancock, Peter, 268

Harman, Jane, 264
Harrelson, Robert, 275
Hathaway, Melissa, 17, 18–19, 20, 22, 43, 108–109, 113, 257, 259–260, 265, 276
Hayden, Gen. Michael, 198
Heartland Payment Systems, 25, 50
Heller, Sen. Dean, 187, 221, 245
Hellmann, Ralph, 147
Hewson, Marilyn. See Lockheed Martin
The Hill, 38, 215, 220, 221, 227, 229
Holder, Attorney General Eric, 198, 199
Home Depot, 2, 4
Homeland Security, Department of (DHS), xi, 2, 6, 11, 13, 18, 19, 20, 27, 28, 32, 34, 37, 38, 42, 45, 46, 48, 56–58, 71, 80, 81, 81–82, 82, 82–83, 83, 84, 85, 86–89, 89–90, 91–92, 93–94, 95, 96, 96–97, 97, 98–99, 100–102, 103, 104, 104–105, 105, 106, 107, 108–110, 119, 130, 144, 148, 149, 150, 159, 171, 197, 209, 223, 224, 229, 231, 232, 238, 243, 245, 254, 255, 256, 259, 261, 263, 267
House Republican Cybersecurity Task Force, x, 29, 59
Hurd, Rep. Will, 103
Hutchison, Sen. Kay Bailey, 34, 36, 47, 147

IBM, xi, 63, 212
Information Security Media Group, 12
Information Technology Industry Council, 97, 191, 192
InsideCybersecurity.com, 5, 11, 51, 52, 57, 58, 59, 61, 63, 65, 68, 76, 87, 93, 96, 105, 115, 118, 120, 123, 135, 148, 151, 164, 173, 180, 193, 200, 212, 221, 232, 275–276, 276
The Interview. See Sony Pictures
Iran, 4, 16, 160, 169, 176, 204, 236, 237, 238, 244, 246

Jackson, David, 205
Jackson Lee, Sheila, 168
Jagielski, Karen, 135
James, Renee, 65
Johnson, Clete, 114, 120
Johnson, Secretary Jeh, ix, 70, 85–87, 107–108, 109, 150, 210, 260
Johnson, Sen. Ron, 5, 218, 226, 235

Josten, R. Bruce, 32, 33
JP Morgan, 5
Justice, Department of (DOJ), 19, 99, 130, 138, 190, 191–192, 193, 198, 241, 242

Kean, Thomas, 263
Kennedy, John F., 160, 201
Kerry, Secretary John, 205
Kolasky, Robert, 57
Knacke, Robert, 210
Kriz, Danielle, 97, 272, 276
Kujawa, Adam, 133

Landfield, Kent, 96
Langer, Jack, 276
Langevin, James, 1, 18, 79, 269, 270, 272
Lawfare, 190
"Lazlo", 126, 266
Lee, Sen. Mike, 187, 220–221, 235
Lehotsky, Steven, 133
Lieberman, Sen. Joseph, 26, 27, 32, 33–34, 34, 34–35, 35, 37, 38, 45, 48, 74, 144, 221, 258
LifeLock, 140, 140–141
Lloyd's, xii
Lockheed Martin, 65, 70, 71
Lofton, Gina, 212
Los Angeles Times, 10–11
Lute, Jane Holl, 83, 163, 272
Lu Wei, 202–203, 204

Magnuson, Laura Lucas, 212
Magri, Joshua, 159
Marinho, John, 125, 126
Markey, Sen. Edward, 147
Mayer, Robert, 80, 113, 114, 115, 115–116, 116, 117, 120, 121, 127, 276
Mayorkas, Alejandro, 231, 232
McAfee, 6, 7, 63, 84, 96
McDonough, Denis, 70
McCain, Sen. John, 3, 18, 34, 36, 37, 39, 86, 106, 183, 185, 201, 235, 236, 243, 264
McCaul, Rep. Michael, 13, 18, 104, 105, 145, 146–147, 149, 150, 152, 156, 167, 168, 169, 173–174, 174, 175, 188, 218, 276
McConnell, Bruce, 19, 20, 27, 37, 42, 45, 46, 83, 276

McConnell, Mike, 16, 17
McGuire, Cheri, 212
Meehan, Rep. Patrick, 149
Menna, Jenny, 92
Mentzer, Tom, 276
Metcalf Incident. *See* Pacific Gas and
    Electric
Micek, Peter. *See* Access Now
Microsoft, 18, 19, 20, 50, 52, 257
Mitchell, Nathan, 60
Moniz, Secretary Ernest, 211
Moore, Samara, 44, 68, 115, 212, 213
Morley, Kevin, 96
Moynihan, Brian, 65
Mulvaney, Rep. Mick, 175
Murkowski, Sen. Lisa, 34

Nakashima, Ellen, 102
Napolitano, Secretary Janet, 82–83, 84,
    144, 160
National Association of Corporate
    Directors, 267
National Institute of Standards and
    Technology (NIST), xv, 1, 2, 26, 28,
    29, 36, 44, 46, 46–47, 48, 49, 49–50,
    50, 51, 52, 53–54, 54–55, 55, 58, 60,
    61, 61–62, 62, 63, 64, 66, 66–67,
    67–68, 68, 69, 69–70, 70, 72, 73, 74,
    75, 75–77, 78, 79, 80, 82, 86, 87, 89,
    90, 93, 97, 98, 113, 125, 126, 130, 131,
    142, 144, 146, 147, 148, 149, 150, 153,
    200, 254, 256, 257, 258, 267, 270, 272,
    273, 276
National Security Agency (NSA), xi, 6, 10,
    11, 19, 30, 82, 99, 143, 146, 147, 164,
    169, 172, 173, 176, 178, 178–179, 179,
    191, 195, 212, 223, 232, 245, 247, 248,
    249, 260, 266
NBC News, xi, xii
Neiman Marcus, 4, 136
Nelson, Sen. Bill, 2, 131, 220
New York Post, ix
New York Times, 22, 37, 73, 143, 178, 179,
    201, 249
Nojeim, Gregory. *See* CDT
Norfolk State University, 211
North Carolina State University, 66, 67
North Korea, 2, 3, 4, 5, 169, 200, 201, 204

Nunes, Rep. Devin, 168–169, 169, 170,
    172, 173, 175, 207, 270

Obama Administration. *See* Obama, Ba-
    rack
Obama, Barack, xii, 1, 3, 4, 5, 6, 7, 12, 13,
    13–15, 15–16, 16, 17, 18, 19, 20, 21,
    21–23, 26, 27, 28, 29, 34, 35, 36, 39,
    41–42, 42, 44, 46, 48, 55, 56, 58, 59,
    65, 67, 69, 70, 71, 82, 84, 85, 100, 105,
    109, 112, 115, 129, 131, 132, 134, 137,
    139, 143, 151, 152, 153, 155, 155–156,
    157, 158, 161, 162, 165, 167, 174, 176,
    177, 180, 184, 188, 191, 194–195, 198,
    200, 201, 202, 203, 204, 205, 207, 211,
    215, 216, 217, 220, 227, 230, 233, 253,
    254, 255, 256, 257, 258, 259, 261, 267
Odderstol, Thad, 90
Office of Management and Budget (OMB),
    42, 87, 103, 253
Office of Personnel Management (OPM),
    102–104, 105, 106, 107, 179, 180, 181,
    184, 197, 198, 199, 201, 202, 204, 205,
    210, 215, 217, 225, 252
Orwell, George, 227
Oxner, Dave, xiii
Ozment, Andy, 85, 101–102, 103, 104,
    105, 106–107, 109, 163

Pacific Gas and Electric, 53
Painter, Christopher, 200
Panetta, Leon, xii
Pascal, Amy. *See* Sony Pictures
Paul, Sen. Rand, 86, 176, 187, 226, 244
Pearson, Harriet, 69
Pelosi, Rep. Nancy, 169, 170
Politico, 36, 73, 74, 121, 125, 252
Ponemon Institute, xi, 164
Postal Service, U.S., 2
PriceWaterhouseCoopers, xi
Pritzker, Penny, 70, 71
ProPublica, 178, 249

Raduege, Harry, 18
Ramirez, FTC Chairwoman Edith, 132,
    134, 136, 137, 138
Ratcliffe, Rep. John, 110, 174, 269
Raymond, Brian, 59
Raytheon, 52

Reid, Sen. Harry, 10, 27, 32, 34, 36, 38, 182, 183, 184, 185, 186, 221, 228, 233, 233–234, 234–235, 235, 236, 237, 238, 244, 250
Reitinger, Philip, 19
Retail Industry Leaders Association, 233
Reuters, 82
Rich, Jessica, 134, 140
Richardson, Michelle. See ACLU
Ridge, Secretary Tom, 140, 263
Rigby, Joe, 65
Rockefeller, Sen. Jay, 10, 25, 26, 32, 33, 34, 36, 47, 59, 72, 114, 136–137, 137, 147, 147–148, 148, 149, 150
Rogers, Rep. Mike, 8, 9, 12, 26, 30, 31, 36, 72, 117, 118, 145, 146, 150, 152, 168, 169, 170, 198, 199
Romine, Dr. Charles, 2, 53, 67
Rosenzweig, Paul, 35
Rottman, Gabriel. See ACLU
Rubio, Sen. Marco, 215
Ruppersberger, Rep. Dutch, 12, 26, 30, 31, 72, 145, 146, 168, 169, 170
Russia, 4, 15, 16, 169, 197, 266

Sage, Ola, 68, 271, 276
Salters, Harold, 160
SANS Institute, 73
Scharf, Charles, 65
Schiff, Rep. Adam, 168, 169–170, 172, 173, 175, 193–194, 194, 204
Schimmeck, Karl, 77, 159, 276
Schmidt, Howard, 20, 42
Schneck, Phyllis, 6, 7, 81, 84, 93, 94, 98, 260
Scholl, Matthew, 49, 53, 55, 75, 276
Schumer, Sen. Charles, 188, 221, 230, 236
Schwartz, Ari, 43, 44, 138, 177
Securities and Exchange Commission (SEC), 76, 130, 132
Securities Industry and Financial Markets Association, xiii, 159
Sedgewick, Adam, 47–48, 49, 49–50, 50, 51, 53, 60, 61, 76, 79, 93, 125, 126, 276
Sessions, Sen. Jeff, 34
Seymour, Donna, 103
Shaw, Donny, 215
Shell, 52

Simpson, Adm. David, 114, 115, 117, 119, 123
Smid, Miles, 54
Snowden, Edward, 6, 8, 9, 10, 44, 47, 143, 146, 149, 152, 172, 178, 179, 180, 249, 250
Snowe, Sen. Olympia, 26
Sony Pictures, 1, 2, 3, 4, 5, 6, 129, 135, 155, 159, 169, 199, 200, 252
Sosenko, Alan, 275
Spaulding, Suzanne, 13, 84, 90, 98, 152
Stanford University, 158, 169
Starks, Tim, 252
State, Department of, 41, 200, 225, 260
Stepanovich, Amie. See Access Now
Stephenson, Randall. See AT&T
Stine, Kevin, 53, 55, 276
Stockton, Paul, 157, 204
Summers, Lawrence, 20

Target, 4, 5, 73, 134, 136, 137
Tester, Sen. Jon, 106
Thompson, Rep. Bennie, 150, 168
Thornberry, Rep. Mac, x, xi, 29
Thune, Sen. John, 136, 144, 147, 148, 149, 237
Time Magazine, 23, 112
Tooley, Matt, 125
Trump, Donald, 253
Turetsky, David, 113, 114

U.S. Chamber of Commerce, 6, 8, 11, 32, 32–33, 33, 37, 37–38, 38, 39, 42, 56, 98, 133, 185, 199, 202, 231, 233, 238, 260, 267
Udall, Sen. Mark, 9, 10
University of California-San Diego, 52, 53
University of South Florida, 75
University of Texas-Dallas, 60
University of Texas-San Antonio, 163–164
U.S. Computer Emergency Response Team (CERT), xiii, 51, 143

Van Wie, Caroline Rose, 118
Verizon, ix, 50
Virginia Tech, 97, 213

Walker, Rep. Mark, 104

Wall Street Journal, 15, 35, 36, 73, 143,
    205, 219, 220
Ward, April, 276
Warren, Sen. Elizabeth, 2
Washington Post, 25, 83, 102, 132, 134,
    146, 195, 203, 237
Weatherford, Mark, 83
Weber, Rick, 52, 61, 275, 276
Westbrook, Jennie, 276
Wheeler, Carole, 112
Wheeler, Thomas, 111, 111–112, 113, 114,
    115, 116, 117, 119, 121, 122, 123–124,
    126
White, Nathan. *See* Access Now

Whitehouse, Sen. Sheldon, 193, 218,
    222–223
Woodson, Randy, 67
Wyden, Sen. Ron,– 9, 10, 100, 170, 177,
    179, 180, 183–184, 184, 186, 188, 190,
    221, 222, 226, 228, 229, 230, 234, 235,
    236, 239–240, 241–242, 245
Wyndham Worldwide, 132–133

Xi Jinping, 202, 203, 205

Yates, Sally Quillian, 191–192

Zelvin, Larry, 99, 109
Zuckerberg, Mark, 203

ABOUT THE AUTHOR

Charlie Mitchell is the editor and co-founder of *Inside Cybersecurity*, the first online news service dedicated to explaining the policy challenges of securing cyberspace. *Inside Cybersecurity* goes inside Congress, the White House, the corporate boardrooms, and security command centers to explain cyber policymaking to a professional audience.

Mitchell also writes a column on cybersecurity for the *Washington Examiner* that is a must-read feature for cyber insiders and concerned citizens alike. He is a regular speaker and panelist at cybersecurity events.

A veteran journalist, Mitchell is the former editor-and-chief of *Roll Call*, the authoritative source of news on Capitol Hill. At *Roll Call*, Charlie built one of the most respected investigative units in the nation and drove a "hometown approach" to covering the life, times, and misadventures of Congress.